Eighteenth-Century
Woodworking Tools

COLONIAL WILLIAMSBURG HISTORIC TRADES
VOLUME III

Eighteenth-Century Woodworking Tools

Papers Presented at a Tool Symposium
May 19–22, 1994

Edited by James M. Gaynor

THE COLONIAL WILLIAMSBURG FOUNDATION
WILLIAMSBURG, VIRGINIA

Colonial Williamsburg Historic Trades is a series of publications dedicated to furthering the interpretive and preservation goals of the Colonial Williamsburg Foundation and promoting the study of technology and processes of traditional trades in the eighteenth century.

Library of Congress Cataloging-in-Publication data

    Eighteenth-century woodworking tools : papers presented at a tool
      symposium, May 19–22, 1994 / edited by James M. Gaynor.
         p.   cm. — (Colonial Williamsburg historic trades)
      Includes bibliographical references
      ISBN 0-87935-110-1
        1. Woodworking tools—England—History—18th century—Congresses.
      2. Woodworking tools—United States—History—18th century—Congresses.
      I. Gaynor, James M.   II. Colonial Williamsburg Foundation.   III. Series: Colonial
      Williamsburg historic trades book.
      TT186.E36   1997
      683'.082—dc21   97-31281
                                                 CIP

ISBN: 0-87935-110-1

Printed in the United States of America

Front cover: Birmingham tools. Folding rule by T. &. G. Cox (ca. 1800); compasses by Sam Ault; timber scribe by T. Symond[s?] dated 1770; gimlet by John Lightfoot; molding plane by George Darbey (1750—1784). The gentleman's claw hammer, drawbore pin, saw wrest, and pincers, although unmarked, are attributed to Birmingham based on their designs. The hammer is ca. 1772; the rest are late eighteenth or early nineteenth century. Hammer OL: 14⅛". G1986-268, 49, gift of Frank M. Smith; 1990-121; 1992-80; W3601593, Stephen C. Wolcott Collection; 1988-490; 1957-123, A2; 1991-159, 1; 1992-115; pincers courtesy, Trip Kahn—Rockhill Research.

Back cover: Detail of interior of the lid of an English joiner's chest, ca. 1790. OL: 44½". Courtesy, Jane and Mark Rees

Contents

Preface

This special issue of *Historic Trades* is composed of papers delivered at a symposium on eighteenth-century woodworking tools hosted by the Colonial Williamsburg Foundation, May 19–22, 1994. The symposium was one of a series of events sponsored by the Foundation in conjunction with the exhibit "TOOLS: Working Wood in 18th-Century America," presented at the DeWitt Wallace Gallery from January 1994 to September 1995. The symposium was held concurrently with the 1994 annual meeting of the Early American Industries Association in Williamsburg.

An introductory session on Thursday evening, May 19, opened the proceedings. Friday's program explored the development, manufacture, and marketing of woodworking tools in England and America. Morning lecture sessions were followed by an afternoon of special presentations, including films of twentieth-century toolmaking in Sheffield, England, prepared and narrated by Mr. Ken Hawley of Sheffield, and demonstrations by members of Colonial Williamsburg's Historic Trades Department. Friday evening's talks focused on planes and planemaking as a case study in tool development and manufacture.

On Saturday, the symposium turned to the relationship of tools to work and products. The morning's lecture sessions were again followed by films and demonstrations, and the day culminated in a panel discussion with Colonial Williamsburg tradespeople and an evening banquet. The symposium concluded on Sunday morning with a panel discussion featuring symposium speakers.

All papers presented at the morning and evening sessions of the symposium are included here, with the exception of Colonial Williamsburg Master Cooper George Pettengell's reminiscences of his apprenticeship experiences at Whitbread's Brewery in London during the 1950s, which were not available in written form. Contributors were asked to select only a few of their many illustrations in order to make publication practical. Roy Underhill's after-banquet group reading of "The Debate of the Carpenter's Tools" is represented by a reprinting of his analysis of that poem as it appeared in *The Woodwright's Workbook* (Chapel Hill, N. C., 1986).

Symposium topics were drawn from the themes of the "Tools" exhibit. Readers who would like further background about these themes may wish to read the exhibit's companion book, *Tools: Working Wood in Eighteenth-Century America,* which is available from Colonial Williamsburg.

Colonial Williamsburg was pleased to host this gathering of historians, collectors, and woodworkers and to participate in the sharing of discoveries and the ongoing search for new areas of exploration. On behalf of the symposium organizers, I thank the speakers and demonstrators, the participants, and the many behind-the-scenes people of the Early American Industries Association and Colonial Williamsburg who made this event and the publication of these papers possible.

Jay Gaynor
Curator of Mechanical Arts

THE DEVELOPMENT, MANUFACTURE, AND MARKETING OF WOODWORKING TOOLS IN ENGLAND AND AMERICA

Woodworking Tools before 1700

By Philip Walker

S ince the period to which these articles are devoted is the earliest during which detailed and illustrated information about woodworking tools and techniques was published, it may be appropriate to take an introductory look at the sources that are available for information about earlier periods.

These sources are, by their nature, indirect in the sense that even when tools are mentioned or illustrated, they were not intended to convey technical information. The reasons for this reticence on such an important subject are probably complex, but suffice it to point out that skilled craftsmen, at most times and in most places, enjoyed a relatively privileged economic and social position. This situation depended on the apprenticeship system being the sole route for passing on the secrets and the skills of the trades, and its beneficiaries had no reason to do anything that might encourage do-it-yourself activities by laymen. Conversely, the literary classes seem often to have felt that matters concerning manual work were beneath their dignity—or perhaps simply beyond their reach!

Thus, in the absence of explicit written records, we must look for clues wherever we can find them. I have grouped the most profitable sources in the six categories that follow together with some examples of the insights that can be obtained.

Surviving tools: The ideal source, provided their dates can be established. Deductions about construction, function, and purpose can be made. Many tools from the sixteenth to the nineteenth centuries actually bear dates (fig. 1), or can be dated from the marks their makers stamped on them. Others come from datable contexts such as ancient Egyptian tombs (fig. 2), the ashes of Pompeii (fig. 3), or the wreck of a ship like the *Mary Rose* (fig. 4).

Marks left by tools: Much can be deduced from such traces: for example, the shape and rate of cutting of augers or saws (fig. 5) and the size and methods of use of axes and adzes (fig. 6).

Fig. 1. Austrian dovetail plane, or *Grathobel,* dated 1607. See G. Heine, "An Historically Important Woodwork Joint—the method of making it in Germany, and some specialised tools," *Tools and Trades,* II (1984), pp. 29–46, for a discussion of the use of these planes. Courtesy, private collection.

Fig. 2. Relief carving from a mastaba of Tiye, Egypt, ca. 2500 B.C., showing joiners at work ripsawing, rubbing down, and boring with a bowdrill. Photograph, courtesy, W. L. Goodman Papers.

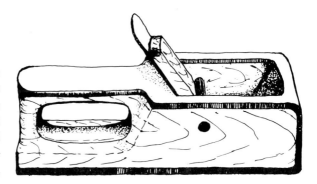

Fig. 3. Reconstruction of a wood-filled iron plane recovered from Pompeii, overwhelmed when Vesuvius erupted in A.D. 79. Drawing by Mary N. Walker.

Fig. 4. Carpenter's tools from the ship *Mary Rose,* which sank in 1545. Courtesy, Mary Rose Trust.

Fig. 5. A chase mortise in a beam of the barley barn, Cressing Temple, Essex, ca. A.D. 1200, showing marks of a spoon auger and a large edge tool—a chisel or twybill. Courtesy, John McCann.

Fig. 6. Marks of an adze (*left*) and of a pitsaw (*right*) on a post in Faulkners Hall, Good Easter, Essex. Courtesy, John McCann.

Language: It is a principle that if a word existed, then the thing to which that word referred must have existed, but this can be misleading unless we can be really sure what the word originally signified. A paper by the late W. L. Goodman, to be published shortly, argues that the ancient Greeks may not have had a word for "plane" after all! The derivation of words can be remarkably revealing, however. The word *auger* was, until the seventeenth century, *nauger,* and that in turn came from the two words in Old English, *nafu gar,* meaning *nave piercer.* So it was a tool large enough to bore a hole that would accommodate an axle, and, incidentally, one that could be worked along the grain of the wood.

Literature: This type of source is splendidly and sufficiently illustrated by Roy Underhill in his presentation of the fifteenth-century "Debate of the Carpenter's Tools." (See pp. 227–244.)

Bureaucratic documents: An account dated 1343 for repairs to Restormel Castle includes the sum of sixpence for an adze to smooth old timber that

Fig. 7. Model woodworkers' workshop from an Egyptian tomb of about 2000 B.C. Photograph, courtesy, W. L. Goodman Papers.

Fig. 8. Memorial to Celerio Palamando, shipwright and oar maker, Ostia, showing a graduated rule, compasses, a double-bitted adze, and two oar blades. First century A.D. Photograph, courtesy, W. L. Goodman Papers.

was so full of nails that the workmen would not set their own tools to it. This confirms the existence and use of the adze (a tool strangely absent from most medieval illustrations). In addition, it proves that workmen did own their personal tools and that old timber was reused. It also provides a value comparison (a man's daily wage then was about fourpence).

Art: The widest and richest source of all. Every sort of figurative representation can be included, from paintings to prints, mosaics to stained glass, carvings to tapestry, marquetry to medallions, and so on. A brief selection could include a 2000 B.C. model workshop from Thebes (fig. 7); a first century A.D. memorial (fig. 8); a wall painting from Pompeii showing a mortise joint being chopped; the Normans building invasion ships in the Bayeux Tapestry; the A.D. 1240 carpenters' window in Chartres Cathedral; a thirteenth-century drawing by Matthew Paris of building work at St. Albans (fig. 9); a 1430 Crucifixion tapestry from La Seo Cathedral at Saragossa; and the 1630 token of the Middelburg carpenters' guild (fig. 10).

Fig. 9. View of building work at Saint Albans Cathedral about 1250 by Matthew Paris, who visited the scene and has conveyed much information about the builders' tools and processes. Courtesy, Board of Trinity College, Dublin.

Fig. 10. The Middelburg carpenters' guild token for 1630. Photograph, courtesy, W. L. Goodman Papers.

Finally, a landmark in the early production of relevant books seems to have been Agostino Gallo's *Le Tredici Giornate* (1566), which included explicit pictures of tools (fig. 11) but did no more than give them names. In the next century came Mathurin Jousse's *L'Art de Charpenterie* (1650) and André Félibien's *Des Principes de l'Architecture* (1676) (fig. 12), followed by Joseph Moxon's *Mechanick Exercises* in the 1680s.

Fig. 11. Plate showing froe, chisel, pincers, and three kinds of saws from Agostino Gallo, *Le Tredici Giornate* (Venice, 1566).

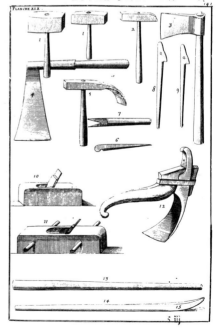

Fig. 12. Plate from André Félibien, *Des Principes de l'Architecture*, 2nd ed. (Paris, 1690). Courtesy, Winterthur Library, Printed Book and Periodical Collection, Winterthur, Del.

The Development of the English Toolmaking Industry during the Seventeenth and Eighteenth Centuries

By David Hey

The English toolmaking industry, centered on Sheffield and Birmingham, is rightly thought of as one that expanded rapidly in the late eighteenth century and that achieved worldwide fame during the nineteenth. The tools that survive—with the exception of those found in archaeological excavations—are of that period. Output in earlier centuries was clearly much more modest. The early history of toolmaking has not attracted much attention from historians, partly because the documentary evidence is about as thin as the material culture. But enough information survives to show that the metalworking districts in and around Birmingham and Sheffield had already gained a national reputation for some of their products by the sixteenth century and that they had already captured the market for certain tools. During the seventeenth century, they began to export some of these tools to America.

London was the ancient center of high-quality metalwares. It has been estimated that there were some ten thousand metalworkers in London in the late seventeenth century. London craftsmen specialized in finishing goods in gold, silver, pewter, copper, brass, tinplate, lead, iron, steel, and combinations of these metals. The city dominated national production in all the finished metal industries, except for goods made of iron and steel, where they faced fierce competition from Birmingham, Sheffield, and, in certain crafts, notably watch- and clockmaking, from southwest Lancashire.

By the mid-sixteenth century, the districts around Birmingham and Sheffield had already captured the national market in the production of agri- cultural edge tools and in the manufacture of cheaper knives and such low- skill goods as nails. In the late 1530s and early 1540s, John Leland toured England and Wales on behalf of King Henry VIII. When he came to Sheffield, he noted that "Ther be many smiths and cutlers" and "veri good smithes for all cuttinge tooles." He made similar comments about the Birmingham area.[1] These two districts had already triumphed over all their rivals and were selling their products in distant parts of the country. In both places, the local labor

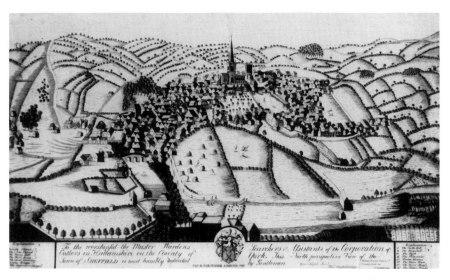

Fig. 1. Thomas Oughtibridge, *View of the Town of Sheffield,* ca. 1737. Taken from Pye Bank, on the northern side of the town, this view shows Sheffield as it was a few years after Defoe had found it "very populous and large," with a population of about 10,000. Courtesy, Sheffield City Libraries and Museums Services.

force had already acquired a tradition of craftsmanship. Making a steel-faced tool demanded high skills that were normally beyond the power of the common smith. The ability to weld steel onto iron to form an even cutting edge, and to work at speed, was a rare one, and the hardening, tempering, grinding, and polishing were fine arts. By the 1670s, the Sheffield district had at least six hundred smithies for the manufacture of knives, scissors, sickles, scythes,

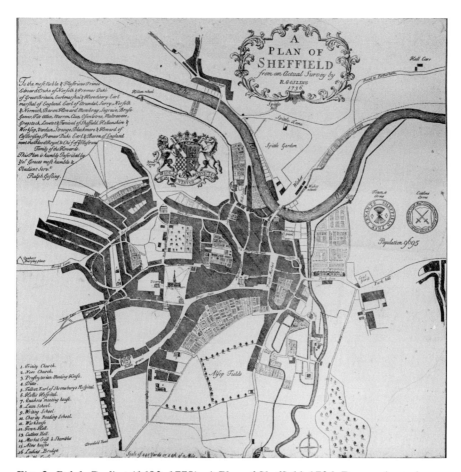

Fig. 2. Ralph Gosling (1693–1758), *A Plan of Sheffield*, 1736. Drawn about the same time as Oughtibridge's view, this is the earliest surviving map of Sheffield. The castle at the confluence of the Rivers Don and Sheaf had long since gone, but the medieval street pattern around the market place was intact. Sheffield was beginning to spread beyond its ancient limits to the northwest of the town, where numerous small workshops were built adjacent to domestic properties. Courtesy, Sheffield City Libraries and Museums Services.

files, awl blades, nails, and other metal goods.[2] When Daniel Defoe visited Sheffield about 1710–1712, he found that the town was "very populous and large, the streets narrow, and the houses dark and black, occasioned by the continued smoke of the forges, which are always at work."[3] A century earlier, in 1608, a noble courtier had written to the Earl of Shrewsbury to say that he was visiting Sheffield, where he expected to be "half-choked with town smoke."[4] Meanwhile, Birmingham and the neighboring district known as the Black Country were attracting similar comments.

Once Sheffield and Birmingham had acquired a tradition of skilled crafts-manship, it is easy to see how they grew to a position of supremacy, but it is more difficult to account for the establishment of metalworking crafts in the first place. These skills had been acquired so far back in time that they predate the surviving documentary evidence. The availability of local iron, and of coal to fuel the metalworkers' smithies, was obviously crucial to the development of metalworking in and around Birmingham and Sheffield, but this was not the reason why these places became the leading centers. By the sixteenth century, the local iron was considered to be of insufficient quality for making tools and knives with sharp cutting edges. By the 1530s, steel was being imported by sea and river hundreds of miles from Bilbao in northern Spain. In the seventeenth century, steel was imported down the Rhine from Germany, and toward the end of the century, bar iron for making steel came via the Baltic and North Seas from Sweden.[5]

What then were the compensating advantages that made it worthwhile and, indeed, commercially viable to import raw materials over such long distances to Sheffield and Birmingham? The principal advantage was that both districts had grinding facilities superior to those possessed by their rivals. In Sheffield, the local sandstones were ideal for making grindstones, and the local rivers and streams that fell quickly from the hills could be dammed at frequent inter-vals. By 1660, Sheffield's five rivers supported forty-one water mills; by 1740, the number had risen to ninety, two-thirds of which were used for grinding those cutting edges that gave Sheffield knives and tools a deserved reputation for quality.[6] No other place in England had such a concentration of water-powered sites.

The capturing of the national market by the Sheffield and Birmingham districts can be illustrated by the agricultural edge-tool industry. By the mid-sixteenth century, almost all the scythes that were manufactured in England

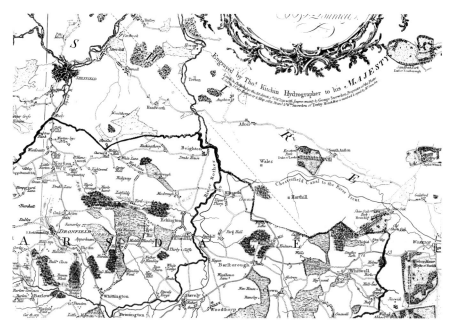

Fig. 3. Peter Burdett (d. 1793), *Map of Derbyshire,* rev. ed., 1791, detail. The parishes of Norton and Eckington, which lay immediately south of Sheffield, were ancient centers for the manufacture of scythes, sickles, axes, and hoes. These were hand forged, then ground to a cutting edge at water-powered grinding wheels on the local streams. Many of these products were exported to America. Courtesy, Sheffield City Libraries and Museums Services.

were made in a few parishes centered on Belbroughton, southwest of Birmingham, and in the parish of Norton, immediately south of Sheffield. These scythes were hand-forged, with the skilled scythesmith being assisted by a scythestriker. The Belbroughton scythemakers sold their wares through much of southern England. The Norton scythesmiths concentrated on markets in northern England and Lowland Scotland. The evidence comes mainly from probate inventories, that is, detailed lists of personal estates drawn up upon death and attached to wills. Thus, in 1541, John Waldern of Belbroughton had 650 scythes valued at 1s. 6d. each, and in 1574, Richard Urton of Norton had 1,200 scythes worth 1s. 7d. each. Transport costs and the middleman's profit inflated these prices by the time they reached the buyer. In the 1640s, Henry Best, who farmed an estate about fifty miles away from Norton, noted that his mowers "usually buy theire sythes att some faires here-aboutes, the price of a sythe is usually 2s.2d. or 2s.4d.; sometimes they may bee bought for 22d. [1s. 10d.] and sometimes againe they cannot bee bought for under 2s.6d."[7]

When William Blythe of Norton Lees died in 1632, he had 1,900 scythes recorded in his inventory. His son and namesake, who died in 1666, had more than 2,000 scythes. Some of these scythes were stored in warehouses in various market towns in northern England. The stock included a number of Scottish scythes. The Blythes were described as yeomen, i.e., superior farmers below the level of the gentry. They seem to have been acting as middlemen in the trade. The early export trade is not documented, but much later, in 1830, William Cobbett visited the parish of Norton and wrote that a "prodigious quantity" of scythes and sickles "go to the United States of America."[8] A striking

Fig. 4. This timber-framed building, which dates from ca. 1500–1550, was the home of the Blythe family who were middlemen in the scythe trade. William Blythe (d. 1632) and his son and namesake (d. 1666) each had about 2,000 scythes ready for sale when inventories of their personal estates were drawn up after their deaths. The building, which stood within the rural parish of Norton, is now a folk museum, Bishops' House, Sheffield. Courtesy, Sheffield City Libraries and Museums Services.

feature of the scythemaking and sicklemaking trades is the continuity of the same families in the trade over several generations. Some of the descendants of the men who were described as scythesmiths in the Norton parish register in the 1560s and 1570s were listed as scythemakers in Gales and Martin's Sheffield *Directory* of 1787, when the trade was still almost exclusively sited in the parish of Norton.

The scythesmiths, like most of the other rural metalworkers of the seventeenth and early eighteenth centuries, were part-time farmers. The scythesmiths were, in fact, the most prosperous of the rural craftsmen. In the late eighteenth century, hand-forging businesses began to be replaced by firms based at water-powered sites where not only grinding but steeling and plating could be performed. The best example is the Abbeydale Works of 1785, which later even cast its own steel. Cast, or crucible, steel had been invented in Sheffield by Benjamin Huntsman in 1742.

The nailmakers were one of the poorest groups. Nailmaking was an ancient rural craft that expanded rapidly in the seventeenth century with the introduction of water-powered slitting mills, which increased the supply of rod iron from which nails were made. Nailmaking was concentrated in the Black Country, south Yorkshire, and south Lancashire, and later in northeast England. The earliest nailmakers were part-timers who also had a small farm, but by the 1720s, the demand for nails was such that many nailers in the Black Country near Birmingham were working full time at their trade. Nails were collected by middlemen known as nailchapmen and sent down the navigable rivers—the Severn, the Trent, and the Mersey—to London, from where they were dispatched to all parts of the country and across the Atlantic. Thus, in 1739–1742 South Yorkshire nails were being sent to Philadelphia, Virginia, Jamaica, the Leeward Islands, and Newfoundland. We must not assume that all the workers were motivated to produce high-quality work. In 1742, a London merchant complained that many of the nails he had received were without heads, others were without points, and some had neither![9]

By the seventeenth century, 60 percent of Sheffield's workforce was employed in the metal trades, chiefly, of course, in the manufacture of knives and scissors. No other town in England at that time had such a specialized workforce.[10] One notable feature of the growth of the metal trades in the seventeenth and eighteenth centuries is the emergence of specialist crafts. We can trace how one of these toolmaking trades got started. In the middle years of

Fig. 5. The making of files became a specialist occupation in Sheffield in the mid-seventeenth century. During the following century it spread to the surrounding villages. The handle of the file cutter's hammer was fitted at an angle to the hammer head to allow a quick wristy action. The file was placed on a lead block during the cutting so that the underside would not be damaged. Courtesy, Sheffield City Libraries and Museums Services.

the seventeenth century, Sheffield had very few specialist filemakers. The three men who are described as filesmiths in the Sheffield marriage register during the 1650s are the first of that trade to be recorded. Cutlers used files continually, but until the middle of the seventeenth century, they probably had made their own stock. Thus, in 1616, Roger Barber, an Eckington cutler, had "4 fyles with some other small tools" valued at 2s.[11] During the later seventeenth century, the number of men who were specialist filemakers grew considerably. In 1682, twenty-one filesmiths were admitted as members of "The Corporation of Cutlers in Hallamshire," i.e., the Cutlers' Company, which had jurisdiction throughout the district around Sheffield. Filecutting must have started as a response to outside demand for its products. Sales were organized through London merchants. When Joseph Brammall, a Sheffield filesmith, died in 1698, he was clearly a small employer or middleman, for he had six hundred dozen files stored in several rooms. His debt book named eight London merchants. The trade continued to grow, so that between October 1, 1728, and September 30, 1733, the Sheffield baptism and burial register named 130 filesmiths, i.e., 6.5 percent of the recorded workforce of the parish. Nowhere else in the country did filemaking become established on such a scale. The earliest reference to a filecutter in the Birmingham district is from 1715.[12] Files are no longer made in Sheffield.

For most of the seventeenth century, the overseas export of Birmingham and Sheffield wares was controlled by London merchants. Tools bought in America that were said to be "from London" may therefore have been manufactured elsewhere. Thus, the Mr. William Sitwell of London whose successors Tappenden & Hanbey advertised "Hoes, Bills, Axes, & other Iron Work for the Plantations"[13] was a member of a family from Renishaw (Derbyshire) who was trading in goods manufactured in the rural area immediately south of Sheffield. During the eighteenth century, Birmingham and Sheffield men broke free from London control and set up as merchants themselves.

The documentary evidence for the manufacture and sale of woodworking tools is thinner than that for scythes or files or nails. There are no references before the middle years of the eighteenth century to specialist sawmakers, chisel makers, or planemakers in Sheffield, as there are to filemakers, scythemakers, sicklemakers, scissorsmiths, shearsmiths, and cutlers. Nor do any local probate inventories[14] list large numbers of chisels, saws, or plane irons. Perhaps the filemakers made such products as well as files, but the evidence is not there. London, of course, long remained a great manufacturing center and is known to have been a source of plane irons and other woodworking tools. Yet such tools were probably being made among the products of local forges near Birmingham and Sheffield. References to the "plating trade" in the Attercliffe Forge accounts in the 1690s may mean chisels, saws, and other tools.[15] Certainly, by the 1740s, Richard Dalton, a Sheffield merchant, was exporting chisels, gouges, awl blades, gimlets, corkscrews, punches, saws, hammers, and foot rules via Hull.[16]

The manufacture of axes, on the other hand, was a rural industry in the same district where scythes and sickles were made. When William Bullock, esquire, of Greenhill in the parish of Norton, died in 1667, the inventory of his possessions noted 199 dozen and 11 odd axes worth £100, 204 dozen of small hoes worth £40 16s., and 122 dozen and a half of larger hoes worth £50. One of his outbuildings was described as the "axhouse."[17] Had it not been for the survival of this document, we would have had little indication that such a business ever existed. William Turner of Mosborough in the neighboring parish of Eckington was described as an axsmith when he died in 1634. He had a medium-sized farm and a smithy, which contained bellows, stithies [anvils], hammers, and tongs, together with some grindstones, but his products were described only in general terms as "wrought and unwrought iron wares that is gone forth and at whome."[18] Between 1632 and 1715, a small number of fathers whose sons were apprenticed to local cutlers are described in the apprenticeship records of the Cutlers' Company as axsmiths; all six of them came from the rural district southeast of Sheffield. Otherwise, the only other known axsmith was Matthew Bird of Sheffield Park, who was buried at Sheffield in 1704. Clearly, the making of axes at this time was not a trade that expanded on the same scale as the making of files, scythes, sickles, or nails, but it was nevertheless a similar trade that depended on arduous hand forging.

The tools that were recorded in probate inventories of woodworkers up and down the country, such as millwrights, wheelwrights, carpenters, joiners, and coopers, were unfortunately rarely specified but were listed simply as "certain tools," "Working tools belonging to his trade," or "a Parcel of Carpenters tools." However, a few inventories are more informative about the finished goods and the types of wood that were being used. Thus, in 1725, John Whitham of Doncaster, a carpenter who was also a small farmer, had some deals [planks or boards of pine or firwood], tools, old wood, and two sash windows in his "Workhouse," a pair of gates, boards, and other wood on the "Back side," some laths and spokes, some ash wood in the lane, and some wood at the sawpit. Likewise, in 1737, the appraisers of the probate inventory of John Chatburn, a Sheffield joiner, listed tools and benches and some unfinished goods in his work chamber, and deals, boards, and planks in his "Wood Chamber," including some from Norway and some English oak and elm. Here we have pictures of typical small craftsmen of the type who were working at the same time in colonial Williamsburg.

The reference to John Whitham's sawpit raises the question of where saws were made and how they were sold to customers. London was an early center of saw manufacture. Odd saws were occasionally noted in the probate inventories of Sheffield cutlers. Thus, Roger Barber, the cutler whom I have already quoted, had a couple of saws in his smithy in 1616. But no specialist sawmakers are noted in Sheffield records until 1747 when Robert Marples baptized a son at Attercliffe. There is then a gap until 1764, when Humphrey Cook apprenticed his son to a local cutler. Another sawmaker, John Tibbits, did the same thing the following year. A few companies listed in the Sheffield directory of 1774 included saws among their products. By the time of the Gales and Martin *Directory* of 1787, ten sawmakers were in business; significantly, they were sited in the newer parts of the town.[19] However, much earlier, in 1594, a correspondent advised that an iron saw could be made locally from a pattern in wood, which he would send to Sheffield. Fortunately, we have the business letters of George Sitwell, a local ironmaster, from 1662 to 1666, which incidentally shed some light on the manufacture of saws at his forge at Pleasley

Fig. 6. Samuel Buck and Nathaniel Buck, *The East Prospect of Sheffield*, 1745, detail. Sheffield was largely rebuilt in brick in the eighteenth century. Samuel and Nathaniel Buckses' view shows a few substantial properties in High Street and many small houses, cottages, and workshops, or "smithies." Courtesy, Sheffield City Libraries and Museums Services.

and their sale via the river ports of Bawtry and Hull to a London merchant, including saws that were made specifically for Barbados. They came in various types—six-foot, seven-foot, cross cut, long, ordinary, peg, whip, and block—and were signed with the marks of their makers. Thus, in 1662, Sitwell sent "12 Dozen more saws whereof 7 Dozen were long saws, and 5 Dozen 6 foot saws." In 1663, he informed his London buyer that his clerk had sent three dozen long saws and three dozen ordinary saws, both marked F:F, and four dozen block saws and six dozen ordinary saws without marks. Sitwell was not above a bit of sharp practice. In 1664, he advised his servant in London that "John Searsey the sawmaker . . . saith he sent two Dozen of saws with the last parcell of myne . . . these are to be delivered to Thomas Cooper the Ironmonger in Woodstreet and he is to pay you for them, they are bound up with hay ropes, and sallow twiggs in the topp of them, if you finde them not readly any two Dozen will serve to deliver, there are more saws comeing."[20]

The correspondence also shows that makers' marks are not always to be trusted. In 1665, Sitwell wrote, "I will write to Mr Hoare to give Mr Haver notice of the saws, but I perceave they have tould you they are F:F: saws, though in truth they are not of Francis but Henry Slanys makeing soe that one may see the folly of men, however I wish as you doe that our Barbados Saws (which are most of this mans makeing) were sould att 40s per Dozen when I come to London."[21]

The story of the English toolmaking industry during the seventeenth and eighteenth centuries is, therefore, one of considerable expansion to meet the demands of the growing population of Britain and America and of increasing specialization in the Sheffield and Birmingham districts so that craftsmen were

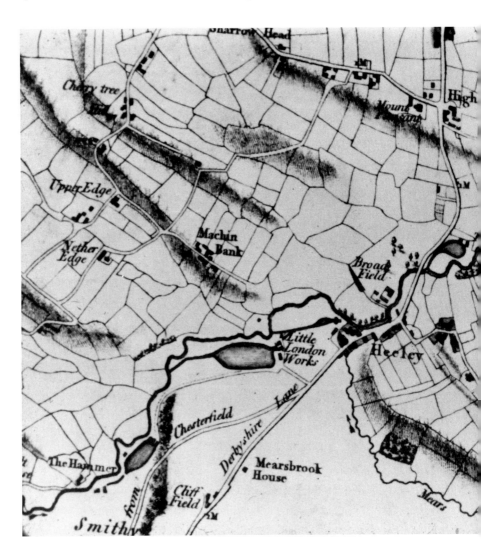

able to devote all their skills to the manufacture of certain tools. The evidence, both from the archives and the material culture, is much thinner than one would like, but perhaps enough survives to show that the districts that became world famous for their tools in the late eighteenth and nineteenth centuries had established their reputations in much earlier times. Long before the foundation of firms such as Law or Kenyon, whose products rightly take a proud place in American collections, the skills of the toolmakers had already been passed down over several generations. Of course, the scale of production was still modest compared with what was to come with the expansion of the industry in the late

eighteenth century. This is reflected in the increased number of tilts [a forge in which a powered, tilt hammer is used] and rolling mills on Sheffield's rivers and in the fact that Sheffield's population in 1736 was only 14,531, whereas in 1851 it had risen to 135,310. Nevertheless, by the end of the eighteenth century, the tools and other products of the districts around Sheffield and Birmingham had long been famous throughout Britain and had already been used by generations of Americans.

Fig. 7. William Fairbank (1730–1801), *Map of the Parish of Sheffield*, 1795, detail. The section of the River Sheaf shows how, by the late eighteenth century, numerous works had been erected along Sheffield's rivers in order to grind cutlery and tools or to forge and roll iron and steel. Some of these sites had been occupied since the Middle Ages, but their capacity had been lately much increased. Courtesy, Sheffield City Libraries and Museums Services.

1. L. T. Smith, ed., *Leland's Itinerary in England and Wales* (London, 1964), II, pp. 96–97, IV, p. 14.

2. David Hey, *The Rural Metalworkers of the Sheffield Region: A Study of Rural Industry Before the Industrial Revolution* (Leicester, Eng., 1972), pp. 10–13.

3. Daniel Defoe, *A Tour Through the Whole Island of Great Britain*, Everyman ed., II (London, 1962), p. 183.

4. Royal Commission on Historical Manuscripts, *A Calendar of the Shrewsbury and Talbot Papers*, II (London, 1971), p. 296.

5. David Hey, "The Origins and Early Growth of the Hallamshire Cutlery and Allied Trades," in John Chartres and David Hey, eds., *English Rural Society, 1500–1800: Essays in Honour of Joan Thirsk* (Cambridge, 1990), pp. 343–362.

6. David Hey, *The Fiery Blades of Hallamshire: Sheffield and Its Neighbourhood, 1660–1740* (Leicester, Eng., 1991), pp. 179–183.

7. Hey, "Origins and Early Growth," pp. 359–362, quotation on p. 361.

8. William Cobbett, *Rural Rides in the Southern, Western and Eastern Counties of England*, ed. G. D. H. Cole and Margaret Cole, II (London, 1930), p. 609.

9. Hey, *Rural Metalworkers*, pp. 31–48.

10. Hey, *Fiery Blades*, chap. 4.

11. Probate inventories, Lichfield Joint Record Office. The probate inventories (for Derbyshire and the Birmingham district) used in this study are housed there and at the Borthwick Institute of Historical Research, York (for Yorkshire).

12. Hey, *Fiery Blades*, pp. 118–122.

13. Tappenden & Hanbey trade card, 85.289, Heal Collection, British Museum.

14. See no. 11.

15. Staveley Iron records, Sheffield Archives.

16. Bagshawe 5/4/2, John Rylands Library, Manchester. I would like to thank Nevill Flavell for this reference.

17. Probate inventories, Lichfield Joint Rec. Ofc.

18. *Ibid.*

19. J. Sketchley, *Sheffield Directory* (Bristol, Eng., 1774); Gales and Martin, comps., *A Directory of Sheffield: Including the Manufactures of the Adjacent Villages* (Sheffield, Eng., 1787; reprint, New York, 1969).

20. P. Riden, ed., *George Sitwell's Letterbook, 1662–66*, Derbyshire Record Society, X (Chesterfield, Eng., 1985), p. 172.

21. *Ibid.*

Eighteenth-Century American Toolmaking

By Paul B. Kebabian

Most woodworking tools used in America during the colonial period were of British origin. I shall consider the reasons for that and describe how the tools used in America changed from imported to local production, a trend that was to lay the foundation for a flourishing American tool industry in the nineteenth century.

Freedom of worship was certainly a motivating force in some of the first voluntary emigration from England. The interest in promoting and establishing American colonies, or provinces, through the first two centuries of colonization, however, was more fundamentally a consequence of the economic policies espoused by England that are identified as mercantilism.[1] This economic philosophy drove the foreign commerce legislation that required colonial possessions—in terms of foreign trade and manufactures—to serve chiefly as suppliers of raw materials rather than as manufacturers of finished goods that would be in competition with production in the home country. Legislation of the British Parliament promoted mercantilism throughout the seventeenth and eighteenth centuries, though with varying effectiveness.[2] For example, as early as 1621, the Privy Council, the body with responsibility for supervising commerce and industry, ordered that all products exported by the Virginia colony were to unload only in England, thus attempting to eliminate export trade with Holland, France, and other nations, as well as with the West Indies.[3] But that effort failed. Only tobacco, the major export of Virginia for the colonial period, was effectively regulated by England's Navigation Acts. As an enumerated item, it had to be shipped to English ports before it could be reexported.

Economic motives for colonization also included the advantages of establishing a ready market for consumption of home manufactures, irrespective of the source of raw materials used; the opportunity to obtain products not readily available at home, such as naval stores of pitch and tar; and the opportunity to control the virtually limitless colonial timber resources, for even at the time, wood was already in short supply in England. It is noteworthy that the more populated coastal settlements of Massachusetts were denuded of salable timber so early that, in 1670, Plymouth colony passed legislation requiring the towns within the colony to share timber, and, in 1672, prohibited timber exports and sales outside the colony for seven years, except in sawn boards, shingles, clapboards, cooperage, etc.[4] The shift from yellow birch to beech for making carpenter's and joiner's planes that took place about 1800 was probably the result of depletion of the yellow birch. Beech had been largely ignored in the northern colonies for toolmaking until that time—though beech was used regularly by planemakers in the Middle Atlantic colonies during the eighteenth century.

Statistical data provide a picture of the country of origin of immigrants to the colonies in the colonial era. As late as 1790, the population of the colonies was still almost 79 percent English, Scottish, and Irish.[5] Such an ethnic distribution inevitably accounted for major influences on the design and technical characteristics of seventeenth- and eighteenth-century woodworking tools. English and Scottish tools were the most consistent prototypes simply because they were the tools that were brought to the colonies by British emigrant carpenters and other workers in wood, and because most toolmakers were of British descent (figs. 1 and 2). Similarly, emigration from the Palatinate to Pennsylvania resulted in Continental forms such as the so-called "goosewing" broad axes made by the Germans in Pennsylvania, horn planes, and planes with decoratively carved surfaces.

Fig. 1. Molding plane made by Thomas Granford, toolmaker of London, ca. 1703. OL: $10^5/_{16}$". Granford is considered one of the earliest English planemakers. He identified his tools by stamping his name, in full, on the toe of his planes. Author's collection.

Fig. 2. Colonial period American molding plane exhibiting the simplicity of line, a tall wedge for positioning the cutter iron, and generously wide chamfering of the upper edges of the stock very similar to English prototypes. This example was made by John Nicholson of Wrentham, Mass., in the second half of the eighteenth century. Author's collection.

Initially, mechanics and artisans, and settlers in general, of necessity brought tools with them. In the early years of colonization, promoters of emigration and writers offering works of travel and description took pains to emphasize the need for carrying both agricultural and woodworking tools when emigrating to America. The Virginia Company, in a broadside of 1622 addressed to prospective settlers, advised taking some thirty-one woodworking tools per family, including a pitsaw, billhooks, felling and broad axes, hand

THE INCONVENIENCIES

THAT HAVE HAPPENED TO SOME PER-
SONS WHICH HAVE TRANSPORTED THEMSELVES

from *England* to *Virginia*, vvithout prouifions neceffary to fuftaine themfelues, hath
greatly hindred the *Progreffe* of that noble *Plantation*: For preuention of the like diforders
heereafter, that no man fuffer, either through ignorance or mifinformation; it is thought re-
quifite to publifh this fhort declaration: wherein is contained a particular of fuch necef-
faries, as either priuate families or fingle perfons fhall haue caufe to furnifh themfelues with, for their better
fupport at their firft landing in Virginia, whereby alfo greater numbers may receiue in part,
directions how to prouide themfelues.

Apparrell.

		li.	s.	d.
	One Monmouth Cap———	oo	o1	10
	Three falling bands———	—	o1	o3
	Three fhirts———	—	o7	o6
	One wafte-coate———	—	o2	o2
	One fuite of Canuafe———	—	o7	o6
	One fuite of Frize———	—	10	oo
	One fuite of Cloth———	—	15	oo
	Three paire of Irifh ftockins———	—	o4	—
	Foure paire of fhooes———	—	o8	o8
Apparrell for one man, and fo after the rate for more.	One paire of garters———	—	oo	10
	One doozen of points———	—	oo	o3
	One paire of Canuafe fheets———	—	o8	oo
	Seuen ells of Canuafe, to make a bed and boulfter, to be filled in *Virginia* 8.s.			
	One Rug for a bed 8. s. which with the bed feruing for two men, halfe is———	o8	oo
	Fiue ells coorfe Canuafe, to make a bed at Sea for two men, to be filled with ftraw, iiij.s.			
	One coorfe Rug at Sea for two men, will coft vj. s. is for one———	o5	oo
		o4	oo	oo

Victuall.

		li.	s.	d.
	Eight bufhels of Meale———	o2	oo	oo
For a whole yeere for one man, and fo for more after the rate.	Two bufhels of peafe at 3.s.———	—	o6	oo
	Two bufhels of Oatemeale 4.s. 6.d.———	—	o9	oo
	One gallon of *Aquanitæ*———	—	o2	o6
	One gallon of Oyle———	—	o3	o6
	Two gallons of Vineger 1.s.———	—	o2	oo
		o3	o3	oo

Armes.

		li.	s.	d.
	One Armour compleat, light———	—	17	oo
For one man, but if halfe of your men haue armour is is fufficient fo that all haue Peeces and fwords.	One long Peece, fiue foot or fiue and a halfe, neere Musket bore———	o1	o2	—
	One fword———	—	o5	—
	One belt———	—	o1	—
	One bandaleere———	—	o1	o6
	Twenty pound of powder———	—	18	oo
	Sixty pound of fhot or lead, Piftoll and Goofe fhot———	—	o5	oo
		o3	o9	o6

Tooles.

		li.	s.	d.
	Fiue broad howes at 2.s. a piece———	—	10	—
	Fiue narrow howes at 16.d. a piece———	—	o6	c8
	Two broad Axes at 3.s. 8.d. a piece———	—	o7	t4
	Fiue felling Axes at 18.d. a piece———	—	o7	o6
	Two fteele hand fawes at 16.d. a piece———	—	o2	o8
	Two two-hand fawes at 5. s. a piece———	—	10	—
	One whip-faw, fet and filed with box, file, and wreft———	—	10	—
	Two hammers 12.d. a piece———	—	o2	oo
For a family of 6. perfons and fo after the rate for more.	Three fhouls 18.d. a piece———	—	o4	o6
	Two fpades at 18.d. a piece———	—	o3	—
	Two augers 6.d. a piece———	—	o1	oo
	Sixe chiffels 6.d. a piece———	—	o3	oo
	Two percers ftocked 4.d. a piece———	—	oo	c8
	Three gimlets 2.d. a piece———	—	oo	o6
	Two hatchets 21.d. a piece———	—	o3	o6
	Two froues to cleaue pale 18.d.———	—	o3	oo
	Two hand bills 20. a piece———	—	o3	o4
	One grindleftone 4.s.———	—	o4	oo
	Nailes of all forts to the value of———	o2	oo	—
	Two Pickaxes———	—	o3	—
		c6	c2	c8

Houfhold Implements.

		li.	s.	d.
	One Iron Pot———	—	o7	—
	One kettle———	—	o6	—
For a family of 6. perfons, and fo for more or leffe after the rate.	One large frying-pan———	—	o2	o6
	One gridiron———	—	o1	o6
	Two skillets———	—	o5	—
	One fpit———	—	o2	—
	Platters, difhes, fpoones of wood———	—	o4	—
		o1	o8	oo

For Suger, Spice, and fruit, and at Sea for 6 men--- | oo | 12 | o6 |

So the full charge of Apparrell, Victuall, Armes, Tooles,
and houfhold ftuffe, and after this rate for each perfon,
will amount vnto about the fumme of——— | 12 | 10 | — |

The paffage of each man is——— | o6 | oo | — |

The fraight of thefe prouifions for a man, will bee about
halfe a Tun, which is——— | o1 | 10 | — |

So the whole charge will amount to about——— | 20 | oo | oo |

*Nets, hookes, lines, and a tent muft be added, if the number of people be grea-
ter, as alfo fome kine.*

*And this is the vfuall proportion that the Virginia Company doe
beftow vpon their Tenants which they fend.*

Whofoeuer tranfports himfelfe or any other at his owne charge vnto *Virginia*, fhall for each perfon fo tranfported before Midfummer 1625.
haue to him and his heires for euer fifty Acres of Land vpon a firft, and fifty Acres vpon a fecond diuifion.

Imprinted at London by FELIX KYNGSTON. 1622.

Fig. 3. This broadside was distributed by the Virginia Company in 1622.
Courtesy, The John Carter Brown Library at Brown University, Providence, R. I.

saws, hammers and nails, augers, chisels, bit stocks, and gimlets (fig. 3).[6] William Wood, publishing twelve years later following a four-year stay in America, also emphasized the need for those emigrating to take agricultural and woodworking tools, even though "all these," he said, "be made in the Country: (there being divers Blacke-smiths)."[7]

At an early date, both the British promoters of colonization and the colonists themselves, through bounties, grants of land, and patents for exclusive manufacturing rights, attempted to introduce the production of raw materials and manufactures. In 1619, the Virginia Company sent 150 men from Warwickshire, Staffordshire, and Essex to the colony to establish an ironworks. The works was completed, only to be destroyed in 1622 in the course of an Indian uprising against the Virginia colonists.[8] The first ironworks in Massachusetts was established in 1643 at Lynn, on the west bank of the Saugus River. This works comprised a furnace, forge, and slitting mill. The Massachusetts General Court granted John Winthrop, Jr., permission to establish a forge at Braintree the following year.[9] It was from such sources, as well as by importing English and Swedish iron from England, that blacksmiths obtained material for the manufacture of tools, implements, and hardware.

Published and archival sources contain frequent references to the seventeenth-century production of iron; they have less to say, however, about the production of tools. But we have good evidence of the possession of tools in many households. Eleven estate inventories from the Plymouth plantation from the very early years—1620, 1631, and 1633—list 129 tools in addition to carpenter Eaton's "toole box."[10] The 1649 estate inventory of Governor John Winthrop of Massachusetts included items such as three joiner's saw plates, two cooper's drawing knives, three braces, one dozen chalk lines, a saw, axes, adzes, awls, files, chisels, a vise, hammer, shears, a grafting saw, two breast wimbles, an iron square, a compass, pincers, and small bits. Strangely absent is the mention of any planes.[11]

Massachusetts records pertaining to Joseph Jenks are almost exceptional in referring to tool "manufacturing" in the current sense of the word. On May 6, 1646, the General Court granted Jenks, "considering ye necessity of raising such manufactures of engins of mils to go by water, for speedy dispatch of much worke with few hands," a fourteen-year patent for use of his new invention. These mills were to be used for the manufacture of "sithes & other edged tooles."[12]

The craftsman's sources for tools in the seventeenth century and into the eighteenth were limited. Imported or locally made tools of his trade might have been available for purchase, or he might have had to make his own. Colonial population centers at this time were concentrated largely in eastern seacoast towns. The in-town craftsman, by the eighteenth century, would have had the opportunity to purchase tools from shops; these tools would have been imported and chiefly of English origin, or made in town by toolmakers and blacksmiths. There was a strong and persistent bias in favor of the imported English tool—well-crafted and made with quality materials and workmanship. It was not until the mid- to late nineteenth century that American saws, for instance, could compete with English imports (in 1830 the total value of American saws manufactured was reported as $5,000; thirty years later, it had grown to $1,237,000).[13] By the third quarter of the nineteenth century, the American woodworking hand tool industry was well established, and its products were outselling foreign imports (fig. 4).

The rural woodworker's source for wooden tools might have been his own handcraftsmanship. If iron parts were required, he might have made them on his own forge (the forge was a common adjunct of a great many farms), or he could have obtained the parts from the local blacksmith. His needs were more likely to be tools for carpentry than for cabinetmaking, and the local black-

Fig. 4. A factory-made plow plane of the Greenfield Tool Co. of Greenfield, Mass., 1851–1883. Fine workmanship, together with the use of rosewood, boxwood, and ivory, contributed to the production of a superior tool. Author's collection.

Fig. 5.
The "Yankee" or
"New England"
felling ax, of which
pre-Revolutionary
examples have been
unearthed,
concentrated
weight in a heavy,
wide poll above the
helve. Author's
collection.

smith could have provided the heavier iron- and steel-based items, such as hammers, axes, and hatchets. In 1731, Governor William Gooch of Virginia informed the Board of Trade in London that the people of New England made "Hoes, Axes, and other Utensils" in their own ironworks.[14]

If it was a question of innovation versus tradition in American toolmaking, certainly tradition won out; innovation was apparently minimal, to judge from the surviving implements. The English woodworking tool persisted as the model for the colonial example through the eighteenth century; it was not until the age of invention during the nineteenth century that patents by the thousands introduced improvements in the design and function of American hand tools, many calling for changes in manufacturing materials. But there were exceptions in the eighteenth century: for example, the American, "Yankee," or New England-style felling ax. This heavy-polled, short-bitted American ax was substantially different from the English and Continental long-bitted felling ax (fig. 5). An illustrated advertisement for the tool appeared in a 1789 Philadelphia newspaper, and examples have been recovered from Revolutionary War sites, which would place the introduction of the tool in the latter part of the eighteenth century. William Douglas, writing in 1760 on the British settlements in North America, commented that "*New-England* perhaps excells in good Ax-Men for felling of Trees, and squaring of Timber."[15] This observation may well have been prompted by observing a new and better tool in the hands of the woodsmen.

Fig. 6. Early eighteenth-century plow planes made by London planemakers Robert Wooding (*top*) and Thomas Phillipson. Author's collection.

Another American innovation was a minor modification of the plow plane. The arms of plow planes of the first English planemakers were probably force-fitted, and subsequently positioned by "keys," or wedges (fig. 6), while the early American tool was conventionally provided with wooden thumbscrew-secured sliding arms (fig. 7). The tool cognoscenti of today have dubbed this style of plow the "Yankee plow."

By contrast with Governor Gooch's comments on New England toolmaking, James Blair, president of the Virginia Council, stated in 1768 that the colonists did "not make a saw, auger, gimlett, file, or nails, iron [or] steel; and most tools in the Country are imported from Britain."[16] Blair may have thought that he was speaking for all the colonies, but we must presume that this observation stemmed from a provincial point of view. Virginia was typical of colonies growing a single cash crop: it was almost totally dependent on the sale of its tobacco in England and relied on the importation of English manufactured goods purchased with the credit tobacco sales earned. Robert Beverley, whose history of Virginia was published in the first quarter of the eighteenth century, described himself as a "Native and Inhabitant of the Place." His presumably realistic images of the colony may be somewhat exaggerated, but they describe well the "colonial" character of the Virginia economy. A chief complaint of Beverley is that the inhabitants produced nothing (other than tobacco) and purchased or traded for their wooden wares, furniture, cabinets, cart wheels, and other necessities that were imported from England—"to the Eternal Reproach of their Laziness." Beverley's closing comment in his book is: "I should be ashamed to publish this slothful Indolence of my Countrymen, but that I hope it will some time or other rouse them out of their Lethargy."[17]

Evidence of tools being made in quantities representing factory production is meager, but blacksmith-toolmakers were to be found in any community where there was sufficient custom to support the trade. Amos Crippen, born in

Fig. 7. Plow planes of Francis Nicholson of Wrentham, Mass., and John Lindenberger of Providence, R. I. Author's collection.

1778 and working in Pittsford, Vermont, was typical. Pittsford was in 1800 a town of 1,400 people. Crippen's daybook for 1803–1805 reveals him making large and small iron pots and a bake pan, for example. He made files, axes, scythes, door latches and hinges, a broad ax for 18s., chains, chisels, a hay knife, and two axes of what he considered higher than average quality that he noted as "warranted" and sold for £1 1s. These tool products were in addition to the day-to-day tasks of welding chain, shoeing horses, repairing ironwork of carriages and wagons, and quite possibly carrying on a second occupation of farmer.[18]

We do know some facts about small-scale manufacturing of tools for sale when considering woodworking planes. This is because American planemakers, starting in the eighteenth century, followed the tradition of English makers in stamping their names and often their town place names on their tools (fig. 8). Research on Francis and John Nicholson, Cesar Chelor, and other eighteenth-century planemakers has contributed greatly to our knowledge of these pioneer manufacturers.

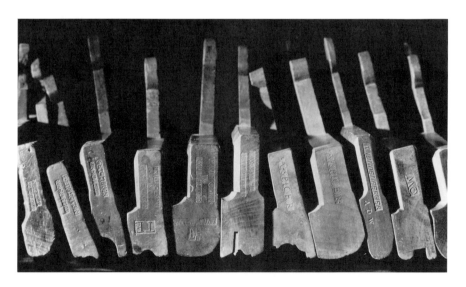

Fig. 8. Individual makers' marks clearly stamped on the fore ends of this group of eighteenth-century molding planes. The makers include Thomas Granford, Francis Nicholson, Cesar Chelor, John Nicholson, A. Smith, A. Spicer, and John Lindenberger. Author's collection.

Newspaper advertisements provide a good source for information on tool-making, distribution, and marketing. Newspapers in the colonies appeared sporadically following the publication of the first successful weekly, *The Boston News-Letter*, in 1704. But by the 1730s, there were ongoing newspapers in Philadelphia, New York, Newport, and Williamsburg. One of the first tool advertisements appeared in the *Boston News-Letter* of February 11/18, 1711/12, offering a warehouse sale of hammers, steel handsaws, and cooper's and joiner's tools, all from London. A reading of a number of these advertisements suggests that the tools typically imported from England were carpenter's and joiner's planes, squares, chisels, drawing knives, files, silversmith's tools, and similar items of moderate shipping weight, and perhaps of more refined manufacture, while the advertisements of the local toolmakers suggest they concentrated on heavier items such as axes and other edge tools, vises, and so forth. On March 4/11, 1716/17 Samuel Bissel, "anvil smith," also placed his advertisement in the *Boston News-Letter* for his manufacture of blacksmith's and goldsmith's anvils, and for bick irons and stakes.

The Pennsylvania Chronicle of September 12, 1734, carried an extensive advertisement of a new Trenton, New Jersey, "Plating and Blade Mill" established by Isaac Harrow, who was manufacturing a broad line of products including many tools: scythes, mill saws, broad axes, handsaws, and cooper's tools. Harrow also manufactured a number of household iron items including pots and pans, the whole being sold, he stated, "at reasonable Rates as any that come from England."

"Just arrived from England" was the self-styled description of William Jasper himself, rather than his wares, when he advertised in 1763 in New York. Jasper announced that he was making a variety of tools, including all kinds of edge tools (which he also ground sharp for customers), saddler's tools, fretsaws, and "likewise draws Teeth with great Ease and Safety, being accustomed to it for many Years." His triple vocation of cutler, toolmaker-tool dealer, and dentist all presumably took place at his business location, which he carefully identified as being in New York, near the Fly, Queen-Street, near the Burling's and Beekman's Slip, next door to Mr. Murray's.[19]

Another category of toolmaker in the eighteenth century was the mathematical instrument maker, capable of constructing sophisticated surveyor's compasses, levels, rules, and a variety of measuring devices. In 1754, James Ham of New York placed an advertisement stating that he made and sold mathematical instruments in wood, brass, or ivory, and that his line included sectors, parallel rulers, plain scales and dividers, gauging rods, bevels, and sliding Gunter's scales.[20]

One can readily see from these advertisements that the colonists were making tools throughout the eighteenth century. But at the same time, the importation and sale of woodworking tools from England did not, apparently, decrease measurably. The establishment of forges and rolling and slitting mills proceeded at an ever-increasing pace, in spite of the resistance of England. The English-appointed governors tended to ignore as not enforceable mercantilist laws such as those relating to the iron industry. The British Board of Trade in 1738 requested that the colonial governors report on colonial trade, manufactures, and commodities. The governor of New York responded only that there were iron and lead mines, "the manufacturing of which have been proposed and the raising of hemp likewise." Reports of 1746 and 1749 contained identical statements.[21] In 1767, Governor Moore reported one manufactory of linen in New York, and that a little foundry had been set up near the city to make small pots, "as yet very inconsiderable."[22] The governors were obviously not reporting what they knew the Board of Trade did not wish to hear.

For the American colonies, the mercantilist system persisted up to the time of the Revolution. A late key example was the Trade and Navigation Act of 1750, the "Iron Act." By its terms, pig iron and bars made in the colonies were permitted to enter England duty free. The following were prohibited: the erection of new rolling and slitting mills and plating forges; the manufacture of hardware; and the export of iron beyond the empire. Its provisions evidently were in large measure ignored.

With the Revolution came a great increase in American manufactures. The Peter Force *American Archives* that document the period of the American Revolution provide valuable insights into the requirements of the Continental Army for tools, especially axes and entrenching tools.[23] Between July 13 and August 12, 1776—less than thirty days—more than 2,200 axes, as well as spades, pickaxes, and some broad axes, were sent to the concentration of soldiers at Forts Ticonderoga and Crown Point. The axes included 1,000 sent from Connecticut that Governor Trumbull noted were ground sharp and with helves.[24] Though some portion of these may have been tools originally imported from

England, both the volume of the shipments and the correspondence concerning the delivery of the tools suggest that many, if not all, were of colonial manufacture.

In 1789, following the establishment of the new constitutional government of the United States, a *Memorial on Manufactures* was addressed to the president and transmitted to the House of Representatives by the tradesmen and mechanics of Baltimore. They requested the imposition of protective import duties to reduce the availability of foreign products and to encourage local manufactures. Appended was a lengthy list of items for which protection was asked, including many woodworking hand tools.[25] Also in 1789, a similar *Memorial*—one of many to be sent forward in the coming years—was submitted on behalf of the mechanics and manufacturers of New York City.[26] These documents confirm the increases in scale of manufacturing that were taking place. The manufacture of woodworking tools in quantity did not take place until after 1800, however; it did not challenge—and ultimately surpass—British and European Continental tool industry exports to this country until several decades into the nineteenth century.

1. Victor S. Clark, *History of Manufactures in the United States*. I: *1607–1860* (New York, 1929; reprint, New York, 1949), pp. 9–12, 14–16.

2. *Ibid.*, p. 25.

3. Great Britain, *Calendar of State Papers, America and West Indies, 1554–1660,* XXVI, Oct. 24, 1621, *ibid.*, p. 12.

4. *The Compact with the Charter and Laws of the Colony of New Plymouth* (Boston, 1836), pp. 164–165.

5. U. S. Bureau of the Census, *Historical Statistics of the United States, Colonial Times to 1970*, Pt. 2 (Washington, D. C., 1975), Series Z 1–19, p. 1168; Series ZZ 20–23, p. 1168.

6. *The Inconveniencies that have happened to some persons which have transported themselves from England to Virginia . . .* (London, 1622).

7. William Wood, *New Englands Prospect* (London, 1634; reprint, New York, 1968), p. 52.

8. J. Leander Bishop, *A History of American Manufactures from 1608 to 1860*, 3rd ed., I (Philadelphia, 1868; reprint, New York, 1967), pp. 468–469.

9. A. B. Forbes, ed., John Winthrop, *Winthrop Papers* (Boston, 1929–1947), IV, *1630–1644*, pp. 465–466; Clark, *History of Manufactures*, I, p. 170.

10. Plymouth Inventories. Lists prepared by Plimouth Plantation for a meeting of the Early American Industries Association, May 1970.

11. Forbes, ed., *Winthrop Papers*, V, *1645–1649*, pp. 333–336.

12. Nathaniel B. Shurtleff, ed., *Records of the Governor and Company of the Massachusetts Bay in New England*, II, *1642–1649* (Boston, 1853–1854), p. 149.

13. U. S. Census Office, 8th Census, 1860, *Manufactures of the United States in 1860* (Washington, D. C., 1865), p. cxciv.

14. Gov. William Gooch to the Board of Trade, Dec. 22, 1731, C.O. 5/1322, fols. 219–221.

15. William Douglass, *A Summary, Historical and Political, Of the first Planting, progressive Improvements, and present State of the British Settlements in North-America*, II (Boston, 1753), p. 52.

16. James Blair to [?], 1768, King's MS 206, British Museum, quoted in Harold B. Gill, Jr., "The Blacksmith in Colonial Virginia," research report, 1965, Colonial Williamsburg Foundation, p. 101.

17. [Robert Beverley], *The History of Virginia . . . by a Native and Inhabitant of the Place*, 2nd ed. (London, 1722), pp. 255–256, 284.

18. Account book of Amos Crippen, Apr. 12, 1802, to May 17, 1810, Collection of the Vermont Historical Society, Montpelier, Vt.

19. Rita Susswein Gottesman, comp., *The Arts and Crafts in New York, 1726–1776: Advertisements and News Items from New York City Newspapers* (New York, 1938; reprint, New York, 1970), p. 200.

20. *Ibid.*, p. 307.

21. E. B. O'Callaghan and Berthold Fernow, eds., *Documents Relative to the Colonial History of the State of New York* (Albany, N. Y., 1853–1887), VI, pp. 127, 393, 511.

22. *Ibid.*, VII, p. 888.

23. Peter Force, comp., *American Archives . . .* , 5th Ser., I (Washington, D. C., 1848), columns 207, 679, 717.

24. *Ibid.*, columns 776, 924, 925.

25. *American State Papers. Documents Legislative and Executive, of the Congress of the United States . . . March 3, 1789, and ending March 3, 1815*, V, Class III. Finance, I, pp. [5]ff.

26. *Ibid.*, p. 9.

Tools for Sale

The Marketing and Distribution of English Woodworking Tools in England and America

By Nancy L. Hagedorn

In today's high-tech, media-oriented society, where we are bombarded daily, hourly—even "minute-ly"—by the seductive ploys of Madison Avenue, few would even consider the possibility that any business or industry could survive, let alone succeed, without effective advertising. High-speed, widespread distribution networks and targeting specific markets are taken for granted and have become almost second nature. What may not be obvious from our vantage point, however, is the importance of marketing and distribution before the age of telephones, television, radio, computers, airplanes, supertankers, super highways, semitrailer trucks, railways, or even canals.[1]

The English tool industry was well established by the mid-eighteenth century and produced an immense array of excellent tools that were readily available to woodworkers in both Britain and her colonies. One important factor in the success of the English tool industry was the marketing system by which its wares were distributed.

By 1750, wholesalers in London, Bristol, and other commercial centers distributed London, Birmingham, Lancashire, and Sheffield products to retailers throughout Britain. One observer noted in 1747 that though the number of wholesale warehouses was relatively small, "almost all of them carry on a very extensive Trade, and are reputed wealthy. It is not easy to conceive, much less to describe, the numerous Articles that pass through their Hands."[2] Many British tool manufacturers and merchants also depended upon overseas sales. London, Bristol, Liverpool, Whitehaven, and Glasgow thrived on international trade, and large quantities of all types of British manufactured goods, including tools, passed through these ports bound for the Continent, Africa, the West Indies, and America.

By the time of the American Revolution, some British manufacturers were heavily dependent on the American trade and feared the economic and social consequences of its threatened interruption. On January 27, 1775, 160 "respectable Merchants and Master Manufacturers, All of whom are immediately interested in the Trade" from the Birmingham region to North America, petitioned the House of Commons about their "uneasy apprehensions" regarding the state of trade to North America. The demand from North America for Birmingham manufactures had very considerably increased during recent years, and many thousands of people found regular employment in making various

Fig. 1. Eighteenth- and early nineteenth-century mortise chisel blades with makers' marks. CWF 1990-238; 1989-284; G1986-268, 68, gift of Frank M. Smith; 1989-267; 1990-239.

Fig. 2. Pliers, tail
vise, hand vise,
dividers, nippers,
and screw plate
by Peter Stubs of
Warrington.
Tail vise, dividers,
and screw plate:
CWF 1990-108;
1985-179;
1953-743. Other
items, courtesy,
private collection.

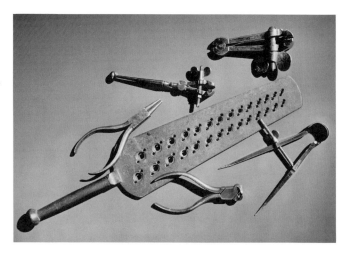

Fig. 2. Pliers, tail vise, hand vise, dividers, nippers, and screw plate by Peter Stubs of Warrington. Tail vise, dividers, and screw plate: CWF 1990-108; 1985-179; 1953-743. Other items, courtesy, private collection.

kinds of goods, including tools, that were exported to the colonies. The concerned citizens noted that the "present stagnation" of their commerce with that country was "already very materially felt," and they feared "that in a short space of time a very numerous body of working people [would] be deprived of the means of subsistence" if the situation did not improve. They trusted the "Honourable House to take their Case into consideration, and grant them such relief" as they judged necessary.[3] Other manufacturing centers no doubt felt similar apprehensions as the clouds of war gathered on the horizon.

English toolmakers and tool merchants employed surprisingly modern techniques to sell their wares both at home and abroad. To build "brand name" recognition, many makers stamped their names on the tools they made and sold (fig. 1). Some makers' names became so well known that the rights to use their marks were sold or passed on to successors and remained in use into the mid-nineteenth century, which makes dating tools bearing those marks extremely difficult. To make matters worse, the names appearing on tools often are those of manufacturers, retailers, or dealers who bought the tools from subcontractors to sell, but did not actually make them. Peter Stubs of Warrington in Lancashire, the well-known maker of watch- and clockmaking tools, for example, purchased many of the tools he sold from "country hands" who contracted to make files and other tools to his specifications. Roughly one-third of the saw files Stubs sold, as well as all of the dividers, vises, and specialized horological tools in his inventory, were made outside of his own shop (fig. 2).[4]

In 1805, he employed twenty-five outside file cutters, fifteen of whom apparently worked exclusively for him.[5] The files bore his name—and reputation for quality—when sold. Each file also bore a letter or numeral identifying the actual subcontractor who made it. Some of these files, notably those marked T in the early nineteenth century (made by Samuel Timmins of Birmingham) acquired a reputation of their own for exceptional quality.[6]

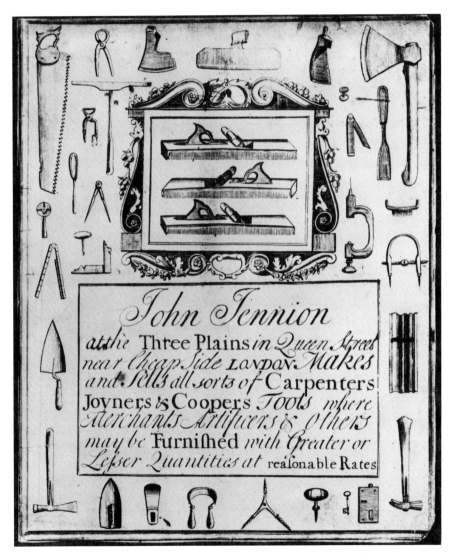

Fig. 3. Trade card of London planemaker John Jennion, ca. 1740. Heal Collection, 118.8. Courtesy, Trustees of the British Museum.

Some toolmakers who operated retail shops specialized in the production of one kind of tool and bought other types to increase the range of wares they offered. John Jennion, a London planemaker, probably specialized in making only the planes and some of the wooden components of the tools depicted on his trade card (fig. 3). In order to appeal to a broader market, he bought the other tools from makers who specialized in their production. Only planes, which were made in his own shop (though not necessarily by him), are known to bear his name. Another London planemaker, George Mutter, put his own name on at least some of the products that he obtained from other specialists for resale, such as a set of eight drill bits that probably were made in Birmingham or Sheffield and that currently are included in Colonial Williamsburg's collection. Christopher Gabriel and Sons, prominent tool dealers and planemakers in London, also bought a variety of products to resell in their shop, and some of them undoubtedly were marked with the Gabriels' name before they were sold.

Many other eighteenth-century marketing techniques were similar to those employed today. Traveling salesmen, or "outriders," representing toolmakers visited prospective customers to show them samples, encourage orders, and collect payments. Toolmakers and merchants handed out illustrated trade cards bearing their names and lists of their wares. Newspaper advertisements announced the availability, quality, and variety of tools for sale. Appealing window displays attracted the casual passerby. City directories listed toolmakers and dealers by name, trade, and location to inform prospective buyers from afar.

Toolmakers produced some of the earliest known English illustrated catalogs. They included engravings of tools and indicated the range of sizes and qualities available. John Wyke, a Lancashire watch- and clock-tool manufacturer, issued the first such catalog in the late 1750s.[7] It contained only the goods sold by his own firm. Later catalogs of Birmingham and Sheffield wares could be used by any manufacturer or wholesaler with the addition of an appropriate price list.

English toolmakers produced not only a vast array of tool types, but offered them in a variety of designs, sizes, and qualities to suit the needs, tastes, and pocketbooks of their customers. Birmingham pliers could be had "black" (unpolished) or finished to a "bright" surface at a higher price. A woodworker buying a chisel could choose between an ordinary one or one that was "best"

Fig. 4. Two gouges and a chisel by Thomas Newbould of Sheffield, marked BEST (ca. 1773). CWF 1957-123, A7-A9.

Fig. 5. Detail of three backsaws showing makers' marks (1790–1820). The saw marks also indicate the type of steel used: spring steel, German steel, or cast steel. CWF 1991-460; 1990-257; 1990-182.

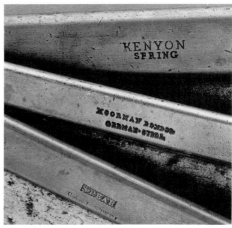

(fig. 4). Retailers offered saws made of different quality steels at a range of prices. Late in the century, handsaws and backsaws sold in London, for example, were priced according to their materials and makers. During the 1790s, the Gabriels' stock inventories listed fourteen-inch sash saws that varied in value from 4s. to 10s., depending on whether they were "common" (probably country made and iron backed), "Kenyon" (made by a well-known Sheffield artisan) and iron backed, "Town" (London made) and iron backed, or "Town" brass backed (fig. 5).[8] Some tools like folding rules came in a truly staggering range of types. John Shaw and Sons of Birmingham had in stock more than ninety different types of wooden and ivory rules in 1805.[9]

Toolmakers and dealers sought to market their wares to general customers as well as to professionals, so catalogs offered special tools for "ladies" and "gentlemen." "Gentlemen's Tool Chests," the eighteenth-century equivalent of a modern handyman's tool set, were sold to homeowners, shopkeepers, and hobbyists. These kits were packaged in wooden chests available in several sizes. They contained anywhere from fifteen to seventy-five tools, plus an assortment of nails, screws, and other hardware. The smallest cost about £1 and the most elaborate about £9 at a time when a London journeyman cabinetmaker could expect to earn one to two shillings a week.[10]

Two gentlemen's tool chests sold by London ironmonger William Hewlett survive in Colonial Williamsburg's collection (fig. 6). One, purchased by an unknown customer on February 13, 1773, is constructed like a fashionable piece of London furniture and is covered with mahogany veneer. Of the fifty-six tools originally sold with the chest, twenty-two remain. They illustrate the widespread distribution network then in place, since they represent the work of toolmakers in London, Lancashire, Birmingham, and Sheffield. Hewlett

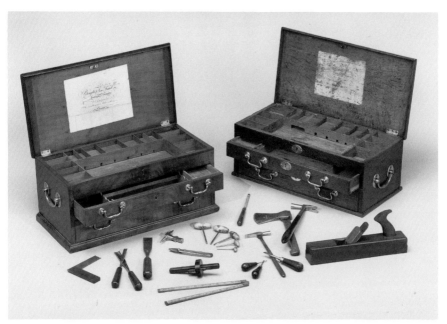

Fig. 6. Two gentlemen's tool chests sold by London ironmonger William Hewlett, one of mahogany (*left*) and the other of oak. The tools shown have survived with the mahogany chest. CWF 1957-123; 1986-247.

sold the second chest at a slightly later date. Its basic design is similar to that of the first chest with nearly identical partitions and compartments. The second chest, however, is made of oak and was constructed using simpler joinery. No tools remain with this chest; its contents undoubtedly were of similar types and origins as those in the mahogany chest, though probably cheaper and of lesser quality. The oak chest probably sold for about 15 percent less than the mahogany one. Even gentlemen apparently had pockets of varying depths.

In America, retail establishments were the most important sources for imported tools throughout the eighteenth century. Many stores carried tools among their general merchandise, while other retailers, particularly those in urban areas, were more specialized. In the South, stores developed somewhat more slowly than in the New England and Middle Atlantic colonies, largely because of the nature of that region's economy and settlement. The southern colonies relied almost entirely on the production and export of staple cash crops such as tobacco and rice. In return, colonists received credit with which they could buy British goods. This cash crop economy, coupled with the relatively slow development of towns and sizable local markets, encouraged southerners to import the vast majority of their small manufactured goods from England throughout the eighteenth century.

Although we know from sources like the Virginia Company's 1622 broadside (see p. 26) and various supply lists that woodworking and agricultural tools figured prominently among the goods sent to Virginia's earliest settlers, the documentary record regarding woodworking tools in early Virginia is relatively sparse until the third quarter of the seventeenth century, when surviving estate inventories begin to list the tools owned by planters and artisans. These inventories reveal that by the 1670s Virginians apparently had ready access to a selection of carpentry and cooperng tools. Although professional carpenters, wheelwrights, and boatbuilders were working in Virginia, they were few in number, and little is known about them or their tools. The tools that appear most commonly in late seventeenth-century records are general-purpose types.

Virginia's economy and society had begun to mature by the turn of the eighteenth century. Population increased, and new towns were established. The demand for houses, mills, vehicles, and furniture—all built of wood—rose. The resulting growth in trades led to a need for more tools, which was met by greater importations of English implements. Most were obtained through wealthy planters who shipped their tobacco directly to agents in England on consignment and imported tools and other goods into Virginia with the credit earned. By at least 1709, this system had ensured that most basic woodworking tools were readily available at short notice to Virginia craftsmen. In May of that year, the York County Court ordered the master of Thomas Ravenscroft to abide by their apprenticeship agreement and provide him with a set of tools worth £5 *within ten days.*[11]

As settlement spread west from the Virginia Tidewater, a system of stores developed. In the 1730s, Scottish merchants sent agents, called "factors," to Virginia to purchase tobacco locally and ship it to Glasgow, which saved small planters the expense and risk of shipping it on consignment. As business grew, many factors found it profitable to set up permanent stores where they purchased the tobacco and sold a wide variety of goods, often on credit. In addition to an impressive array of foodstuffs, fabrics, clothing accessories, and housewares, these stores carried hardware and tools, sometimes in astonishing varieties and quantities. The Scots were so successful that many English merchants followed suit. Some opened stores of their own, while others went into the wholesale business or cargo trade, supplying the vast quantities of goods required by retail stores. By the 1760s, these stores became the principal source of imported tools for many Virginians.

Most rural Virginia storekeepers stocked a basic assortment of imported tools, and local woodworkers could obtain hammers, saws, chisels, planes, and other common tools through them. Some urban stores, such as John Greenhow's in Williamsburg, specialized in more complete selections of trade tools. In 1767, Greenhow advertised "tools and materials for all kinds of tradesmen."[12] Savvy merchants like William Allason of Falmouth, Virginia, kept abreast of the latest tool developments and knew the best wholesale sources from which to obtain the best English implements at the lowest cost. Axes, adzes, hatchets, saws, and complete "sets" of joiner's tools came from London; Liverpool supplied cutlery of all sorts, including edge tools; nails and hoes could be had in Glasgow; and all types of ironmongery and tools were available in Bristol.[13]

From a practical standpoint, it was unnecessary to extend most British domestic marketing techniques to America. Orders placed by Americans were usually quite general, specifying types and sizes but rarely mentioning other details or makers' names. As one Philadelphia merchant remarked, he was not "particular in fixing the Prices or paterns of many Articles, but . . . trust to thee [his agent] to send them on as reasonable Terms as Possible & of the newest Patterns."[14]

Store documents and newspaper advertisements, however, provide some tantalizing clues to the specific makers of tools imported into North America and the success of English makers' attempts to build brand name recognition beyond their local markets. James Cocke & Company (1740–d. 1789) of Williamsburg, Virginia, for example, ordered two dozen "John Greens best Firmers [chisels]" from John Norton and Sons of London in 1772.[15] Cocke (or his customers) apparently preferred chisels made by Green, an edge tool maker located on Burgess Street in Sheffield during the mid-1770s. Thirty years later, Gerrit H. Van Wagenen, a New York hardwareman, advertised that he had for sale "a handsome assortment of Carpenters and Cabinet makers Planes of Stothert's make"—presumably George Stothert (1784–1818) of Bath, England.[16]

Philadelphians may have been more name conscious than other early Americans—at least many of the eighteenth-century newspaper references to specific toolmakers appear in the Philadelphia papers. Mid-century Philadelphia merchants advertised saws made by Smith, White, Dallaway, and Lume, probably William Smith (1718–1749) and Robert Dalaway (?–1776) of Birmingham (fig. 7); augers and gimlets by Vincent, probably Hugh Vincent (1719) or his successor of Birmingham; and edge tools by MOORE, undoubtedly Robert Moore (possibly father and son, 1721–1776), probably also of Birmingham (fig. 8).[17] Since most advertisements failed to mention specific makers, the repeated appearance of these names indicates that both Philadel-

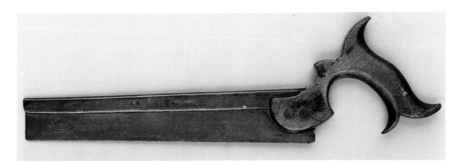

Fig. 7. Dovetail saw by Robert or William Dalaway (1746–1809). CWF 1990-100.

Fig. 8. Edge tools marked ROBERT MOORE. Moore was a mid-eighteenth-century maker, probably of Birmingham. Mortise chisel, CWF 1989-284; socket gouge, 1993-68; plow iron, 1988-492, 10; skew chisel, 1982-230.

phia retailers and their customers were familiar with them and attached some importance—probably a reputation for high quality—to them.

Similar evidence survives outside of newspaper ads. In 1760, a chest of joiner's tools ordered by Philadelphia merchant William Wilson for joiner Richard Johns included a handsaw, a panel saw, a tenon saw, a sash saw, and a dozen small keyhole saws—"all of white's best sort," three dozen of "Moores best plain Irons," and a great variety of planes, which were to be "of John Ridgus's make," probably John Rogers of London.[18] About a half-century later, Philadelphia ironmonger William Hallowell, Jr., was also quite specific about the makers of iron wares and tools that he ordered from Benjamin Stokes of Birmingham in April 1801. The files he ordered were "to be stampt IK" and the saws were "to be of Kenyon make" (both probably John Kenyon, merchant, filesmith, and sawmaker of Sheffield), "the Chissles & plain Irons to be of Weldons make" (possibly Bishop, Weldon, and Carr, the turn-of-the-century successors to William Weldon of Sheffield), and the shoe knives were to be stamped HOWE[19] (fig. 9). Few surviving American records give this kind of detail about the marks, or "brands," preferred by early American woodworkers.

Fig. 9. Edge tools made by
Weldon of Sheffield,
probably William Weldon
(1774–1787)
or his successors.
Carving tool,
socket mortise chisel,
mortise chisel, and
large plane iron:
CWF 1952-277, 148;
1990-158; 1987-750;
1992-81. Gouge, courtesy,
Malcolm G. MacGregor.
Small plane iron, courtesy,
Martyl and Emil Pollak.

The eighteenth-century English toolmaker best known in the colonies was quite possibly a sawmaker named White, whose name appears repeatedly in newspapers and store records throughout the colonies. "WHITES saws" were advertised and sold not just in Philadelphia, but also in Virginia. In fact, White's is one of very few makers' names that appear in the surviving records for mid-eighteenth-century Virginia. Anthony Hay and Christopher Ford of Williamsburg, both woodworkers, advertised and sold "*White's* Steel Plate Saws of all Sorts" in 1755, a professional endorsement undoubtedly aimed at the local craftsmen who were their customers.[20] Local storekeepers also kept White's saws in stock. Francis Jerdone of Yorktown, Virginia, not only sold White's saws to local craftsmen like Yorktown carpenter John Richardson, who purchased panel, sash, and tenon saws of White's make between December 1750 and July 1751,[21] but also supplied them wholesale to other merchants like John Thomson and Company and Taylor and Power of Hanover County and Pattison and Apperson of New Kent and James City Counties (fig. 10).[22]

White's saws, known for their quality, were quite expensive. A "common" handsaw sold wholesale for only 2s. 3p., while one of White's best steel plate handsaws cost three times as much at 7s. 6p.—a discrepancy only partly explained by differences in materials. An artisan could purchase one retail at 13s. 7p., a considerable investment of two to four days' wages for most common journeymen.[23] Even runaways apparently preferred White's saws. One frustrated master, Thomas Clemson, waxed poetic about the White's saw with which his runaway servant, Joseph Willard, absconded. As Clemson noted of Willard,

> He with him took
> (If that you will be pleas'd to look)
> A Handsaw, made of London Steel,
> And stamped with White, near to the Heel.[24]

Ironically, nothing is currently known about White except the popularity of his saws in mid-eighteenth-century America, and, until lately, no saws of his make were known to survive. Given the rarity of early documented English saws, this is not surprising. Recently, however, during a research trip for the tools exhibit, an early handsaw and backsaw came to light in the collections of the Stanley-Whitman House in Farmington, Connecticut. Both were

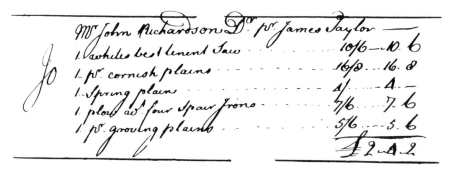

Fig. 10. Daybook entry for tools, including "1 whites best tenent Saw," sold to Yorktown carpenter John Richardson by storekeeper Francis Jerdone, July 1, 1751. Jerdone Papers, Account Book of Francis Jerdone, 1750–1752, Earl Gregg Swem Library, College of William and Mary, Williamsburg, Va.

Fig. 11. English backsaw marked WHITE [with crown], owned by Judah Woodruff of Farmington, Conn. Courtesy, Stanley-Whitman House, Farmington, Conn.

used by eighteenth-century carpenter and joiner Judah Woodruff. They are two of the earliest known surviving English saws. The handsaw marked Smith (probably William Smith, 1718–1749, Birmingham) was a wonderful find, but even it pales beside the excitement of deciphering the backsaw's seemingly illegible mark. After lengthy and frustrating study, the light suddenly hit the mark just right and the name WHITE leapt off the blade! To date, this saw is the only known example marked with White's name (fig. 11).

American orders, whether from individual planters and tradesmen or from merchants and storekeepers, generally were sent to English agents, who gathered the tools required from nearby dealers and retailers, packed them, and shipped them to their customers. Some suppliers seemed to specialize in providing needed goods for export merchants. The London firms of Tappenden and Hanbey and James Sharp and the Glasgow establishments of William McAuley and Archibald and William Coats often served as sources of tools and ironmongery for merchants supplying Virginia storekeepers.

English merchants and retailers may have found catalogs, directories, and trade cards useful in making their purchases and attracting customers, but it would have served little purpose to distribute these publications widely in America. Still, there is evidence that at least some American storekeepers and merchants had reference to sample cards and possibly catalogs when writing up their orders. William Hallowell's ironmongery orders, for example, refer to specific card numbers for many items, including bung drawers, bits, sawsets, hand vises, pincers, penknives, scissors, awl blades, compasses, and hammers.[25] Standard sizes denoted by numbers were also well known by the mid-eighteenth century.[26]

Once the tools arrived in America, some retailers adopted the new marketing techniques employed by their English counterparts. Newspaper advertisements notified interested customers of the latest goods "Just Imported, and to be SOLD,"[27] emphasizing the tools' English origins and quality. Not all storekeepers advertised in the papers, however. In Williamsburg, store ads became much more prevalent after mid-century, and even then smart store-keepers who wanted to get the most for their money advertised only during the spring and fall when the General Court was in session and their invento-ries were well stocked with the latest fashions.[28] Many storekeepers also no doubt displayed the new wares in their shop windows. John H. Norton spent more than £87 to build a new store in Winchester, Virginia, in April 1786. The building featured "3 outside doors with glass," five large windows, and more than one hundred lights of sash.[29] Inside such retail establishments, shelves, counters, and "show boxes" allowed goods to be displayed to best advantage.[30]

American toolmakers and retailers also attempted to build name recogni-tion and followed the English practice of marking their wares with their names and frequently their locations. Some American toolmaker-retailers like the Boston planemaker Levi Little (1770–1802) may have attempted to obscure the British origins of their wares by stamping their own names directly over those of the English makers. Others, like the Philadelphia ironmongers T. Poultney & Sons, took a slightly less direct approach and merely added

Fig. 12. London molding plane by George Mutter (1766–1799), retailed and marked by the Philadelphia ironmongers T. Poultney & Sons, probably before 1798. Courtesy, Alan G. Bates.

their stamp to that of the original maker (fig. 12). New York merchant Thomas Grant (d. 1802) not only marked the planes he sold with his own name, but apparently customized them for his patrons by adding their initials (fig. 13).[31]

Despite attempts of American toolmakers to make their wares attractive and competitive in terms of price, variety, and quality with the products of British manufacturers, few were successful during the eighteenth century. Even reasonably well-established American toolmakers, like planemakers, sometimes imported English tools and planes for resale to supplement their own stock, and nearly all continued to use imported English blades. Most American craftsmen lived within reach of a store that offered at least a basic assortment of imported English tools for sale, and they continued to buy them. The sophisticated distribution systems of the eighteenth-century North Atlantic world ensured that familiar, high-quality, reasonably priced English tools of the newest types and designs would continue to be found in most American tool kits until well into the nineteenth century.

Fig. 13. Molding plane sold by New York planemaker Thomas Grant with a boxed set of crowned letter stamps similar to those he probably used to mark it with his customer's initials, P S. Plane, courtesy, Martyl and Emil Pollak. Letter stamps, CWF 1988-426.

1. This article has been adapted from James M. Gaynor and Nancy L. Hagedorn, *Tools: Working Wood in Eighteenth-Century America* (Williamsburg, Va., 1993), pp. 17–24.

2. *A General Description of all Trades, Digested in Alphabetical Order* (London, 1747), p. 18.

3. Swinney's *Birmingham and Stafford Chronicle,* Feb. 2, 1775, included in Boulton Papers, "America" box, Birmingham Archives, Birmingham, Eng. Edmund Burke, MP, apparently defended the petition in Parliament, for on Feb. 8, 1775, "The Merchants & Manufacturers, who have had a principal share of the American trade from this town & neighbourhood," wrote him a letter to thank him. The signatories included S. Freeth and R. Rabone. Lloyd's *Evening Post,* Feb. 13–15, 1775, Boulton Papers. Those who signed the actual petition included Matthew Boulton, John Fothergill, Thomas Green, and Joseph Green. Item #2, *ibid.* Later, in May 1786, the Birmingham Commercial Committee was actively involved in obtaining repeal of the "Law prohibiting the Exportation of our Tools & utensils" to America. Item #10, "Birmingham Commercial Committee" box, 1783–1801, *ibid.*

4. E. Surrey Dane, *Peter Stubs and the Lancashire Hand Tool Industry* (Altringham, Eng., 1973), p. 83.

5. *Ibid.,* p. 84.

6. *Ibid.,* p. 87.

7. Theodore R. Crom, *Trade Catalogues, 1542–1842* (Melrose, Fla., 1989), p. 150.

8. William Louis Goodman, "Gabriel & Sons, Stock Inventories," *Chronicle of the Early American Industries Association,* XXXVI (1983), p. 60.

9. Stock list of John Shaw and Sons, ca. 1805, MSS DB/24/401, pp. 152–157, Records of John Shaw and Sons, Wolverhampton Borough Archives, Wolverhampton, Eng.

10. Robert Campbell, *The London Tradesman. Being a Compendious View of All the Trades, Professions, Arts, both Liberal and Mechanic, now practised in the Cities of London and Westminster* (London, 1747; reprint, New York, 1969), pp. 171–172.

11. Italics mine. York County, Va., Deeds, Orders, and Wills, XIII, 1706–1710, p. 221.

12. *Virginia Gazette* (Williamsburg) (Purdie and Dixon), June 4, 1767.

13. Goods that come from London, Invoice and Inventory Book for Falmouth Store, 1769–1774, Allason Papers, Library of Virginia, Richmond, Va.

14. William Hallowell, Jr., to Benjamin Stokes of Birmingham, Apr. 4, 1801, Spruance Library, Bucks County Historical Society, Doylestown, Pa. I would like to thank Trip Kahn for bringing this document to my attention.

15. Invoice of James Cocke and Company, Dec. 3, 1772. John Norton and Sons, folder 79, Norton Papers, CWF.

16. *Mercantile Advertiser* (New York, N. Y.), June 4, 1801.

17. All references are from the *Pennsylvania Gazette* (Philadelphia). Saws: Aug. 9, 1739, Jan. 28, 1746, June 25, 1747, Jan. 3, 1749, Nov. 9, 1749, Sept. 6, 1750, and Dec. 25, 1750. Augers and gimlets: Jan. 28, 1746, Oct. 15, 1747, and Jan. 3, 1749 (marked HV). Edge tools: Nov. 9, 1749.

18. John Ridgus is probably John Rogers of London (1734–1765). List of a Chest of Joiners Tools to be Shipt pr William Neale for accot of Wm. Wilson (being for Richard Johns), Letter and Order Book, William Wilson, Philadelphia, 1757–1760, New York Public Library, in Charles F. Hummel, *With Hammer in Hand: The Dominy Craftsmen of East Hampton, New York* (Charlottesville, Va., 1968), pp. 32–33.

19. Order for goods to be sent, enclosed in Hallowell to Stokes, Apr. 4, 1801, Spruance Lib.

20. *Va. Gaz.*, Mar. 21, 1755.

21. Entries for Dec. 15, 1750, and July 2, 1751, Journal, 15 Sept. 1750–2 June 1760, Francis Jerdone Papers, 1749–1773, Lib. of Va.; Account Book, 1750–1752, Jerdone Papers, Lot 1, bound volumes, Earl Gregg Swem Library, College of William and Mary, Williamsburg, Va.

22. John Thomson and Company, entries for Dec. 13, 1750, and July 2, 1751, Journal, Jerdone Papers; Taylor and Power, entry for Nov. 1, 1749, Francis Jerdone Cargo Wastebook, 1748–1749, CWF; entry for Sept. 9, 1750, Journal, Jerdone Papers; Pattison and Apperson, entry for Nov. 1, 1751, *ibid.*

23. See entry for Taylor and Power, Sept. 9, 1750, and cash account for July 1751, Journal, Jerdone Papers.

24. Clemson's entire ad, which is quite lengthy, is in the form of a poem. *Pa. Gaz.*, Aug. 7, 1746. See *ibid.*, Feb. 7, 1740, for another runaway, carpenter Michael Berry, who also absconded with a "new Handsaw of White's, stamped on the Handle in several Places with T S." "TS" apparently were the initials of the owner and master, Thomas Sugar.

25. Order for goods to be sent, enclosed in Hallowell to Stokes, Apr. 4, 1801, Spruance Lib.

26. Many storekeepers like Francis Jerdone regularly ordered tools sized by number. See inside front cover of Jerdone Cargo Wastebook.

27. *Va. Gaz.*, Mar. 21, 1755.

28. Mary Goodwin, "The Colonial Store," research report, CWF, 1966, p. 74.

29. J. H. Norton, Dr. to Jacob Bougher for Building a Store, Apr. 1786, folder 170, Norton Papers.

30. Reuben Berry constructed a "show box" for the Boyd's Hole, Va., store of John Glassford and Company in 1769. John Glassford and Company Records for Virginia, Boyd's Hole Store, Ledger 3, 1769–1770, fol. 5, Lib. of Cong.

31. Emil Pollak and Martyl Pollak, *A Guide to the Makers of American Wooden Planes,* 3rd ed. (Mendham, N. J., 1994), 170–171.

"He wants a Sett of Tools"

The Acquisition and Ownership
of Tools in Virginia

By Jan K. Gilliam

Newspapers, probate inventories, store accounts, and merchandise orders all demonstrate that a wide range of eighteenth-century Americans acquired tools. Tradesmen required a supply of tools to keep them in business, but everyone needed at least some tools in order to survive in the colonies. Although this article focuses on Virginia, similar patterns of ownership and acquisition were common to the other colonies.[1]

Tools were an important factor in the settlement of Virginia from the colony's earliest days. The colonists needed tools to build their houses, cultivate their land, make their clothes, construct the barrels in which they stored and shipped their food and tobacco, and undertake a variety of other daily tasks. During the first quarter of the seventeenth century, tools were considered so valuable that the colonial government passed laws imposing strict punishments for those who lost, abused, or traded them without authorization. As late as 1701, during the construction of the first Capitol in Williamsburg, Henry Cary, the builder, petitioned and obtained the government's permission "to sel at his discretion any of the Tooles &c. which were Come in for Supplying the Workmen to be Imployed in building the Capitol."[2]

Ships sailing from England to Virginia to establish settlements carried not only colonists, but supplies as well. The tools provided for such projects as colonizing Berkeley Hundred and Smythes Hundred included both agricultural tools and tools for trades such as carpentry, coopering, and tailoring. While well-organized efforts ensured that groups arrived with the appropriate tools, others came to Virginia less well equipped to cope with the new environment. As the Virginia Company's 1622 promotional broadside noted, colonists could not survive without the proper tools (see p. 26). The broadside warned that some immigrants had not adequately prepared themselves for the move, and thus had hindered themselves and the development of the colony. To correct this problem, the Virginia Company felt compelled to publish a comprehensive list of items that were necessary to sustain life in the colony. This list delineated the necessary number of each item to be taken by a single person, family, and larger groups. For a family of six, the required tools consisted of specific numbers of saws, hoes, axes, hammers, chisels, and augers. Not surprisingly, these tools were general-purpose domestic, agricultural, and woodworking implements that allowed the settlers to maintain their households and farms.[3] Without these basic tools, survival would have been difficult at best.

Not only did the supply of tools have to be carefully monitored, so did the people engaged in the trades. In 1621, Governor Francis Wyatt was instructed "To put prentices to trades, and not let them forsake their trades for planting tobacco, or any such useless commodity."[4] Those skilled in particular trades were in demand. The need was so great at times that special measures were taken to ensure that tradesmen came to Virginia. Convicted Englishman Stephen Rogers, sentenced in England to hang for killing a man, was "reprieved in the interest of Virginia because he was a carpenter."[5] Wyatt's instructions further directed him to oversee the building of houses and mills and the development of other sites.[6] This demand for improvements required the presence of tradesmen equipped with the tools necessary to accomplish the work.

Well into the beginning of the eighteenth century, the government recognized tools as significant assets. Official guidelines emphasized the role tools played in the ability of each individual to earn a living and the importance of

Fig. 1. Along with written documents, some of the best evidence for the use of tools in Virginia are fragments of tools recovered archaeologically. The tools pictured here, primarily English imports, were all found on Williamsburg archaeological sites.

that to the colony. *The Office and Authority of a Justice of Peace*, printed in Williamsburg in 1736, contained useful information and cases for local justices "Collected from the Common and Statute Laws of England, and Acts of Assembly, now in Force; And adapted to the Constitution and Practice of Virginia."[7] In this manual, George Webb included a section on matters relating to debt. If a man appeared in court for debt, all his possessions could be taken to satisfy his obligations except "Beasts of the Plough, and the Tools or Instruments of a Man's Trade or Profession. . . . A Horse, when a Man, or Woman is riding on him; an Ax in a Man's Hand, cutting Wood, &c. are also priviledged for that time."[8] It was pointless to take a man's tools since that would deprive him of the means of paying off his debts. If in prison, the debtor had to supply the sheriff with a complete account of his estate so that any of the items could be sold to pay his creditors, all items, that is, except "his necessary Apparel and Utensils of Trade."[9] It was important to the welfare of the colony that its members be productive citizens.

Most households had at least a basic set of woodworking tools. When someone died, court appointees compiled an inventory of the deceased's household goods and equipment. Today, these documents provide evidence for the kinds of items owned by the early colonists (fig. 1). At his death in the 1640s, John Kemp of Norfolk County had "old smiths tooles, as hamers files, a scruplate [screwplate] & tapps and old gouge & Chisells" and "a parcell of old Carpenters tooles."[10] Taken together, the most commonly recorded implements formed a basic kit for woodworking and usually included a hammer, an

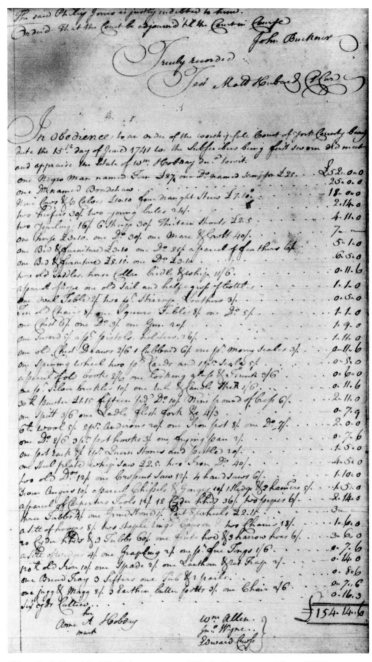

Fig. 2. Like this 1741 inventory of York County resident William
Hobday, many inventories provide information about tool ownership,
listing tools by name or trade and giving values for the tools. York
County, Va., Records, Wills and Inventories, XIX, 1740–1746, p. 47.

ax, a saw, a drawknife, and a few other general-purpose tools. These kits did not correspond to any particular trade; rather, they reflected their owners' needs to accomplish a variety of daily tasks to maintain a household.

Wills also contain evidence of tool ownership. In 1695, James Thelaball left a cross cut saw and iron wedges to one son, while to another he bequeathed "One toole Chest and all the twoles therein."[11] In New England, many seventeenth-century wills reveal that tools passed from one generation to the next.

The numbers and types of tools recorded in inventories and wills demonstrate the diversity of tool ownership. Where a colonist lived and his wealth and standing in society affected the quantity and variety of tools he might eventually own. Small farmers had different tool needs from planters with large estates, and both had different needs from those of urban tradesmen. A tradesman with little money might make do with a few general-purpose tools and purchase others only as the need arose, while those who could afford to do so might purchase entire sets at one time. Individuals who continued in a family trade might inherit the required tools of that trade and avoid large expenditures for tools. Slaves generally were supplied with tools by their masters.[12]

Eighteenth-century probate inventories, like those of the century before, reveal the widespread ownership of tools in Virginia (fig. 2). Individuals possessed implements ranging from a few basic tools to quite extensive kits, depending on the deceased's occupation, wealth, and other circumstances. Unfortunately, the most frequent ways of referring to such tools are also the most tantalizing and frustrating for the modern researcher: "A set of carpenters tools." "A parcel of coopers tools." "A chest of joiners tools." "A parcel of old tools." While helpful in some respects, this type of entry makes one want to know exactly what a "set" or "parcel" was. In rare instances, more detailed documents suggest possibilities. For example, a fairly complete list of tools is given in the 1750 inventory of Stephen Minor of Frederick County. It begins with a jointer, two fore planes, two jack planes, and five smoothing planes, and continues on to enumerate other planes as well as saws, chisels, gouges, files, and other tools.[13] This inventory gives at least a hint of what lies behind the simple entry of "parcel" or "set." Another way of determining the probable size of a group of tools is to study the value assigned by the inventory takers and compare it to the value of individual tools or known groups. The values of unspecified groups generally ranged from a few shillings to a few pounds. This suggests that these tool groups often consisted of a few more expensive, newer tools or several less expensive, older tools. Such conclusions, while better than nothing, must be considered with caution.

One way to obtain tools was to make them oneself. Most young men learned a trade through an apprenticeship. During this training, the apprentice learned how to use tools, and, in some cases at least, how to make some of them (fig. 3). Making squares, bevels, gauges, and tool handles during his apprenticeship not only taught the young woodworker necessary skills but also

Fig. 3. Apprentices learned woodworking skills by making some of their tools (*left*) while they acquired other, commercially made, tools through purchase or as freedom dues at the end of their term (*right*).

provided him with tools that traditionally were not commercially available. Some indentures formalized this practice in the written agreement between master and apprentice. North Carolina wheelwright and joiner Robert Hogston promised in 1777 to assist his apprentice, Thomas Cathey Braty, "in making the working Tools belonging to the said Trades."[14]

Freedom dues obtained at the end of the training process might also provide tools. John Miller, an orphan bound out in 1725/26 to learn the trade of joiner in Lancaster County, Virginia, was promised "necessary tools for his trade" at the completion of his apprenticeship.[15] Twenty years later, John Garrow of York County, an apprentice carpenter, received "as many Carpenters tooles as will build a common Clabboard House."[16] Apprentices whose dues did not include tools often were granted money with which they could purchase necessary components of their basic kit. Alternatively, tools might be provided by a bequest or as a gift from a generous relative. In 1773, Robert Hart ordered from John Norton & Sons of London a group of tools for a relation who was "an apprentice to a House Carpenter and who is free of his servitude next Christmas, he wants a Sett of Tools for that business not to exceed 7£ or 8£."[17]

Not all apprentices were so fortunate as to have their tools freely given to them. Following the unexpected death of his master in 1726/27, Jonathan Parish had to sue the estate for his tools. The Lancaster County Court awarded Parish "a set of Carpenters tools for course [coarse] work vizt. a good froe, broad ax, handsaw, adz, Inch auger, hamer, drawing knife, two Chizells, gouge, a rule & pr of Compasses & two gimblets."[18] From this list it appears that the tools provided in these freedom dues probably were the type usually obtained from commercial sources. These commercially made tools, along with those an apprentice made during his training, provided him with the basic kit of tools necessary to make a start in his chosen trade.

Once out on their own, many journeymen no doubt found themselves in need of a greater variety of tools or, eventually, having to replace others that had been broken or used up. There were many ways an artisan could do this. He might make the simpler tools himself. One of the most straightforward ways was to go to the local store and purchase them. Accounts and advertisements indicate that many stores carried a great variety of tools in a range of sizes. Advertisements in colonial newspapers like the *Virginia Gazette* often began with "Just imported and to be sold," which alerted readers that they were likely to find sets of trade-specific tools as well as individual tools available from the local merchants (fig. 4).

If a tradesman did not have cash, he might barter his services for the tools he wanted. In 1769, Reubin Berry, a cabinetmaker near Boyd's Hole, Virginia, made a "Show Box for the Store" of John Glassford and Company and earned a credit of 12s. 6d. Berry used the credit to obtain tools and other goods.[19] Negro Jack, a slave in Colchester, Virginia, did odd jobs in exchange for credit at his local store. During a two-year period, Jack received credit of more than £2 for making "1 Pine Table," constructing pigeonholes and bookshelves for a desk, moving fences, and assisting with storing supplies. He used his credit to purchase a variety of goods and tools, including gimlets, a whipsaw file, glue, and a plane iron.[20]

Another means of obtaining tools was, of course, to send directly to England for them. Men such as George Washington, Thomas Jefferson, and Peyton Skipwith sent detailed instructions about the types and numbers of tools they wanted. Peyton Skipwith, owner of Prestwould plantation in Mecklenburg County, Virginia, ordered "Sundry Joiners Tools to be sent in a compleat Tool chest to hold not only the tools now ordered but such too as I already have by me with the usual places within to contain Saws little places for Screws Chizels Gouges and other small tools of different sizes &c. &c. with a strong Lock wth 2 Keys to it." Skipwith enumerated each of the tools that should be included in this group, from the three sets of bench planes and a brace to hammers and joiner's hatchets[21] (fig. 5).

Juſt Imported, and to be SOLD, by the Subſcribers in
WILLIAMSBURG,

A LARGE Aſſortment of Carpenters, Joiners, and Cabinet-Makers Tools, conſiſting of *White's* Steel Plate Saws of all Sorts, Glue Jointers, long Planes, Bench Planes, Tooth and Smoothing ditto, Moulding Planes of all Sorts, Plane Irons, Chiſſels, Formers, Scribing Gouges, Raſps, Files, *Turkey* Oil-Stones, *German* Slates, and Variety of other Things.   *Chriſtopher Ford,* Jun.
                                                                      Anthony Hay.

Fig. 4. This advertisement from the *Virginia Gazette* alerted readers to the great variety of new tools they could purchase from Hay and Ford. Although many shops advertised their wares, few provided such detail as this notice. *Virginia Gazette*, Mar. 21, 1755.

Memorandum of Sundry Joiners Tools to be sent in a compleat Tool chest, to hold not only the tools now ordered but such ... as ... already have by one ... with the several places within to contain same little ... for Screws Chizels Gouges and other small tools of different sizes &c &c with a strong Lock with a Key to it — in order to save freight — other Goods if any to come may be put in the empty places in the said Chest

2 Setts of Bench-Plains
1 compleat Brace of the best sort and Bits to it of every Size and Kind
½ Breaking Plains from 1 Inch to ⅛ of an Inch
1 Sash Circle
½ ⅜ Inch Oge
3 Moving-Plains with Sets of Irons compleat
1 Moving Filister — which is made to move by a Brass Screws and so
1 Set of Sash-Plains work on ¾ of an Inch with answering filister to work from the front side
½ ¼ of an Inch quarter Round
½ ½ filli Do
1 Raising Plain
½ 1½ Inch and ½ ¾ Inch Iron with a Rabbit Plains
1 Pair of Groving-Plains to work Floors of 1⅛ Inch thick
½ 1⅛ hollow to Rose Stair Steps
1 Set of Mortising Chizels for making Door Locks &c to come neatly ... &c
2 good Iron Blades Squares for the purpose of laying up the ...
2 Drawing Knives with different mouldings in them for the purpose of working sliding Chair Carriages
1 Small and 1 Large Stroke-shave
1 Dozen of fine Raising Chizzels from 2 Inch broad to ¾ of an Inch
1 Set of ... for making ... and Doors
½ ¾ Inch ... and head
½ ¾ Inch Astrichel
½ 1 Inch Bollution
1 Cornish Plain 3½ Inches wide and Bed-mould to suit it
2 Dozen Flat Handsome files
1 Box &c for Saw miller Saws
3 Hand hammers of different sizes and one Middling size ... for Blacksmith use
2 ... Steel Plate Saws for a Saw Mill
1 Small Coffee grinder sort.
3 best Carpenters broad Axes largest size for strong able Men to work with (those generally sent being ... too light ... over The Blade)
2 neat joiners Hatchets

Direct orders like Skipwith's came from large-scale, wealthy planters who had agents and credit in England. The tools they requested generally were intended for use by employees, servants, or slaves who were trained in particular trades. The plantation system allowed some slaves to specialize in various trades, with their masters supplying appropriate tools. In 1819, Thomas Jefferson requested that three carpenters be sent to work at Poplar Forest where building of his house was underway. Since the carpenters would need only a few tools they were to "bring them on their shoulders. They will need 2 hand saws, 2 jack planes, 2 pr. chissels broad and narrow, some augers for common framing, an foot adze, and one of the narrow adzes which were made here to dig gutturs in the joists. These things divided among three will weigh little."[22] These tools would have come from the supply Jefferson kept at Monticello.

As the inventories indicate, most of these tools remained the property of the planter and not the slave who used them. In 1728, Nathaniel Harrison owned tools for coopering, carpentry, wheelwright's work, and joinery. These tools were divided up under shop headings or were noted as being stored in a shop barn, a dry store, or a store shed.[23] Most likely, these tools were parceled out to the slaves as they were needed and returned to storage when not in use. Fifty years later, Thomas Lord Fairfax also owned an impressive number and variety of tools, some of which were kept at the quarters where slaves lived.[24] This practice of supplying tools for slaves was common in Virginia.

Other gentlemen ordered tools as the need for certain items arose. In 1737, William Beverley ordered from Perry, his agent in London, a whipsaw and twelve files, two broad axes, two adzes, two drawing knives, a set of cornice planes and irons, and a set of house carpenter's augers.[25] These were probably to supplement a supply of tools Beverley already had on hand.

While most of the tools found in American woodworkers' kits were imported, there often were local makers of at least some types of tools. Toolmakers in New England were well known for their skills, but even in Virginia, where toolmaking was never widespread, some were skilled in the toolmaking trades. In 1775, Robert Carter noted in his daybook that a man in Frederick County made files and rasps from "the finest of each to the coarsest."[26] Samuel Daniel, a blacksmith and chairmaker in Middlesex, advertised in 1775: "On proper encouragement, I will oblige myself to supply my county, and a large number more, with all kinds of PLANTERS and CARPENTERS TOOLS, no ways inferiour to those imported" (fig. 6).[27] Local forges like James Hunter's on the Rappahannock River made axes, hoes, and other useful iron wares.

New tools could be bought from local stores, ordered directly from England, or purchased from local makers, but there was also a ready market for secondhand tools. Notices of estate sales appeared in the newspapers almost as frequently as store ads. Usually entire estates, from houses and land to household furnishings and business accouterments, were offered for sale upon the death of their owners. These sales often provided an opportunity to purchase secondhand tools and implements. Occasionally, official court records include a detailed account of who bought what. Tools seem to have been purchased piecemeal by individuals buying one or two tools each.

Although most public sales occurred because of the death of the owner, some served to satisfy debts. Even though the official manual for justices stated that the tools of a man's trade were exempt from seizure, the actual court records tell a different story. Tools were indeed used to settle debts on occasion. Witnesses in debt cases often stated that they had tools owned by the defendant in their possession, which were then taken and sold to pay the plaintiff. In most cases, the witnesses had only one or two of the defendant's tools. These

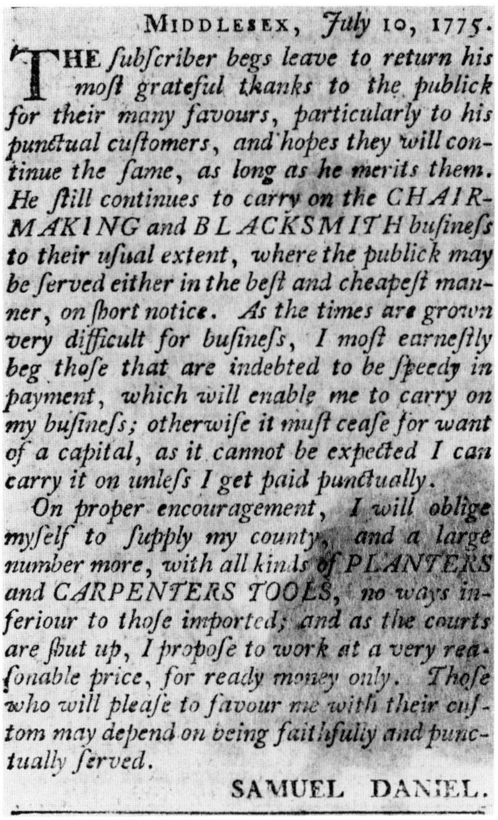

MIDDLESEX, *July* 10, 1775.

THE *subscriber begs leave to return his most grateful thanks to the publick for their many favours, particularly to his punctual customers, and hopes they will continue the same, as long as he merits them. He still continues to carry on the CHAIR-MAKING and BLACKSMITH business to their usual extent, where the publick may be served either in the best and cheapest manner, on short notice. As the times are grown very difficult for business, I most earnestly beg those that are indebted to be speedy in payment, which will enable me to carry on my business; otherwise it must cease for want of a capital, as it cannot be expected I can carry it on unless I get paid punctually.*

On proper encouragement, I will oblige myself to supply my county, and a large number more, with all kinds of PLANTERS and CARPENTERS TOOLS, no ways inferiour to those imported; and as the courts are shut up, I propose to work at a very reasonable price, for ready money only. Those who will please to favour me with their custom may depend on being faithfully and punctually served.

SAMUEL DANIEL.

Fig. 6. Samuel Daniel used the newspaper to encourage local customers "and a large number more" to purchase tools of his own making. *Virginia Gazette* (Purdie), July 28, 1775.

Fig. 7. Public auctions were advertised frequently in the newspapers and gave tradesmen access to a variety of used tools. *Virginia Gazette* (Purdie), Dec. 12, 1777.

To be SOLD by publick auction, for ready money, on Monday the 2d of February next, at the subscriber's shop in Williamsburg,

VARIOUS sorts of household and kitchen furniture, a complete chest of cabinet makers tools, turning laths and work benches, some mahogany and walnut plank, desk mountings, locks, and several sorts of materials for carrying on said business, looking glasses of various sizes, a small quantity of quicksilver, with all other materials for silvering of glass. The sale to begin at ten o'clock, and continue till all is sold off.   RICHARD HARROCKS.

N. B. Any person inclinable to purchase by private bargain may know the terms by applying as above, and possession may be had immediately. The purchaser, if unacquainted with the method of silvering glass, may have proper instructions *gratis*.

All persons who have any just claims against the subscriber are desired to bring in their accounts, and those indebted are requested to pay off their respective balances.

tools, when sold along with other items seized by the sheriff, were enough to satisfy the debts.[28] Not everyone waited for the sheriff to close in. William Byrd III, a planter constantly in debt, advertised in 1761 the upcoming sale of a large quantity of tools as well as five hundred slaves "among which are Tradesmen of all Sorts."[29]

Another source for secondhand tools was the sale of tools by an owner who was going out of business. When Williamsburg cabinetmaker Peter Scott decided to move to England in 1755, he offered for sale two Negro cabinetmakers, pieces of cabinetwork, and the tools and materials for the business. Scott never left for England, however, and his goods were not actually sold until after his death some twenty years later.[30] John Clark of Richmond, Virginia, also planned to leave the colony. He advertised in March 1776 that he intended to sell his house lot and dwelling, which included rooms "in Order for a Cabinet-Maker's Shop, for which it has of late been used" and "the Benches and Tools, which are sufficient to employ six Hands," plus a quantity of stock and hardware.[31] Someone with the capital to invest could buy not only the tools of his trade but also an entire business.

While most sale ads tended to list tools with little descriptive detail, some gave more specific information. In 1777, Richard Harrocks sold at public auction in Williamsburg a complete chest of cabinetmaker's tools, turning lathes, workbenches, wood, and materials for carrying on the business (fig. 7). In the same year, the goods of the late Joshua Kendall, a house carpenter and joiner who had come to the colony with Lord Botetourt and set up on his own in Williamsburg, were sold. They included "A chest of complete carpenters and joiners tools, with all the household furniture."[32]

Secondhand tools were available in other ways. There were pawn shops and dealers in secondhand tools in England (fig. 8). Similar sources for used tools probably existed in the colonies, though we have little information about them and they were likely smaller and less substantial operations.

Some tradesmen stated the desired disposition of their tools in their wills. If tools were to be sold, the money from the sale became a means of support for the deceased's family. In such cases, the sons generally were not old enough to enter into a trade and therefore the tools were more useful to the family as a source of ready cash. In 1755, William Whitehurst of Norfolk County requested that all his working carpenter's tools be sold to provide schooling for his son. Another father recommended that his shop and tools be rented out to support his wife and children, or, if this was not sufficient, to sell them outright.[33]

Many other tradesmen desired that their tools be passed along to the next generation. These bequests encouraged children to carry on the family trade. Some fathers even made this a condition of the inheritance, and if not complied with, the tools were given to others or were sold. Wills also indicate that sons often were already in the family business. One New England father left to his son the tools "which are now in his [the son's] possession and occupation."[34] A Virginia father left his son his smith's tools, provided that he stay

Fig. 8. Trade card of Dupear's General Tool Warehouse, London, ca. 1810?. Heal Collection, 118.3, courtesy, Trustees of the British Museum.

and work on the plantation until his mother's death. Another left his "well beloved son Thomas" all of his cooper's and carpenter's tools.[35] In 1777, Charles Grim of Winchester, Virginia, bequeathed his house and all his joinery tools to his son Charles. He also desired that "my son Charles shall take to him after my discease his Brother George and his Sister Caty Grim and he shall give them education so far as to read and write and shall larne his Brother George Grim the art and mistery of the joiners trade."[36] As these kits passed from generation to generation, they were added to when the needs of the new owner changed and as tools were used up, broken, or became obsolete.

As has been demonstrated, tools, both new and used, were readily available in the colony and from abroad. Some enterprising individuals, though, employed less honorable methods in acquiring their tools (fig. 9). In May 1770, the *Virginia Gazette* announced the arrest of

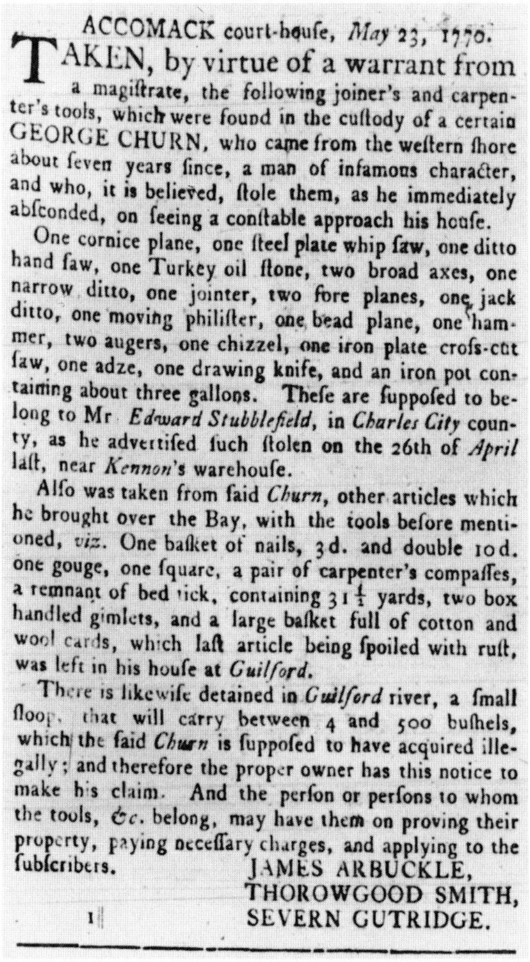

ACCOMACK court-houfe, *May* 23, 1770.

TAKEN, by virtue of a warrant from a magiftrate, the following joiner's and carpenter's tools, which were found in the cuftody of a certain GEORGE CHURN, who came from the weftern fhore about feven years fince, a man of infamous character, and who, it is believed, ftole them, as he immediately abfconded, on feeing a conftable approach his houfe.

One cornice plane, one fteel plate whip faw, one ditto hand faw, one Turkey oil ftone, two broad axes, one narrow ditto, one jointer, two fore planes, one jack ditto, one moving philifter, one bead plane, one hammer, two augers, one chizzel, one iron plate crofs-cut faw, one adze, one drawing knife, and an iron pot containing about three gallons. Thefe are fuppofed to belong to Mr *Edward Stubblefield*, in *Charles City* county, as he advertifed fuch ftolen on the 26th of *April* laft, near *Kennon's* warehoufe.

Alfo was taken from faid *Churn*, other articles which he brought over the Bay, with the tools before mentioned, *viz.* One bafket of nails, 3 d. and double 10 d. one gouge, one fquare, a pair of carpenter's compaffes, a remnant of bed tick, containing 31¼ yards, two box handled gimlets, and a large bafket full of cotton and wool cards, which laft article being fpoiled with ruft, was left in his houfe at *Guilford.*

There is likewife detained in *Guilford* river, a fmall floop, that will carry between 4 and 500 bufhels, which the faid *Churn* is fuppofed to have acquired illegally; and therefore the proper owner has this notice to make his claim. And the perfon or perfons to whom the tools, *&c.* belong, may have them on proving their property, paying neceffary charges, and applying to the fubfcribers.   JAMES ARBUCKLE,
                                THOROWGOOD SMITH,
          1   SEVERN GUTRIDGE.

Fig. 9. Tools were valuable assets to those who made a living using them, and their theft was cause for concern and action. *Virginia Gazette* (Rind), June 7, 1770.

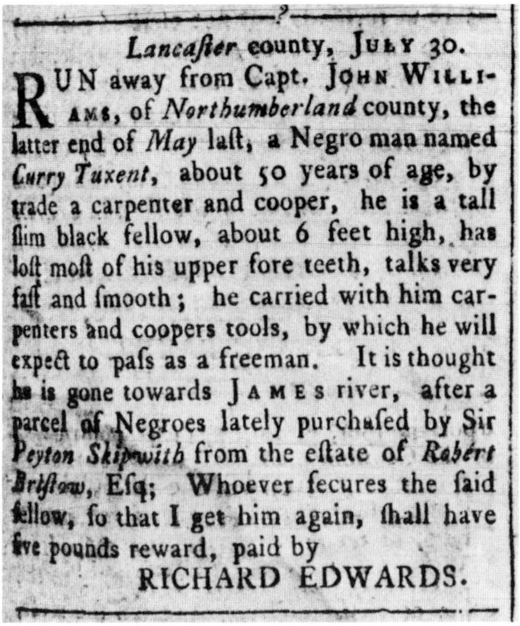

Fig. 10. Many runaway slaves were identified in notices by their clothing or their skills. Those slaves who practiced a trade might use tools and skills to pass as free men. *Virginia Gazette*, Aug. 4, 1768.

Lancaſter county, Ju**L**Y 30.
RUN away from Capt. J**O**H**N** W**IL**L**I**-
AM**S**, of *Northumberland* county, the latter end of *May* laſt, a Negro man named *Curry Tuxent*, about 50 years of age, by trade a carpenter and cooper, he is a tall ſlim black fellow, about 6 feet high, has loſt moſt of his upper fore teeth, talks very faſt and ſmooth; he carried with him carpenters and coopers tools, by which he will expect to paſs as a freeman. It is thought he is gone towards J**A**M**E**S river, after a parcel of Negroes lately purchaſed by Sir *Peyton Skipwith* from the eſtate of *Robert Briſtow*, Eſq; Whoever ſecures the ſaid fellow, ſo that I get him again, ſhall have five pounds reward, paid by
RICHARD EDWARDS.

George Churn, "a man of infamous character," who was found with numerous joiner's and carpenter's tools believed to have been stolen. The tools included a cornice plane, other planes of various types, saws, and axes. The men who apprehended Churn believed the tools belonged to a Mr. Edward Stubblefield, as he had advertised earlier that such tools had been stolen from him in April. He could get them back by proving they were his and paying the necessary charges. By the middle of July, Mr. Stubblefield had apparently not come forward to claim his tools. The subscribers appealed to him in an open letter published in the *Gazette* stating that they were sure the tools were his and they needed him to present himself in order to convict Churn. Furthermore, "If villains were thus to elude the law, and triumph over justice, every prudent man would be cautious of paying the least attention to yours, or any other stranger's advertisement."[37] It is hoped that justice was served on Mr. Churn, but no more was heard from either party.

Notices of tools stolen by runaway slaves and indentured servants appeared in newspapers throughout the colonies. Many runaway ads noted the fugitives' trades and indicated that they had taken with them sundry tools of those trades (fig. 10). Slave owners alerted the public that the slave might use the stolen tools to try to pass as a freeman. It is interesting to consider that the tools allowed their possessor a measure of freedom. With training and tools, a slave or servant could aspire to earn a decent living on his own. Ben, a thirty-five-year-old runaway slave, might have held such hope. He was by trade a carpenter who also knew "something of the cooper's business." When he ran, he took with him tools of both trades, causing his master to believe that he would "endeavour to pass for a freeman."[38] Another runaway, Will, was a cooper and carpenter, although according to his master not particularly adept at either trade, as well as a turner. He took several of his tools with him, but his master noted that Will might try to sell them since they would be troublesome to carry. This particular notice refers to the tools as "his" tools, though in most cases there is no qualifier.[39] Considered with other evidence, it seems that tools taken by slaves were considered the masters' property, as were the slaves themselves.

Fig. 11.
Eighteenth-
century American
tradesmen had
several ways of
acquiring tools
like these that
belonged to
Thomas Nixon of
Framingham,
Mass. Their tool
kits consisted of
tools that were
locally made as
well as imported.
Courtesy,
Framingham
Historical and
Natural History
Society,
Framingham,
Mass.

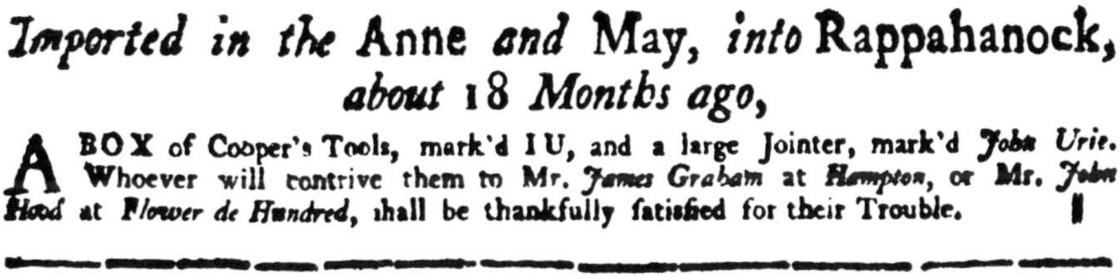

Imported in the Anne *and* May, *into* Rappahanock,
about 18 *Months ago,*

A BOX of Cooper's Tools, mark'd I U, and a large Jointer, mark'd *John Urie.*
Whoever will contrive them to Mr. *James Graham* at *Hampton,* or Mr. *John
Hood* at *Flower de Hundred,* shall be thankfully satisfied for their Trouble.

Fig. 12. Some owners marked their tools with their name or initials. In case of
theft or misdirection, these marks made it possible to identify the owner and return
the tools. *Virginia Gazette,* Dec. 29, 1752.

In the case of indentured servants, it is more difficult to determine whether
the tools were the master's or were actually owned by the servant. In 1738,
four servants ran away from their master. One was a plasterer and another a
middle-aged convict, a joiner by trade. Both men took various tools of their
trades with them.[40] If they made it to freedom, these men could have set themselves up in their trades and might have succeeded in making a new life for
themselves.

The threat of theft may have been one reason why some tool owners identified their tools with personal marks. Some marks were strictly utilitarian,
consisting of a stamp of the owner's initials or his name. Tools in a chest from
Framingham, Massachusetts, owned by Thomas Nixon and later his son War-
ren, are stamped with the initials TN, while Dominy tools from the Winterthur
collection bear their owners' names or initials (fig. 11). Since these groups of
tools were passed down in the family, the initials help determine which tools
were owned by which generation. This practice of marking tools would have
helped men like the unfortunate Mr. Stubblefield prove ownership of their
lost or stolen tools. In 1752, a box of cooper's tools marked IU was imported
to Virginia along with a large jointer marked with the full name of John Urie
(fig. 12). Apparently these tools never made it to their proper owner because
two gentlemen advertised in the *Gazette* that they were still seeking the tools
eighteen months after they had supposedly arrived.[41] Some tools bear inscrip-
tions of names and dates that are decorative and perhaps reflect the owners'
pride in their tools.

During the colonial period, tools played an important role in the colonists' lives. Some colonists used tools only occasionally to accomplish house-

hold chores, while others needed them daily to earn a living. Colonial Virginians had access to tools from a variety of sources. They could purchase them new from stores or directly from England, or buy them used from a local tradesman. They might create some of their own tools or inherit tools from their relatives. Others had tools supplied to them or stole them from their masters. It is evident that a majority of people in Virginia came into daily contact with tools. Study of these tools helps us learn more about the tools themselves and also about their owners and users from some two hundred years ago.

1. This paper has evolved from the research I did in conjunction with the book *Tools: Working Wood in Eighteenth-Century America* by James M. Gaynor and Nancy L. Hagedorn (Williamsburg, Va., 1993) and the accompanying exhibit of the same title. With the permission of the authors, I have borrowed extensively throughout this article from pp. 22–31 of the book.

2. "Building of the Capitol," *William and Mary Quarterly,* 1st Ser., X (1901), p. 80.

3. Jay Gaynor, "'Tooles of all sorts to worke': A Brief Look at Common Woodworking Tools in 17th-Century Virginia," in *The Archaeology of 17th-Century Virginia,* ed. Theodore R. Reinhart and Dennis J. Pogue (Richmond, Va., 1993), pp. 313–314.

4. "Instructions to Governor Wyatt," in William Waller Hening, ed., *The Statutes at Large; Being a Collection of All the Laws of Virginia, from the First Session of the Legislature, in the Year 1619* (New York, Philadelphia, and Richmond, Va., 1819–1823), I, p. 115.

5. "Virginia Threads for the Future Historian," *WMQ,* 1st Ser., II (1893), p. 61.

6. "Instructions to Governor Wyatt," in Hening, ed., *Statutes at Large,* I, p. 115.

7. George Webb, *The Office and Authority of a Justice of Peace* (Williamsburg, Va., 1736; reprint, Holmes Beach, Fla., 1969), title page.

8. *Ibid.,* p. 141.

9. *Ibid.,* p. 190–191.

10. Inventory of the estate of John Kemp, Lower Norfolk County, Va., Deeds & Wills, 1646–1651, p. 96, transcription in research files, CWF. My research for the tool project included surveying court records of a few sample Virginia counties to determine the numbers, types, and frequencies of tools occurring in them. My conclusions here are based on this unpublished research.

11. Will of James Thelaball, proved Sept. 1693, in notes for "The Church in Lower Norfolk County," *Lower Norfolk County Virginia Antiquary,* III (1899–1901), p. 143.

12. Inventories of the wealthier planters in Virginia frequently list a large number and variety of tools. This stock of tools was for use by slaves/servants working the plantations. Some of the wealthy planters also imported tools in quantities larger than those needed for their own use. The surpluses were used to stock plantation "stores" from which their less well-to-do neighbors could obtain needed implements.

13. Inventory of Stephen Minor, Aug. 17, 1750, Frederick County, Va., Records, Will Book, I, 1743–1751, pp. 408–410, microfilm, Lib. of Va.

14. Apprenticeship indenture of Thomas Cathey Braty, July 30, 1777, Rowan County, N. C., Court of Pleas and Quarters, microfilm, North Carolina Department of Archives and History, Raleigh, N. C.

15. Apprenticeship indenture of John Miller, Jan. 12, 1725/26, Lancaster County, Va., Records, Order Book, VII, 1721–1729, p. 150.

16. Apprenticeship indenture of John Garrow, Mar. 16, 1746/47, York Co. Recs., Deeds, V, 1741–1754, p. 208.

17. Robert Hart to John Norton & Sons of London, Nov. 17, 1773, folder 98, Norton Papers.

18. John Parish judgment, Mar. 8, 1726/27, Lancaster Co. Recs., Order Book, VII, p. 229.

19. John Glassford and Co. Recs., Boyd's Hole Store, Ledger 3, fol. 5.

20. Colchester Store, Ledger Book D, 1763–1764, fols. 175, 226; Ledger Book E, 1765, fols. 10, 11, 145, 152; Ledger Book F, 1766, fols. 97, 113; Ledger Book G, 1766–1767, fol. 97, *Ibid.*

21. "Memorandum of sundry Joiners Tools," undated manuscript list of tools, Skipwith Papers, Box 21, folder 37, Swem Lib.

22. Thomas Jefferson to Edmund Meeks, Poplar Forest, July 19, 1819, Jefferson Papers, Massachusetts Historical Society, Boston, Mass., transcription by Cinder Stanton, Monticello.

23. "Harrison of James River," *Virginia Magazine of History and Biography,* XXXI (1923), pp. 370–375.

24. "An Inventory of the Estate of the Right Honorable Thomas Lord Fairfax, Deceased," *ibid.,* VIII (1900), pp. 14–15.

25. "Some Letters of William Beverley," *WMQ,* 1st Ser., III (1895), pp. 223–225.

26. Robert Carter Day Book, 1775, XIII (1773–1776), MSS Division, Duke University Library, Durham, N. C., pp. 68–71.

27. *Va. Gaz.* (Purdie), July 28, 1775.

28. In my study of the Frederick Co., Va., Order Books for 1743–1764, I found several cases that involved the collection and sale of tools to satisfy debts.

29. *Va. Gaz.*, Jan. 16, 1761.

30. *Ibid.*, Sept. 12, 1755.

31. *Ibid.* (Dixon), Mar. 9, 1776.

32. *Ibid.* (Purdie), Dec. 12, 1777, Aug. 15, 1777.

33. Will of William Whitehurst, 1755, Norfolk Co. Recs., Will Book, I, 1755–1772, p. 17; Will of Joshua Baker, 1764, Frederick Co. Recs., Will Book, III, 1761–1770, p. 307.

34. Robert Blair St. George, "Fathers, Sons, and Identity: Woodworking Artisans in Southeastern New England, 1620–1700," in *The Craftsman in Early America*, ed. Ian M. G. Quimby (New York, 1984), pp. 98–100, 116–117, quotation on p. 117.

35. Will of John Chinnswith, Nov. 3, 1770, Frederick Co. Recs., Will Book, IV, 1770–1783, p. 62; Will of Thomas Ward, Mar. 15, 1745, Norfolk Co. Recs., Wills & Deeds, I, 1736–1756, p. 129.

36. Will of Charles Grim, Aug. 16, 1777, Frederick Co. Recs., Will Book, IV, pp. 391–392.

37. *Va. Gaz.* (Rind), June 7, July 19, 1770.

38. *Ibid.* (Purdie and Dixon), Mar. 22, 1770.

39. *Ibid.* (Rind), Nov. 15, 1770.

40. *Ibid.*, Apr. 21–28, 1738.

41. *Ibid.*, Dec. 29, 1752.

The Archaeological Evidence of Tools Used in Seventeenth- and Eighteenth-Century Virginia

By David Harvey

A dreadful storm and hideous began to blow from out the north-east, which, swelling and roaring as it were by fits, some hours with more violence than others, at length did beat all light from Heaven; which, like an hell of darkness, turned black upon us.
William Strachey, July 14, 1610[1]

On July 24, 1609, a small fleet of nine ships was overtaken by a terrible hurricane. The flagship, the *Sea Venture,* a vessel of three hundred tons burden, was sailing from England to Jamestown, Virginia, with 150 people and provisions for the fledgling Virginia colony. The storm raged for four days and the battered ship accumulated more than ten feet of water in her bilge. The sinking ship luckily lodged between two rocks on the shoals just off shore of Bermuda.[2]

William Strachey's account of the *Sea Venture*'s story, written on July 14, 1610, is thought to be the basis for *The Tempest* by William Shakespeare.

Fig. 1. The common types of tools used by shipwrights to construct vessels such as those built by the survivors of the *Sea Venture* are depicted in this sixteenth-century Continental engraving by Theodore de Bry. "A Medieval Shipyard" in *Nec Mora Continuo*. Courtesy, Mariners' Museum, Newport News, Va.

The shipwrecked sailors and settlers made a life for themselves, salvaging what they could from their ship and finding ample food sources on the island. The important and most interesting aspect of this story for us today is that they had the tools and the artisans to build two small pinnaces from the oak salvaged from their wrecked ship and the native island cedars. They ingeniously built a kiln, roasted native limestone, slaked the limestone with water, and "tempered" it with tortoise oil to use as a "tar" to close and seal the seams in the hull.[3]

We know that the artisans who built those two small pinnaces encountered many troubles in working the island's native cedar wood: "The most part of her timber was cedar, which we found to be bad for shipping for that it is wondrous false inward, and besides it is so spalled or brickle that it will make no good planks; her beams were all oak of our ruined ship"[4] (fig. 1).

This is also a story of plots and intrigues among the shipwrecked. We only know about the actual tools they possessed because of the intrigues of "one Henry Paine, the thirteenth of March, full of mischief, and every hour preparing something or other, stealing swords, addices [adzes], axes, hatchets, saws, augurs, planes, mallets, etc., to make good his own bad end."[5]

The sailors and settlers set sail to Jamestown, Virginia, in the *Deliverance* and the *Patience* built of their own hands. They made landfall on the Virginia Capes ten months after they had left England. They arrived in Virginia to find the colony in the midst of being abandoned during the infamous "Starving time" of 1610.[6]

Without the tools and the skilled hands to utilize them, the shipwrecked settlers would scarcely have been able to survive on the island, let alone leave it. This story is a dramatic testament to the fact that England was exporting an entire wood- and metalworking culture to the shores of Virginia in the age of Shakespeare.

In the late 1970s, the Bermuda Maritime Museum conducted archaeological excavations on the *Sea Venture* site. All that remained were fragmentary portions of the hull and scattered shards of pottery and glass. If our only source of knowledge about this site was archaeological, I would have no story to tell you today. And yet, there are marvelous instances of archaeological preservation. For example, the underwater excavation of the sunken *Mary Rose* has added immeasurably to our knowledge of the world of Henry VIII back to the very day the ship sank on July 19, 1545.[7]

What is the place of archaeological sites and artifacts in the world of tool scholarship? What can we learn from finding tools in the shadowy, stained soils where buildings once stood and people once lived and worked?

First, archaeologically recovered tools are of primary importance for they tell us irrefutably that individual tool artifacts belong to a specific place and time. Archaeological sites are assemblages of numerous material artifacts in intimate association with each other in soil or seabed layers. Because of this, varied and discrete criteria (such as ceramics, glass, and coins) can be utilized to date tool artifacts. Archaeological tools can often provide the "missing link" to constructing tool typologies because of the survival of well-provenanced tools and tool types. There are many examples of tool types that have survived in the ground and have no existing counterparts in provenanced tool collections. Often there is a dearth of documentary information for specific historical periods and locales. This lack of evidence creates a natural niche for the study of well-preserved artifact collections.

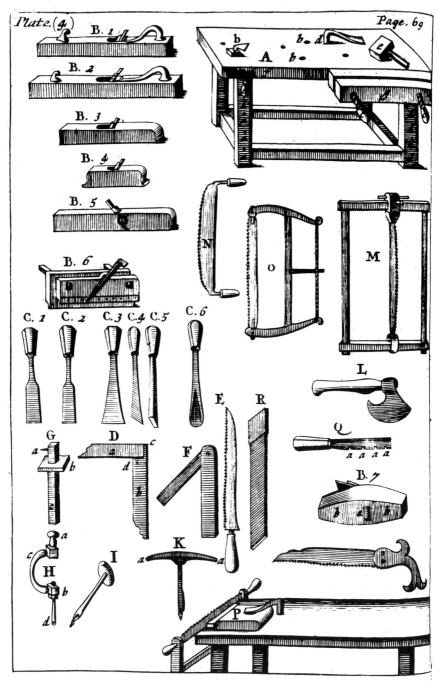

Fig. 2. Joinery tools illustrated in Joseph Moxon, *Mechanick Exercises: or, The Doctrine of Handy-works,* 3rd ed. (London, 1703), the first English book of trade practices, originally published 1678–1680.

Second, archaeological tools are an often neglected resource that can tell anthropologists and historians about historic and prehistoric work patterns and the cultural exploitation of natural resources. Tools enable the generic and specialized craft activities that impact the historic landscape.

Third, archaeological tools are a wonderful resource to help us understand the quality of tools as a class of manufactured goods. The scientific analysis of archaeological tools can tell us of the quality of the raw materials and the successes and failures of toolmaking artisans in fabricating a functional product. Archaeological tools also offer a wonderful glimpse into the world of tool use and misuse in the hands of past peoples.[8]

If one reads the site reports of American historical archaeologists, one encounters the unstated notion that "a tool is a tool is a tool." One will read endless pages on architectural features, soil stratigraphy, ceramic vessel analysis, and faunal analysis, but tools are scarcely mentioned, and, if so, only in passing.

I find this puzzling. Lithic tool artifact research has developed typologies, materials identification with its attendant trading pattern implications, and use-wear analysis as standard methodologies of prehistoric American archaeology. Extensive archaeological research has been devoted to ancient and medieval metal tool artifacts. It is surprising that archaeologically recovered historic American tools are too often intellectually abstracted into what an English colleague calls "those little brown bits."

I would like to make the case for studying those "little brown bits," because, as a scholarly resource, they have much to tell us about the world of tools in early America and the past peoples who made and used them.

I just want to offer a caveat before I begin to review the results of our archaeological research. When examining archaeological sites and artifacts, be ever mindful of this question: "Why did these objects get buried in the ground?"

The Colonial Williamsburg Archaeological Tool Survey

The Colonial Williamsburg archaeological tool survey began in June 1987. It is an ongoing research project. Although the study of archaeological tools has long been a part of Colonial Williamsburg's research efforts, particularly in the historic trades program, this tool survey project was the first systematic effort to study and record seventeenth- and eighteenth-century tools in archaeological site collections in Virginia and Maryland.

The site assemblages that we surveyed ranged from the early fortified compounds and houses of the first quarter of the seventeenth century to the slave quarter sites and large plantation complexes of the second half of the eighteenth century.

We have found that there is little to say about urban contexts. Although a wealth of tools have been excavated from Jamestown Island, few of the artifacts have good archaeological provenances. The further reassessment of the Jamestown Island sites, which is now underway, could result in more data about these tool artifact resources. The town of Williamsburg has surprisingly little to offer us in terms of tool artifact finds. It seems that urban craftsmen were less prone to lose or discard the tools of their trades.

For the purposes of this paper, I will review only the artifactual evidence from the major classes of woodworking tools, and I will limit the temporal span of the archaeological sites to the period of 1625 to 1750, focusing on those of the seventeenth century, from which the accompanying charts of tool types were composed (figs. 3–10).

The first class of woodworking tools that we examined comprises felling axes. In the thriving tobacco agriculture of the Chesapeake region, felling axes were the primary land-clearing and lumbering tool. We have found two distinct ax pattern groupings and a group of miscellaneous ax patterns: pointed ear, rounded ear, and miscellaneous felling axes. In figure 3, the artifacts are chronologically arranged from left to right within the tool groupings.[9] The variation in the flare of the ax blades doesn't seem to be temporally oriented. Also, all of these archaeological ax pattern types coexist in both time and place. Two ax types were found within the fortified compound at Jordan's Point (1620–1635; near Hopewell, Virginia). Both the pointed ear ax and the rounded ear ax were in use in this compound at the same time. We also have evidence that these ax pattern forms were used for extended periods. A pointed ear pattern ax from one of the root cellars of the Utopia II slave quarter site (1730–1770; near Williamsburg, Virginia) is similar in form to its Jordan's Point counterpart buried in the ground one hundred years earlier. We have also documented several mortise axes in our survey, such as an example from the Kingsmill Tenement site (1625–1650; near Williamsburg, Virginia).

When we examined archaeological broad axes, we encountered a consistently surprising feature: almost all of these axes are double-beveled (fig. 4). This means that the axes were multifunctional: they would both chop and rough-square the sides of logs. This evidence conflicts with the traditional view that broad axes have a single bevel and are used just for squaring.[10] We know

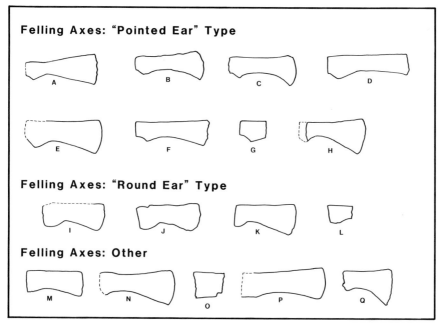

Fig. 3. *Felling Axes.* A: Martin's Hundred (1738A), 1620–1645; B and C: Jordan's Point (44PG302/F-110 EU#766), 1620–1635; D: Kingsmill Tenement (KM562D), early to mid-seventeenth century; E. Jordan's Point (44PG300/1E 106), 1620–1635; F and G: Mathews Manor (Weber Collection), mid-seventeenth century; H: St. Mary's City (STI-13-1468MM/AH), 1635–1700, broken through eye; I and J: Jordan's Point (44PG302/F-110S EU#766), 1620–1635; K: Flowerdew Hundred (44PG86), probably 1620–1630 (surface find); L: Martin's Hundred (2076B), 1620–1640, eye fragment; M: Harbor View Fort (SK192/19Y), 1620–1630; N: Jordan's Point (44PG300/7E 195), 1620–1635; O: Martin's Hundred (2080A), 1620–1640, eye fragment (original blade configuration unknown); P: Jordan's Point (44PG300/1E 68), 1620–1635; Q: Drummond site (GL242), 1680–1710 (possibly to ca. 1720) (all approx. $\frac{1}{16}$ scale). Figures 3–10 are reprinted from Jay Gaynor, "'Tooles of all sorts to worke': A Brief Look at Common Woodworking Tools in 17th-Century Virginia," in *The Archaeology of 17th-Century Virginia,* ed. Theodore R. Reinhart and Dennis J. Pogue (Richmond, Va., 1993), p. 322–345. They were prepared by Dennis J. Pogue for the original publication.

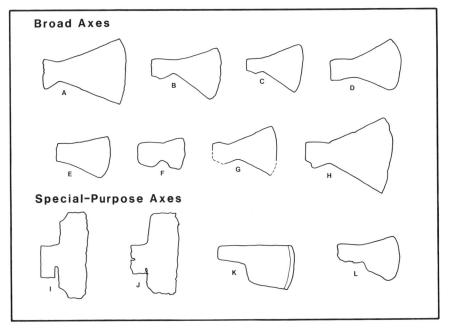

Broad Axes

Special-Purpose Axes

Fig. 4. *Broad Axes.* A: Martin's Hundred (1755E), 1620–1645, broken through eye; B: Martin's Hundred (ax: 4115A #92, socket: 4143A #2), ca. 1620; C: Martin's Hundred (2115A), 1620–1640; D. Chesopean site (44VB48), probably 1625–1650; E: Pettus site (KM152C), mid- to late seventeenth century, blade only; F: Jordan's Point (44PG332/1B), 1620–1635, most of blade missing; G: Jordan's Point (44PG300/1F), 1620–1635, a hewing ax with one side flat. H: Mathews Manor (WS203, Weber Collection), mid-seventeenth century (all approx. $\frac{1}{16}$ scale). *Special Purpose Axes.* I: Cooper's ax, Martin's Hundred (1771J), 1620–1640; J: Cooper's ax, Mathews Manor (WS238, Weber Collection), mid-seventeenth century; K: "Bearded" ax, Causey's Care (44CC178/2), pre-1665, eye broken off. L: Jordan's Point (44PG300/1E 61N), 1620–1635 (all approx. $\frac{1}{16}$ scale).

that these axes were used here in Virginia, and we also have direct evidence that they were fabricated here as well. Several locally made axes were excavated from the Chesopean site (1625–1650; near Virginia Beach, Virginia). We are certain of this because archaeologists also found the drift tool that a blacksmith used as a mandrel to define the form of the eyes of these axes. We have also encountered special-purpose axes. One is a bearded ax from the Causey's Care site (1665; near Hopewell, Virginia). Another is a hatchet from the Drummond site (1680–1720; near Jamestown, Virginia).

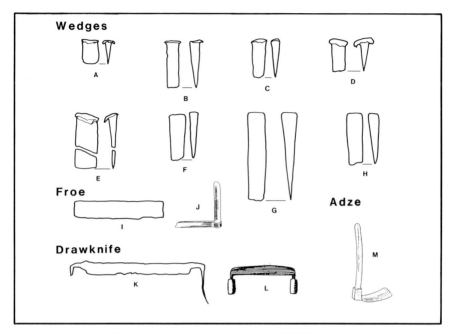

Fig. 5. *Wedges.* A: Flowerdew Hundred (44PG65/193N3D-4), "Enclosed Compound," 1618–1660; B–D: Martin's Hundred (1738A, 1752, 1731), 1620–1645; E: Flowerdew Hundred (44PG65/122, 123-40), "Enclosed Compound" (surface), 1618–1660; F: Causey's Care (44CC178/39/2P), pre-1665; G: Pettus site (KM151C), mid- to late seventeenth century; H: Kingsmill Tenement (KM353B), early to mid–seventeenth century (all approx. $\frac{1}{16}$ scale).
Froe. I: Pasbehay site (JC298/105G), 1625–1650 (approx. $\frac{1}{16}$ scale); J: illustration adapted from Joseph Smith, *Explanation or Key, to the Various Manufactories of Sheffield* (Sheffield, Eng., 1816) (not to scale). *Drawknife.* K: Causey's Care (44CC178/39/1/2L), pre-1665 (approx. $\frac{1}{16}$ scale). L: illustration from Moxon, *Mechanick Exercises* (not to scale). *Adze.* M: illustration adapted from Peter Nicholson, *Mechanical Exercises* (London, 1812) (not to scale).

Relatively few splitting tools are found on Virginia archaeological sites. Wedges are the most common splitting tool artifacts (fig. 5). Wedges were heavily used. There is extreme mushrooming of the head in an example from the Fortified Area, Flowerdew Hundred (1618–1660; near Hopewell, Virginia). This is an almost-universal feature of these tools. Small, five-inch-long wedges are most typical, while we have only two examples of long wedges, such as a wedge from the Pettus site (mid- to late seventeenth century; near

Williamsburg, Virginia). We have encountered only one froe in our entire survey—a very early example from the Pasbehay site (1625–1650; near Jamestown, Virginia).

Since we know from documentary sources that the technology of wood splitting dominated the woodworking landscape in Virginia, why don't we find more splitting tools when sites are excavated? We suggest that logs would be preprocessed on the site of their felling. They would be split up into manageable sizes before transportation back to house or barn, much as a hunter dresses his kill before walking home.[11] One of the few intact adzes comes from the same site as that eighteenth-century pointed ear ax—from one of the root cellars of the Utopia II slave quarter site.

Figure 6 shows the saw types. Cross cut saws are the most common type we have identified. Wooden handles were fitted onto the upturned tangs, and a man on each end would alternate strokes to cut across logs. In the two cross cut saw fragments from the Basse's Choice site (1620–1640; near Smithfield, Virginia) sheet-metal stops have been riveted to each blade end just before the handle tang. These stops would prevent the ends of the saw from being dragged through the log during sawing. Traditionally, cross cut saws were sharpened with symmetrical teeth so that the saw cut on both of the strokes. This has been one way that small fragments of these saws have been identified. The early seventeenth-century examples from Basse's Choice, however, have asymmetrical teeth sharpened to cut in one direction, while the example from the Causey's Care site has symmetrical teeth. This suggests that identification by tooth patterns, which can be altered by resharpening, must be used cautiously in determining saw typologies.[12] We have encountered a few examples of pitsaw and frame saw fragments in the archaeological collections. These saws were used to produce more accurately dimensioned lumber than could be achieved through splitting. Pitsaw fragments can be identified from the tooth pattern and by the taper in the width of the saw as found in the two examples from the Causey's Care site.

Only a few handsaw fragments have survived archaeologically. This is probably because such thin sheet metal deteriorates rapidly in the ground. At the Kingsmill Tenement site, there was a remarkable survival of a compass saw. Another remarkable survival is a tanged handsaw from the Jordan's Point site. It is similar to the one depicted in Joseph Moxon's *Mechanick Exercises* (fig. 2), with a decorative ogee pattern on its nose. An identical example of this saw type has been excavated from the Clifts Plantation site (1635–1650) on the Northern Neck of Virginia. There are saw blade fragments recovered from the foreshore of the Thames that have an ogee nose form similar to that found on the early Virginia saws. Do all of these saws represent a Continental type, perhaps Dutch, that would have been available in Virginia before the adoption of the English Navigation Acts?[13]

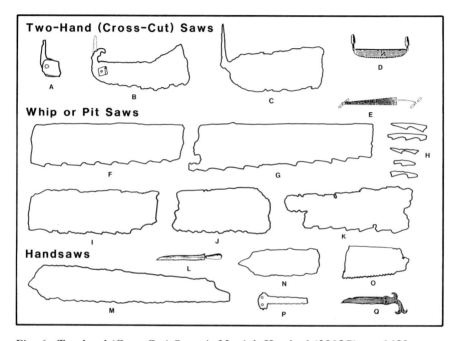

Fig. 6. *Two-hand (Cross Cut) Saws.* A: Martin's Hundred (3012C), ca. 1620; B: Basse's Choice (IW13/102A), 1620–1640, one of two end pieces, possibly from same saw, that survive; C: Causey's Care (44CC178/39/2P), pre-1665 (all approx. $^1/_{16}$ scale); D: illustration from Moxon, *Mechanick Exercises* (not to scale). *Whip or Pit Saws.* E: illustration adapted from Smith, *Explanation or Key* (not to scale); F: Causey's Care (44CC178/39/6L), pre-1665; G: Causey's Care (44CC178/39), pre-1665; H: Tooth fragments, Flowerdew Hundred (44PG65/190–191), "Enclosed Compound," 1618–1660; I: Causey's Care (44CC178/39), pre-1665; J: Causey's Care (44CC178/6/8H), pre-1665; K: Pettus site (KM54A) mid- to late seventeenth century (all approx. $^1/_{16}$ scale). *Handsaws.* L: illustration adapted from Moxon, *Mechanick Exercises* (not to scale); M and N: Jordan's Point (44PG302/F–110 EU#766), 1620–1635; O: Jamestown (COLO J 10374, Project 103, Feature 40, Fill), no date, but probably early seventeenth century; P: Compass saw, Kingsmill Tenement (KM353C), early to mid-seventeenth century (all approx. $^1/_{16}$ scale); Q: illustration from Moxon, *Mechanick Exercises* (not to scale).

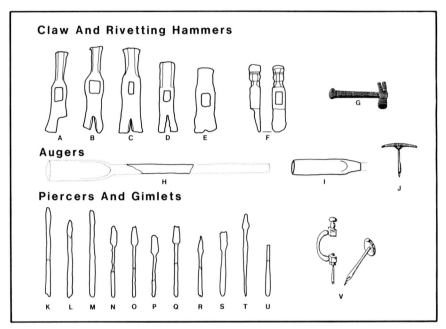

Fig. 7. *Hammer Heads.* A: The Maine (GL109A), pre-1626; B: The Maine
(GL13B), pre-1626; C: Flowerdew Hundred (44PG64/2C/SWQ), "Temporary
Pit Dwelling," 1618–1630(?); D: Kingsmill Tenement (KM376B), early to
mid-seventeenth century; E: Kingsmill Tenement (KM415A), 1690–1710;
F: Flowerdew Hundred (44PG66/508A1-53), "Flowerdew Town" earthfast
structure, 1690–1730 (all approx. ⅛ scale); G: illustration from Moxon, *Mechanick
Exercises* (the odd perspective shows both the top of the hammer head and the
straps and handle) (not to scale). *Augers.* H: Jordan's Point (44PG300/7/E),
1620–1635, encrusted and configuration approximate; I: Kingsmill Tenement
(KM393A), 1635–1650 (this site may have eighteenth-century contamination)
(all approx. ⅛ scale); J: illustration from Moxon, *Mechanick Exercises,* of what
appears to be a Continental-type auger (not to scale). *Piercers and Gimlets.* K:
Martin's Hundred (3013G), ca. 1620; L: Boldrup Well (44NN40/7V), 1630s; M:
Kingsmill Tenement (KM393F), 1635–1650; N: The Maine (GL110A), pre-1626;
O: The Maine (GL127A), pre-1626; P: The Maine (GL124A), pre-1626;
Q: Flowerdew Hundred (44PG65/190/53-22), "Enclosed Compound,"
1618–1660; R: Martin's Hundred (2103B), 1620–1640; S: Causey's Care
(CC178/6/36C), pre-1665. T: Kingsmill Tenement (KM415A), 1690–1710;
U: Flowerdew Hundred (44PG65/190KZ-48), "Enclosed Compound," 1618–1660
(all approx. ⅛ scale); V: illustrations of piercer (*left*) and gimlet (*right*) from
Moxon, *Mechanick Exercises* (not to scale).

Figure 7 shows the typology of hammers and boring tools. In Moxon's view of a claw hammer, a pair of iron straps was used to mount the hammer head to its wooden handle. We have encountered few surviving archaeological hammer strap fragments, but we have encountered a number of claw hammer heads. There are two early examples excavated from the Maine site. They both have octagonal faces, rectangular eyes, and flared split claws. This form does not seem to change much at all, even well into the late eighteenth century, when we see these hammers depicted in English tool catalogs. A more unusual form is a rivetting hammer from the Fortified Area, Flowerdew Hundred. The narrow peen of this hammer was almost certainly used for driving small brads into restricted locations. Interestingly, similar decorative treatments of the head can be seen in examples recovered from the foreshore of the Thames.

Braces and bits, along with gimlets and augers, were a necessity for joined wood construction. Although no braces have been found in archaeological excavations, there is a profusion of bits and gimlets such as the examples from the Martin's Hundred site (1620; near Williamsburg). We have found that the bit tangs are a flat rectangle, rather than square, in section. This seems to be a distinctive feature of all the seventeenth-century examples that we have studied. Bits and gimlets are small and, therefore, easy tools to misplace and lose, which probably explains their numerous presence in the archaeological collections.[14] In contrast we have found only a couple of augers, such as an example from the Jordan's Point site.

By far, the most common class of tools that we have documented in our survey of the archaeological collections are chisels (fig. 8). The Moxon plate (fig. 2) shows that tanged chisels were widely available in numerous sizes, and our archaeological examples confirm this. Tanged chisels were used for the light-to-moderate work of shaping and cleaning up wood joints for close fitting. The tanged chisel that was excavated from the Jordan's Point site is typical of the examples we have seen. We have discovered several intriguing examples of tanged chisels with three-sided bolsters, such as one excavated from the Fortified Area, Flowerdew Hundred. Examples of this seventeenth-century type have also been documented in St. Mary's City, Maryland. The lack of a bottom bolster facet doesn't seem to be a functional element, but it is almost certainly an idiosyncratic one.[15]

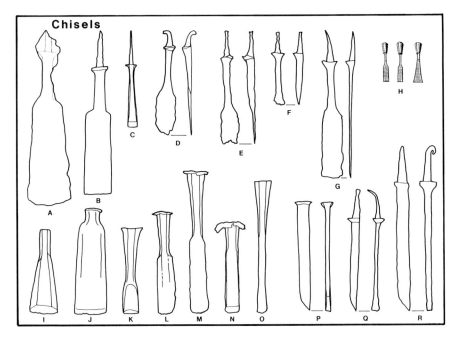

Fig. 8. Tanged Chisels. A: Jordan's Point (44PG302/F-320 EU#889), 1620–1635, tang-end encrusted and bolster-and-tang configuration approximate; B: Causey's Care (CC178/50A), 1680–1710; C: Drummond site (GL250B), 1680–1710; D: Jamestown (COLO J 5278, 96:100–152), no date. E: Jamestown (COLO J 1862, B87, Depth 4–5 feet), no date; F: Flowerdew Hundred (44PG66/578J2-412), "Flowerdew Town" earthfast structure, 1690–1730; G: St. Mary's City (ST1-23/72C/JF), 1678–ca. 1720 (all approx. ⅛ scale); H: illustrations of tanged chisels from Moxon, *Mechanick Exercises* (not to scale). *Socket Chisels.* I: Portion of shank and blade only, Flowerdew Hundred (44PG65/193F/M–17), "Enclosed Compound," 1618–1660; J: Portion of shank and blade only, Pettus site (KM82P-2), mid- to late seventeenth century; K: Pettus site (KM110A), mid- to late seventeenth century (this piece is actually a gouge); L: Drummond site (GL235M), probably late seventeenth century; M–O: Kings Reach (18CV83), 1690–1715 (all approx. ⅛ scale). *Mortise Chisels.* P: Drummond site (GL222V), 1650–1680; Q: Flowerdew Hundred (PG3/25), Flowerdew Hundred Plantation (surface), date unknown; R: Causey's Care (CC178/39/4B), pre-1665 (all approx. ⅛ scale).

We have found numerous examples of socket chisels in the archaeological collections. Socket chisels had a wooden handle fitted into the socket cavity that allowed them to withstand heavy blows applied with a mallet. All of the socket chisels from the seventeenth century that we have examined have a hexagonal socket form. A mid-eighteenth-century socket chisel that was excavated from one of the root cellars at the Utopia II slave quarter site has a visible weld seam running along the underside of the hexagonal socket. Hexagonal socket chisels also have been collected from the foreshore of the Thames. They are a great example of a form that dominates the archaeological record, but is rare in aboveground antiques.[16]

The miscellaneous archaeological tool category includes the least represented, and often unique, examples of their types (fig. 9). A complete grindstone was excavated from the Drummond site. Saw wrests are found occasionally, such as two examples from Flowerdew Town (1690–1730) at Flowerdew Hundred. The tanged versions would have had wooden handles and would be suitable for setting teeth on heavier saws; the smaller, round wrests have an integral metal handle and are of a size to set handsaws. Plane irons have been excavated from a variety of Virginia archaeological sites. Almost all of them are for bench planes. A specialized plane iron, for cutting three-eighths-inch tongues for tongue-and-groove joints, was excavated from the Fortified Area, Flowerdew Hundred. This implies that a sophisticated form of joinery was being practiced on this site, probably architectural woodwork.[17] Another unique find is a bench hook that came from the Flowerdew Town site, Flowerdew Hundred. It is a unique example of this tool type and is very similar to what Moxon depicts in his illustration of the joiner's bench (fig. 2). Tooth marks from these tools survive on seventeenth- and eighteenth-century furniture, but to date, this is the only extant archaeological example of which we are aware. Reproductions of this bench hook were made by blacksmiths at Colonial Williamsburg and are now used in the Hay Cabinetmaking Shop.

Compasses, such as the example from Jamestown, are well represented in the archaeological record from a variety of seventeenth- and eighteenth-century sites (fig. 10). These tools may have been easily misplaced or lost, as we suspected in the cases of bits and gimlets. Lathing hammers, such as an example from the Causey's Care site, exist in such large numbers and from such a large variety of sites, including urban Williamsburg, that we wonder about

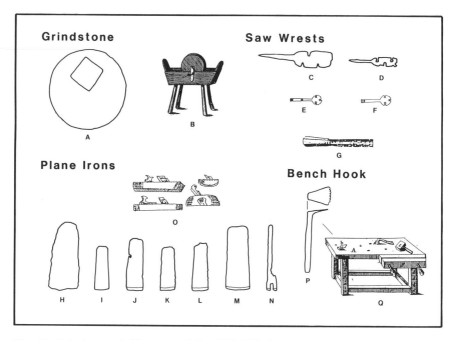

Fig. 9. *Grindstone.* A: Drummond site (GL442), late seventeenth century (approx. $\frac{1}{16}$ scale); B: illustration from Moxon, *Mechanick Exercises* (not to scale). *Saw Wrests.* C: Causey's Care (44CC178/39/2P), ca. 1665; D: Flowerdew Hundred (44PG66/508V2A3-27), "Flowerdew Town" earthfast structure, 1690–1730; E: Drummond Site (GL250B), 1680–1710; F: Flowerdew Hundred (44PG66/508B1-92), "Flowerdew Town" earthfast structure, 1690–1730 (all approx. $\frac{1}{16}$ scale); G: illustration from Moxon, *Mechanick Exercises* (not to scale). *Plane Irons.* H: Jordan's Point (44PG302/F-320 EU#889), 1620–1635; I: Flowerdew Hundred (44PG64/179Q), "Dwelling House," 1624–1660; J: Chesopean site (44VB48) (dug in the 1950s), probably 1625–1650; K: Flowerdew Hundred (44PG64/179Q), "Dwelling House," 1624–1660; L: Causey's Care (CC178/39/1L), ca. 1665; M: Causey's Care (CC178/6/8H), ca. 1665; N: Flowerdew Hundred (44PG65/193L1-6), "Enclosed Compound," 1618–1660 (all approx. $\frac{1}{16}$ scale); O: illustration from Randle Holme, *The Academy of Armory, or, a Storehouse of Armory and Blazon . . .* (Chester, Eng., 1688) (not to scale). *Bench Hook.* P: Flowerdew Hundred (44PG66/508B3/CD1-1), "Flowerdew Town" earthfast structure, 1690–1730 (approx. $\frac{1}{16}$ scale); Q: illustration from Moxon, *Mechanick Exercises,* showing bench hook at *b* (not to scale).

their use. As lathing hammers, the small hatchet end would be used to cut thin lath strips to the required lengths, and the hammer would be used to drive the nails. But the widespread distribution of these tools begs us to wonder if they weren't used as the common utility hammers of their day, doing everything from splitting kindling to pounding back loose boards.[18]

The majority of the tools we have seen in the archaeological collections show signs of heavy use and outright failure. Imagine if carpenters used the

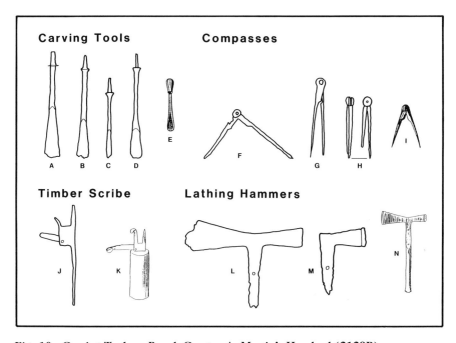

Fig. 10. *Carving Tools or Bench Gouges.* A: Martin's Hundred (2129B), 1620–1640; B: Martin's Hundred (3011E), ca. 1620; C: Martin's Hundred (4115E #145), ca. 1620; D: Martin's Hundred (4065 #1), ca. 1620 (all approx. $\frac{1}{8}$ scale); E: illustration from Moxon, *Mechanick Exercises* (not to scale). *Compasses.* F: Martin's Hundred (3135A), ca. 1620; G: Martin's Hundred (4115A #125), ca. 1620; H. Martin's Hundred (3011H), ca. 1620 (all approx. $\frac{1}{8}$ scale); I: illustration from Moxon, *Mechanick Exercises* (not to scale). *Timber Scribe.* J: Pettus site (KM116), mid- to late seventeenth century (approx. $\frac{1}{8}$ scale); K: illustration by Jay Gaynor (not to scale). *Lathing Hammers.* L: Causey's Care (CC178/50B), pre-1665; M: Kingsmill Tenement (KM353C) early to mid-seventeenth century (both approx. $\frac{1}{8}$ scale); N: illustration by Jay Gaynor (not to scale).

Fig. 11. The shattered poll of the Harbor View Fort ax, 1620–1630. Note that pieces of metal have actually been punched out with no sheer edges and that there are large transverse fractures. This is indicative of a very brittle failure. Photograph by author.

poll of their ax instead of a wooden maul to drive pegs into heavy framing! The likely result is seen in an ax that was excavated from the Martin's Hundred site. The ferrous metal in the ax has completely failed across the wrought-iron grain of the ax poll. Such transgranular failures are typical of what we see in these archaeological tools and are probably attributable to the low-quality iron used to fabricate the tool. Another example of an ax failure was excavated from the Kingsmill site. The Kingsmill ax has completely split along its weld. The steel bit insert is visible in the end of the split.

An ax that was excavated from the Harbor View Fort site (1620–1630; near Suffolk, Virginia) is the only damaged archaeological tool we have been able to sample for metallurgical analysis. The poll of the Harbor View Fort ax is shown in figure 11. It is about as brittle a metal failure as one is liable to encounter. It appears that the bottom of the poll was actually punched out of the body, as if a hammer blow was delivered to thin and brittle cast iron. A small sample was removed from the edge of this massive failure for metallurgical analysis. The photomicrograph of the ax poll sample is shown in figure 12 (magnified one hundred times). The sample was polished flat and etched with a reagent, which visually defines the structures within the iron. The gray band in the center of the sample is a large, two-phase slag inclusion. There are also twin lines within the iron grains; these lines, called Neumann bands, indicate that this piece of iron was excessively cold worked.

If phosphorus is present in iron it will remain unetched, hence light colored, as opposed to the darker bands in the structure of the iron. Only one-tenth of 1 percent phosphorus in iron can cause it to be "cold-short," or extremely brittle, if it is pounded upon at room temperature. The slag in iron mostly consists of silicate glass and is brittle. If slag is present in large quantities, it can lead to mechanical splitting and cracking.[19] Further analysis needs to be conducted on the samples from this ax, and we need to start collecting samples from other damaged archaeological tools.

An adjunct metallurgical research project on aboveground antique tools in the Colonial Williamsburg collection was recently undertaken by Dr. Michael Notis and Ms. Donna Belcher of Lehigh University. They found a remarkable consistency of materials and hardening/tempering procedures in the small sample group of hand tools from the Colonial Williamsburg tool collection, dated between 1730 and 1830.[20]

Fig. 12. Photomicrograph of a tiny sample removed from the Harbor View Fort ax poll (enlarged 100 times). The bright areas are ferrous metal with the intragranular pattern produced by an etchant that shows phosphorus segregation. The gray area is a large two-phase slag inclusion (SiO_2 + FeO) within the metal. Either an excess of slag or the presence of phosphorus can lead to a massive metal failure such as the one this tool artifact suffered. Photograph, courtesy, Robert Edall, NASA.

Fig. 13. Reconstructed slave quarter at Carter's Grove. This type of split-wood architecture dominated the landscape of seventeenth- and eighteenth-century Virginia.

Perhaps archaeological tools were disposed of because they cracked and broke. The materials from which they were made were not suited for recycling. This raises a whole host of questions about the range of quality in seventeenth- and eighteenth-century hand tools.

Many of the tools that we have encountered in our study were used by the newly arrived settlers in Virginia to build the earthfast wattle and daub huts of Jamestown. This earthfast building tradition continued into the early years of the eighteenth century.[21] In the last decades of the seventeenth century, the massive importation of African slaves had begun. They were housed in quarters throughout the countryside near the places where they worked, such as the site reconstructed at Carter's Grove plantation (fig. 13). The quarter buildings were typically log construction or rough hewn logs, with clapboard roofs. Within the quarter rooms, slaves dug multiple root cellars for the storage of a variety of materials; archaeological finds include ceramics, glass, buttons, metal objects, and especially tools.[22] Even in the city of Williamsburg, there were rough buildings, such as the reconstructed James Anderson Blacksmith Shop, built almost entirely of split clapboards. When we look at this historical continuum of hewn- and split-wood architecture, along with the fact that split-wood shingles and barrel staves followed closely after tobacco as major exports from Virginia, we can begin to understand how pervasive the experiences of using these simple but effective tools were, in this place, more than three hundred years ago.

Although we have surveyed hundreds of tool artifacts in our research, our aim has been to use our understanding of them—these "little brown bits"—to further our understanding of the artisans who made these tools and the peoples who used them.

Fig. 14. The people who used these tools changed over time. The majority of the labor force during the first three-quarters of the seventeenth century were indentured laborers of Anglo-European descent. They gave way to the massive importation of African slaves during the eighteenth century. The eighteenth century also saw the rise of a distinct artisan class practicing specialized and sophisticated trades in cities by the time of the American Revolution. Photograph by author.

1. Louis B. Wright, ed., *A Voyage to Virginia in 1609* (Charlottesville, Va., 1964), p. 4.

2. *Ibid.*, pp. 15–16.

3. *Ibid.*, p. 55.

4. *Ibid.*, p. 57.

5. *Ibid.*, p. 47.

6. *Ibid.*, pp. 58–72.

7. Peter Throckmorton, ed., *The Sea Remembers* (New York, 1987), pp. 8–13, 142–144. See Margaret Rule, *The Mary Rose: The Excavation and Raising of Henry VIII's Flagship* (London, 1982).

8. Jay Gaynor, "'Tooles of all sorts to worke': A Brief Look at Common Woodworking Tools in 17th-Century Virginia," in *The Archaeology of 17th-Century Virginia*, ed. Theodore R. Reinhart and Dennis J. Pogue (Richmond, Va., 1993), p. 347.

9. *Ibid.*, pp. 322–323.

10. *Ibid.*, pp. 321, 325.

11. *Ibid.*, p. 329.

12. *Ibid.*, p. 330.

13. *Ibid.*, p. 346.

14. *Ibid.*, p. 320.

15. *Ibid.*, p. 334.

16. *Ibid.*, p. 346.

17. *Ibid.*, p. 342.

18. *Ibid.*, pp. 347–348.

19. Robert B. Gordon, "Strength and Structure of Wrought Iron," *Archaeomaterials*, II (Spring 1988), pp. 119–220. This is a classic paper showing the relationship between microstructure and composition to measurable mechanical properties in a number of historic wrought-iron samples.

20. Donna L. Belcher, "A Metallographic Study of 18th Century Woodworking Tools from the Williamsburg Collection" (master's thesis, Lehigh University, 1994).

21. Cary Carson et al., "Impermanent Architecture in the Southern American Colonies" in *Material Life in America, 1600–1860*, ed. Robert Blair St. George (Boston, 1987), pp. 113–158.

22. William M. Kelso, "Archaeology of Chesapeake Common Folks: Artifacts of Definition and Change Among Rich and Poor at Kingsmill and Monticello, 1650–1810," in *Common People and Their Material World: Free Men and Women in the Chesapeake, 1700–1830*, ed. David Harvey and Gregory Brown (Williamsburg, Va., 1995). See also William M. Kelso, *Kingsmill Plantations, 1619–1800: Archaeology of Country Life in Colonial Virginia* (Orlando, Fla., 1984); and Leland G. Ferguson, *Uncommon Ground: Archaeology and Early African America, 1650–1800* (Washington, D. C., 1992).

PLANEMAKING: A CASE STUDY

From Granford to Gabriel

Some Aspects of Planemaking in England in the Eighteenth Century

By Jane and Mark Rees

The student of English planemaking faces certain difficulties. We have planes from the *Mary Rose* wreck that date from 1545, but we have no planes that we can date between then and the end of the seventeenth century.

Compared with the planes made by the commercial makers of 1700 and later, both the form and quality of the *Mary Rose* planes are very varied (fig. 1). This indicates that these were the products of craftsmen making planes for their own use or, at best, for a very limited local market. The technology of planemaking is, however, clearly well developed; there are examples of bench-mouthed, eyed, and side-mouthed planes. Present are not only bench planes of various lengths but also planes to cut hollows and rounds, an ogee, a rabbet plane, and, perhaps most exciting of all, an early example of a plow plane.

By the beginning of the eighteenth century, the existence of a wide variety of types of planes was confirmed by Moxon, who described five types of bench planes and six types of molding planes. A less well-known source is *The Academy of Armory* by Randle Holme published in 1688.[1] This extraordinary book was intended to assist in the design of coats of arms, but strayed into matters

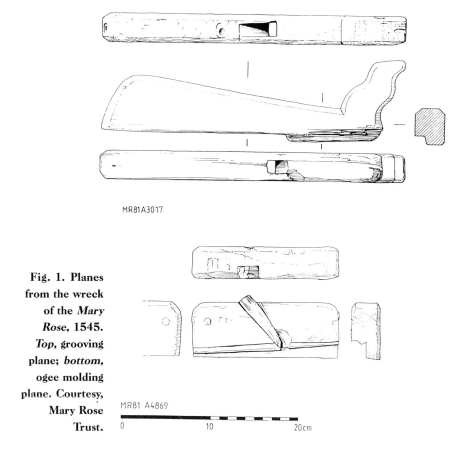

MR81A3017

MR81 A4869

0   10   20 cm

of etiquette including such topics as suitable menus for entertaining the king
when he came to visit!

More importantly for our purposes, Holme enumerates various trades,
their tools, and their specialist terms in the process of discussing whether such
tradesmen may consider themselves to be gentlemen. Incidentally, in the better trades they were! While some of his text appears to be derivative of Moxon,
the engravings, though small, are closely observed and do not seem to be derivative. He lists some types of planes that are not in Moxon: the miter,
bolection, back ogee, cornish (that is, cornice), fillister, and the intriguing
scurging plane, perhaps a type of scrub plane.

Commercial Planemaking

Both Moxon and Holme were writing in the 1680s, which is contemporary with what we now believe to be the start of commercial planemaking. The change from craftsman planemaking to commercial planemaking had important effects on the product. The planes produced commercially are of a more standardized nature. A plane by John Davenport, possibly the earliest identified planemaker, is shown in figure 2. Throughout the eighteenth century, the variability of design that is to be found in molding planes decreases so that, by 1800, both molding planes and bench planes had become almost totally standardized, and there is little or no variation between any of the makers.

Why had this come about? The reason is that, contrary to what might be supposed at first sight, the design of the molding plane is a functional answer to the challenge of producing a tool that works well, fits the hand nicely, and, as much as anything in an increasingly commercial trade, was relatively easy to make.

Fig. 2. A molding plane to cut a form of ogee, 10½" long, by John Davenport, possibly the earliest named planemaker. Courtesy, private collection, photograph by Jane Rees.

There is no doubt about the form and style of the molding plane of 1700 as we have a reasonable number of examples. The typical plane was 10½ inches long with heavy ½-inch-wide chamfers and a wedge that terminated in a full round head and a long neck. To us these planes have a laid back appearance; or seem reminiscent of old ladies with long necks!

Slowly, as the century progressed, the length of the molding plane decreased, each successive generation making them a little shorter, until around 1760 the standard length of 9½ inches was reached. The driving forces for this change were, we think, economy and the discovery that the shorter planes worked just as well. Why the shrinkage stopped at 9½ inches is perhaps more interesting (fig. 3). While at 9½ inches the molding plane was about as short as practical for a cut of normal size, the likely reason why planes became standardized at this length was that, by 1760–1770, the large numbers being made effectively set a standard that became so accepted no maker could ignore it. This was standardization brought about, not by endless committees, but by the marketplace!

This is not the place to undertake a detailed examination of the changes in style of molding planes during the century. This has been covered in *British Planemakers from 1700*.[2] We remain wary of the use of small matters of style to

Fig. 3. Molding planes by Robert Wooding (1706–1739), William Madox (1748–1775), and Christopher Gabriel (1770–1822) illustrating the reduction in the length of planes during the eighteenth century. Authors' collection, photograph by Jane Rees.

Fig. 4. Panel
fielding plane by
Robert Wooding
ca. 1720. Note the
round-topped
wedge and iron.
Courtesy, private
collection,
photograph by Nigel
Macbeth.

date or provide provenance for molding planes, and there are other matters
relating to the trade that made them, their use, and their relation to the products made with them that deserve more attention from researchers.

We can be less certain about the form of the bench plane of 1700 as we
have no examples that can be dated before 1750. We do, however, have a few
examples of near-bench planes. These are panel fielding planes that date from
around 1720–1730. The example shown in figure 4 is possibly even earlier. It
is by Robert Wooding and is of particular significance as it is the only English
plane known to us with a bench-type escapement and a round-topped wedge,
although the existence of the round-topped wedge in English planes has been
deduced from the illustrations on the Jennion trade card (see page 40). This
style, which so neatly matches the round-topped irons of the period, must have
quickly faded, for by 1750, and possibly earlier, the square-topped wedge had
become standard.

The word *planemaker* has been much bandied about without a great deal
of effort to define what it means. We find that many people have a vision of
a man, a dog, and a boy apprentice eking out a living in a quaint, dusty

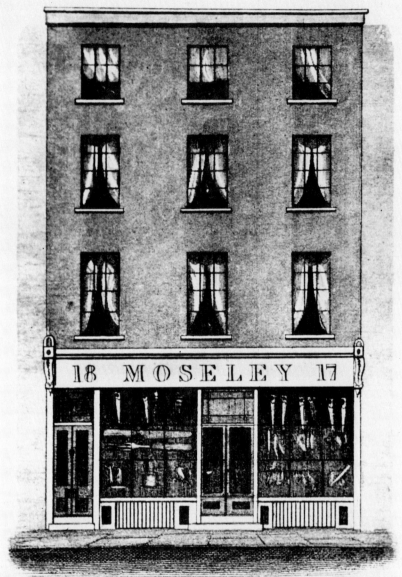

Fig. 5. Trade card of John Moseley, New Street, London, showing the retail shop in New Street. Although this card probably dates from the 1820s, this is the same premises (renumbered) that he had occupied since the last quarter of the eighteenth century. Courtesy, Guildhall Library, Corporation of London.

workshop and selling planes to workmen who knew where to find them and knocked on the workshop door. But this is a fantasy.

We must also differentiate between the man who ran a planemaking business, marketing products and putting his name on them, and the planemaker-tradesman who actually worked at the bench. They might be one and the same, but in general they were not. Even by the early years of the eighteenth century, it is apparent that planemaking and selling was a business that had developed beyond the stage of a man, a boy, and a canine friend.

Thomas Granford, the earliest "planemaker" identified with any certainty, listed in his 1703 advertisement "all sorts of Joyners and Carpenters Tooles. . . . You may also be furnished with several sorts of materials related to building."[3] This is already beginning to sound like the local hardware store.

The celebrated Jennion trade card, dating from circa 1735, again illustrates a wide range of tools and a lock and key, indicating that hardware was among the range of goods he sold. The trade card of William Emmett of Plymouth, believed to date from 1731, lists a huge range of tools, including "all sorts of planes." Here is evidence that some of the tool-selling trade had developed to the point at which little, if any, of the goods being sold were made by the vendor.

The John Harris-George Stothert firm in Bath (1777–1857) and the John Moseley firm in London (1778–1910) are good examples of leading firms that certainly had strong retail sides to their businesses but also were manufacturers of planes in premises closely connected to their shops (fig. 5).

The earliest of the London planemakers, such as Granford, Wooding, and Jennion, were located within the City of London. The next generation of makers were not situated in the City but were grouped in two main areas, Westminster, near the Abbey, and the Old Street area, just north of the City. As early as 1750, four makers, John Rogers in Tufton Street, William Madox in Peter Street, Richard Burman in Marsham Street, and Thomas Okines, were already established in Westminster, and before the end of the century, Joseph Sym, John Green, John Hazey, John Haydon, John Brough, and James Higgs were all working in Westminster. Thomas Okines and some other Westminster makers indicated their location in the King's City by placing a crown above their name.

Richard Horwood's map of London, first published in the 1790s, shows that the Westminster area was still but a street or two from the edge of town

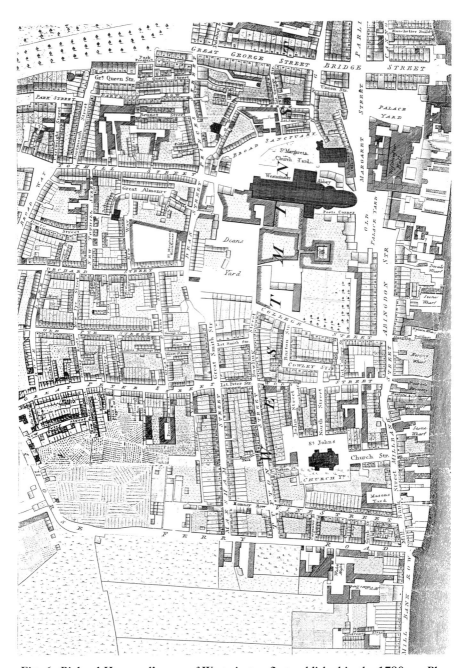

Fig. 6. Richard Horwood's map of Westminster, first published in the 1790s as *Plan of the Cities of London and Westminster* . . . (London, 1799). Courtesy, Museum of London.

(fig. 6). The comparative isolation from the retail shopping areas of London—these were still in the City and the Strand—would suggest that these makers were changing to manufacturers selling to the wholesale market in preference to retailing themselves. There is some evidence to support this view, including the American order of 1760 to John Rogers,[4] and, perhaps more telling, the very large number of planes produced by William Madox. His was plainly no one man, a boy, and a dog type of business.

Before turning to the Old Street area of London, we need to look at the picture in the provinces. It is not until the 1740s that a number of provincial planemakers can be identified, in the towns shown in figure 7. There is no doubt that the making of planes was common in the provinces before this date, but these are the earliest makers yet discovered. They include Thomas Moody in Worcester, who then moved to Birmingham, and George Darbey, who was also working there by 1750. Perhaps more surprising are Sam Penn of Midhurst and Robert Bloxham of Banbury, both working in minor provincial towns at a time when we have no identified makers in some of the larger cities.

By the end of the eighteenth century, there were makers operating in almost all the major provincial cities. Those working in the smaller provincial

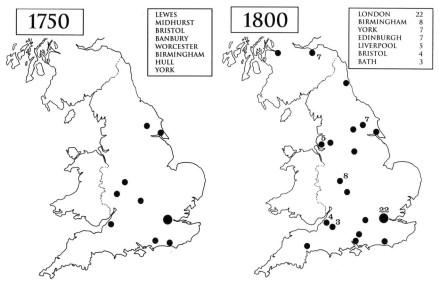

Fig. 7. Maps showing the location of planemakers in England in 1750 and 1800, including the numbers working in the principal centers in 1800.

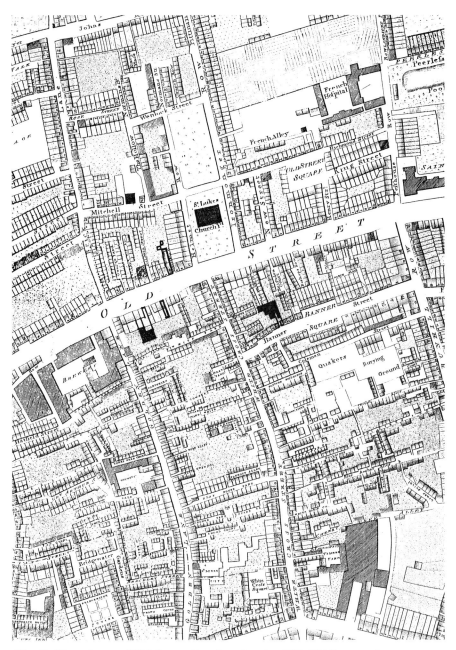

Fig. 8. Map of part of Old Street, London, showing 100 Old Street, where
Christopher Gabriel worked from 1779 to 1794. Almost opposite, at Number 20,
were the premises of William Moorman, sawmaker. In 1794, the Gabriel business
moved to Nos. 31 and 32 Banner Street, which can also be seen on this map.
Richard Horwood, *Plan of the Cities of London and Westminster.* Courtesy,
Museum of London.

towns had ceased, and the industry was expanding in the centers that eventually came to dominate the trade: York, with seven makers and the location of the very extensive John Green business; Birmingham, where, by 1800, eight makers were operating; and the Bristol-Bath area. However, London remained a principal center of British planemaking until the end of the nineteenth century.

Returning to London, the other area that seems to have been attractive to planemakers was just north of the City running up to Old Street (fig. 8). This area was much favored by the cabinetmaking and joinery trades, and, even today, woodworking firms, timber suppliers, and ironmongery merchants are still plentiful. John Cogdell and Robert Fitkin were working here from the 1750s. Other toolmakers included William Moorman, smith and sawmaker,

who had premises at 20 Old Street with works adjacent. By the time the third edition of Horwood's map was published in 1813, these works were one of the very few business premises large enough to be indicated by name.

Almost opposite, at Number 100, Christopher Gabriel lived and worked (fig. 9). He had started in business in this area in 1770 and four years later moved to Golden Lane. In 1779, when the business was really beginning to prosper, he moved around the corner to a newly built house at 100 Old Street. From Horwood's map we know exactly where Gabriel worked. Old Street received much attention from both the Luftwaffe and the postwar developers, so we were amazed to dis-

Fig. 9. Portrait of Christopher Gabriel, planemaker, 1746–1809. Oil painting, approximately 12" by 10". Courtesy, private collection.

cover that the only remaining eighteenth-century houses were in the block where Gabriel worked. His house, Number 100, has gone, but Number 99, the next-door house, and the rest of the block to Number 96 still stand, giving a good idea of the size and extent of the properties. Between 1789 and 1793, John Fitkin, planemaker, worked here in Number 98.

The Gabriel Ledger

Gabriel is the only eighteenth-century planemaker about whom we have sufficient information to build a good picture of the man, his premises, and his trade. Due to a unique survival—the Gabriel Ledger—we have an insight into the business of a man who was perhaps the most prominent planemaker in London at the end of the eighteenth century (fig. 10).[5]

Amazingly, the ledger has not remained with the family since the eighteenth century. It somehow passed into the hands of an antiquarian bookseller from whom it was purchased by a family friend in the 1950s for 10s. 6p. and given to the then Christopher Gabriel. The ledger started life in 1758 as the school copybook of the twelve-year-old Christopher, who was living in Falmouth in Cornwall. He copied many sums into the book. Much later, at Christmas 1770 to be precise, Mr. Gabriel, now twenty-four years of age and recently married, started to write details of his wealth into the spare pages, and he continued this practice, with some gaps, until 1794.

Fig. 10. A page from the Gabriel ledger showing the end-of-year accounts for 1782 and 1783, written by Christopher Gabriel. Note the 1782 reference to a "Flat Plane Rume" and a "Molding Plane Rume." Courtesy, private collection.

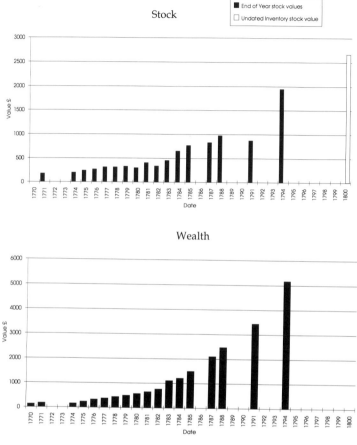

Fig. 11. Graphs showing the end-of-year value of Christopher Gabriel's stock and the growth of his wealth.

From these figures, we know that he prospered. In twenty-four years he had accumulated wealth of more than £5,000. As a typical tradesman's wage at the time was £50 per year, this represents a very considerable store of wealth. From the stock levels and the debts that were owing to him, it can be seen that, at first, growth was slow, but, after 1780, it started to accelerate (fig. 11). As Gabriel prospered, he began to purchase properties: in 1785, a house in Cannon Street, and, in 1788, the house at Number 100 Old Street. Other properties followed, including Numbers 31 and 32 Banner Street, occupied in 1794 by his sons Thomas and Christopher who had joined him in the business. These purchases were recorded in the ledger.

The Inventories

Perhaps more important than the accounts in the ledger are two inventories of his plane and tool stock. One is dated July 1791. The other is undated, but most likely is for 1799. These inventories are detailed and give a good idea of the nature of his trade.

The 1791 inventory has six hundred entries, and the total value, with the timber in stock, is £810. The goods in each room are listed in an apparently haphazard order—Gabriel presumably started in one corner and worked around the walls (fig. 12). This inventory was taken only a year or two before the business was transferred across the road to Banner Street. With some goods stored in sheds detached from the premises, it would appear that they were bulging at the seams. Mr. Gabriel and his family were living on the upper floors of the premises, but after the move to Banner Street in 1794, the sons lived with the business and father moved to a new house in Islington, then a village to the north of Old Street.

The areas used for business are listed as the warehouse, closet on stairs, the room, loft over shop, upper shop, second shop and yard, and also two sheds nearby. Incidentally, in the 1782 end-of-year account, Gabriel referred to a flat plane room, a molding plane room, and a wareroom. We think the last refers to a retail shop.

It is clear that planemaking was Gabriel's principal business activity, but he also sold everything that the woodworker needed including chalk lines, folding and ivory rules, pincers, glue pots, axes and hatchets, black lead pencils, bookbinder's screws, and even three bed winches.

His stocks were large. For example, he had fifty-eight dozen two-inch plane irons, and more than two hundred dozen toothing plane irons of eight different sizes. In all, there were about 9,700 plane irons. Also in stock were 1,300 chisels and gouges. The message is that this was a substantial operation possibly selling some items on a wholesale basis. Indeed, it is no surprise to discover that, in 1796, when Joseph Seaton of Chatham wanted to buy his son Benjamin a comprehensive set of cabinetmaker's tools he went to Christopher Gabriel (fig. 13).[6]

Fig. 12. A page from the 1791 inventory showing the variety of goods Christopher Gabriel stocked and the brevity of the descriptions, which require considerable care in deciphering. Courtesy, private collection.

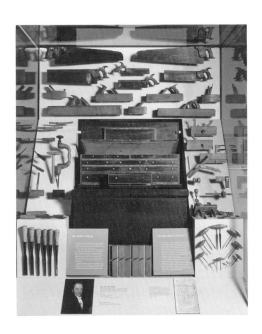

Fig. 13. The Benjamin Seaton tool chest as it appeared in the exhibit "Tools: Working Wood in 18th-Century America." Courtesy, Guildhall Museum, Rochester, Kent, Eng.

Working Methods

The quantities of finished planes in stock in the 1791 inventory seem quite modest. There were, for example, six jack planes and twenty try planes but only one moving fillister and four sash fillisters. There were, however, huge quantities of wood billets already prepared to the stage where they were allocated for specific types of planes: 2,800 woods for rabbets, 9,200 for molding planes, and 5,900 for bench planes. It is therefore clear that Gabriel "cultivated," that is, broke down, the wood into pieces suitable for the various types of planes at an early stage (fig. 14).

At the end of the inventory there is a list of monies that Gabriel owed, mostly to trade suppliers. Prominent are several Sheffield firms: John Kenyon sawmakers, who made the saws in the Seaton chest; and the firms of Hannah Green and Jane Green & Sons, both principal edge tool makers and also the makers of many of the chisels in the Seaton chest.[7]

Of interest are the firms of Sheppard & Bill of Wolverhampton and London, wholesale ironmongers and most likely the suppliers of the brass fittings used on planes, and Thomas Hattam of the Barbican, ironmongers and braziers whom Gabriel almost certainly also supplied with planes. He was also

Fig. 14. A page from the 1791 inventory showing some of the wood billets already "cultivated" to the stage where they have been allocated for specific types of planes. Courtesy, private collection.

buying from his neighbor just across the road, the sawmaker William Moorman & Son, as well as other London sawmakers. This shows that although the Gabriel business was large enough to be buying direct from the principal edge tool manufacturers of the time, some goods were coming via wholesalers.

Plane irons and other edge tools evidently traveled in casks, as there is reference to a cask of irons, and there were several empty ones in the yard. The molding plane irons are listed by size. They are described as soft irons, sized from ¼ inch to 2¼ inches. Again, the quantities are large, in total 1,600. They would have been filed to shape as required and then hardened.

Conclusion

To what extent was Gabriel typical of London planemakers at the end of the eighteenth century? The answer, we think, is not very typical. With few exceptions—and John Moseley is perhaps the most obvious—most makers did not prosper to the extent of the Gabriels. However, the Gabriels are typical in that they combined other business activities, particularly tool selling, with planemaking, a pattern that can be seen throughout the trade starting from the time of Thomas Granford.

1. Randle Holme, *The Academy of Armory, or, a Storehouse of Armory and Blazon . . . * (Chester, Eng., 1688; reprint, Menston, Eng., 1972).

2. W. L. Goodman, *British Planemakers from 1700*, 3rd ed. rev. by Jane and Mark Rees (Needham Market, Eng., 1993).

3. *The Post Man*, May 6–8, 1703, reprinted in "Letters," *Chron. Early Amer. Industries Assn.*, XXXIII (1980), p. 70.

4. List of a Chest of Joiners Tools, Letter and Order Book, William Wilson, in Hummel, *With Hammer in Hand*, pp. 32–33.

5. For a detailed discussion of the Gabriel business, see Jane and Mark Rees, *Christopher Gilbert and the Tool Trade in 18th Century London* (Needham Market, Eng., 1997).

6. Jane and Mark Rees, eds., *The Tool Chest of Benjamin Seaton, 1797* (Bournemouth, Eng., 1994).

7. *Ibid.*

Planemaking in Eighteenth-Century America

By Donald and Anne Wing

Why should anyone spend time studying people who made wooden planes two and a half centuries ago?

The answer, aside from the obvious reasons for studying history in general, is that planemaking in colonial America was essentially the beginning of hand tool production. Certainly, blacksmiths and others were producing tools right from the first settlements, but wooden planes were the first tools, and, indeed, were among the first objects of any kind to be commercially produced and stamped systematically with the name and very frequently the place of residence of the maker—the first instances of makers advertising and marketing their locally made products. From this small start the hand tool industry developed.

Researching these early makers is a real challenge. Unlike the educated clergymen and government leaders of their day, planemakers were generally yeomen, men who owned farms and worked hard for their living. Most seem to have been able to read and write (books are included in the inventories of their estates, they served as town officers, etc.) but were much too busy with the necessity of sheltering, feeding, and clothing themselves and their families

117

to indulge in the luxury of keeping diaries or writing prolifically to their friends. Thus we do not have the paper trail of a Thomas Jefferson to give us insights into their lives. We have to rely on wills, land deeds of the makers and their abutters, newspaper ads, contemporary ledger entries, and the like to piece together what information we can.

The pioneer in this research, Jack Kebabian, was intelligent and erudite—and very fortunate. He was intelligent enough to recognize more than twenty years ago that some planes had characteristics similar to other eighteenth-century antiques with which he was familiar; scholarly enough to begin searching early records to identify their makers; and his good fortune was that he began with Francis Nicholson of Wrentham, Massachusetts. In one "fell swoop" he discovered the still earliest documented American planemaker, a generational link between makers represented by Francis's son John Nicholson, and the first black planemaker, the slave Cesar Chelor, whom Francis set free upon his death.[1] Any one of these discoveries would have been a major coup, but to find all three in the first stab at this research is incredible. We all owe a great deal to Jack Kebabian's scholarship, enthusiasm, and willingness to share his knowledge. Ken Roberts's contributions to the study of planemaking in America are to be noted also; he was the first to undertake the task of listing all American makers and has inspired many other researchers.

"Eighteenth-century" planes were not all made between 1700 and 1800. Styles changed gradually, and so for the purposes of this paper, "eighteenth-century" planes will include those made from approximately 1680 to 1820. There was no magic, deliberate style change as the century turned at midnight.

The map, figure 1, emphasizes the fact that most of what we know about eighteenth-century planemaking relates to New England.[2] The dots show the planemaking centers from about 1750 to 1810, most of which are concentrated close to Providence, Rhode Island. One must realize that the expansion of American planemaking began essentially in this region. There were other important makers, of course, with Thomas Grant and James Stiles in New York City and a group that followed Samuel Caruthers in Philadelphia.

A few planemakers were located in the Hudson River valley, where James Stiles moved from New York City, and the Connecticut River valley, where Henry Wetherel relocated from Norton, Massachusetts, and Leonard Kennedy

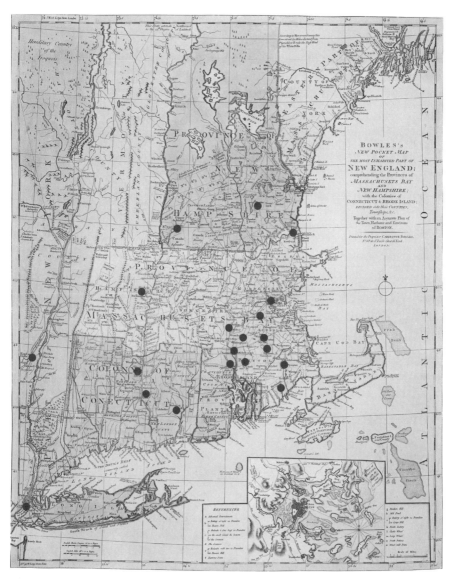

Fig. 1. Towns in which major eighteenth-century planemakers were located are shown by the dots; the majority were in southeastern New England. Those in the Connecticut and Hudson River valleys and New Hampshire indicate the expansion of the trade in the last quarter of the century. Carington Bowles, *New Pocket Map of the Most Inhabited Part of New England in 1780* (London, ca. 1780). Reproduced from a map in the Library of Congress, courtesy, Historic Urban Plans, Inc., Ithaca, N. Y.

settled at the end of the eighteenth century. Also, John Sleeper moved from Newburyport, Massachusetts, to New Hampshire, and other rural and coastal makers began to migrate farther inland.

There are several reasons for this initial concentration of planemakers in New England, and more specifically in southeastern Massachusetts. The availability of bog iron and of the appropriate timber are primary among them. Further, the rapidly increasing number of wood-framed houses, barns, and rural churches contributed to the demand for wooden planes and stimulated some modifications from the traditional British patterns to suit the building needs.

Of equal importance is structure of society. Boston was the only large town in New England at that time. A man who owned a farm and had some training in working wood could make planes for himself and perhaps a few extras to trade with neighboring farmers and craftsmen. If he lived near a main road, he could dispatch some planes with the passing peddler.

On the contrary, the South, with its large plantations and mostly single-crop economy, was dependent on the mother country for manufactured goods. If a craftsman on a southern plantation needed a plane, he would most likely either buy an imported one from a merchant or make it himself. The busy New England trading village was absent in the South.

In the Middle Colonies, a different element was present: the influence of the major cities of Philadelphia and New York. Woodworkers there relied more on imported planes early on. By the decade before the Revolution, however, making planes became an occupation more structured than in New England, with merchant-manufacturers such as Caruthers, Armitage, and Martin in business in Philadelphia and Grant and Stiles in New York. With more contact with the mother country, these makers tended to follow British patterns fairly closely.

Three areas will be addressed in this summary of eighteenth-century planemakers: first, the planes themselves; second, the production and marketing of planes; and third, the men who made them.

First, regarding these objects, these planes: that planemaking in America grew out of British planemaking is readily apparent. One can see a bit of Dutch influence, but the styles of British and American planes are so similar and the ties between the two countries so strong that this connection is overwhelm-

Fig. 2. Similarities between the earliest examples by Londoner Robert Wooding (ca. 1679–1727), *left,* and southeastern Massachusetts maker Francis Nicholson (ca. 1683–1753) include shoulder details and wide, flat chamfers. CWF 1986-34; private collection.

ingly obvious—as it is in furniture, clothing styles, and the like. Some makers like Thomas Napier worked on both sides of the Atlantic.

The earliest marked English and American planes are quite similar. While Londoner Robert Wooding died in 1727,[3] almost the same time that Francis Nicholson was probably beginning serious production in Wrentham, Massachusetts, the two examples of these men's early planes, shown in figure 2, are close to identical, sharing the unmistakable characteristics of late seventeenth- and early eighteenth-century planes. Both are well over 10 inches long (the standard later became 9½ inches), with similar wide, flat chamfers and notching at the shoulder. We still do not know where Francis Nicholson received his woodwork training around 1700. It appears that the planes he was making by 1728 would have been copied from those produced almost a generation earlier. Akin to the lag in furniture styles, this was due to the time involved for English patterns to reach the outlying regions of New England and to be accepted as the proper style.

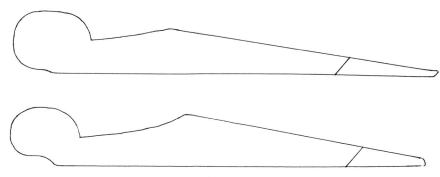

Fig. 3. Two examples of molding plane wedges by Joseph Fuller of Providence, R. I. (1746–1822), show the development of relief for iron adjustment. The top is from his first period, ca. 1770, the bottom from his second, ca. 1785. Fuller's later wedges were conventional, with no relief at all.

New England planes, including and perhaps led by Francis Nicholson's, soon began to develop an appearance of their own. One clear difference is in the wood; New Englanders usually used yellow birch rather than beech, the wood favored in England and, during the nineteenth century, in the United States. This was due to availability rather than to a conscious desire to be different, no doubt. Birch was plentiful near the coastal plain; beech was not in wide use until there were settlements well inland, where it grows in higher elevations. Birch has an open, shorter grain; it is slightly harder and takes a better finish than beech.

Wedges of New England planes developed a "relief" on the back (fig. 3) to make tapping the iron less likely to cause damage to the back of the wedge. This seems to be a feature developed in the Wrentham-Providence area, in contrast to the British imports and other American planes.

Another feature that distinguishes New England-made planes from their British counterparts is the decorative "flute" appearing below the shoulder, first as an elongated chamfer slope and then with a more defined scallop. Compare the early Francis Nicholson plane in figure 2 with that of Aaron Smith of Rehoboth, Massachusetts, in figure 4. With certain makers, especially in the Middleboro and Norton, Massachusetts, areas, a small hole drilled through the upper body near the toe, perhaps for an apprentice to pull (as on the larger crown molding planes) seems to be a standard feature (fig. 5). Joseph Fuller of Providence apparently offered two grades of planes, his standard and a more "deluxe" model with a beaded edge to the shoulder (fig. 6).[4]

Several explanations for these transatlantic dissimilarities have been offered, all of which are probably true to some degree. The differences in the wood used have been discussed above. Another key is the lack of a highly regulated apprenticeship system in America. The English system of a seven-year service to a master was centuries old and was enforced fairly strictly. A much less formal system existed in America, which is a constant source of frustration to researchers. Through others' writings and the American apprenticeship indentures that we have examined, however, it is evident that apprenticeships here were very often less than seven years, probably because of the shortage of skilled labor. With less formal training and no firm guild rules to follow, planemakers were much freer to put their individual variations on a plane. London planes made in the second quarter of the eighteenth century, for example, have a sophisticated look not found in America until the latter part of the century.

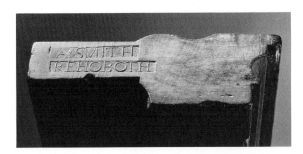

Fig. 4. Decorative fluting on plane ends that developed in the latter half of the eighteenth century is shown in this plane by Aaron Smith (1769–1822) of Rehoboth, Mass. Authors' collection.

Fig. 5. Only one plane with Joseph Fuller's unique USA stamp is known. This singular example, combined with his early name stamp and misspelled PROVIDANCE, may indicate a date of 1776. Courtesy, Martyl and Emil Pollack.

Another explanation is that American planemakers, in a growing sense of independence, were purposely striving for a different look from British planes. As more British laws restricting trade were passed, and with growing resentment toward the mother country, it is possible that the colonists wanted their products to look unique—an early version of today's "Buy American" campaign. Joseph Fuller took the American look to extremes with the stamp in figure 5.

Finally, early Dutch planes had more carving and embellishments than contemporary British ones. It is possible, even likely, that the decorative fluting by American makers was influenced by these Dutch planes at least a bit; after all, the Pilgrims and others had spent some time in Holland in the early part of the seventeenth century, and Holland was an important participant in world trade throughout the eighteenth.

Curiously, these unique features started to disappear after the Revolution, although there is no precise cutoff date. Planes of Joseph Fuller of Providence illustrate these style changes: from circa 1770, with slight wedge relief and no fluting; to circa 1780, with heavy relief and fluting; to circa 1800, with no wedge relief and no fluting. The progression of Fuller's more rural neighbor, Aaron Smith of Rehoboth, followed closely, indicating competition for the same market and a possible link between the two makers.[5]

Fig. 6. Early planes by Leonard Kennedy (1767–1842) of Hartford, *top*, had a more refined, "British" appearance than those by contemporary Massachusetts and Rhode Island makers like Joseph Fuller. Authors' collection.

Ebenezer Clark of Hartford, Connecticut, was advertising in 1796 tools that were "made in the neatest manner from English patterns,"[6] most likely made by Leonard Kennedy.[7] In figure 6, one can easily see how "British" Kennedy's plane looked compared to the example by Fuller. By the 1820s, wooden planes looked virtually the same in both countries. They were made of beech, were 9½ inches long, and had no wedge relief. It is almost as if, once the political bond had been broken, it was acceptable and even desirable to imitate the British planes, which had been more standardized and "refined" looking throughout the eighteenth century. Leonard Kennedy of Hartford used a very "British" style right from the 1790s, and one might speculate that he could have been trained in Philadelphia or New York. There is little similarity to the other New England makers' styles.

Rural American planemakers were slower than the British to adopt the standard length of 9½ inches. Although the planes of even early makers like Francis Nicholson show a shortening in length from well over 10 inches to about 9⅝ inches, it was a good thirty to forty years after British standardization that all Americans conformed.

In addition to the decorative idiosyncracies of early American planes, some new types of planes appeared in this country. The "stick and rabbet" plane (fig. 7), combining the rabbeting and molding functions of two distinct planes,

Fig. 7. Single "stick and rabbet" sash planes were more prevalent in America than in England, where a sash molding plane and a separate rabbet plane would be used for making window muntins. Authors' collection.

Fig. 8. Characteristics of the "Yankee" plow plane, such as this example by E. Clark of Middleboro, Mass. (second half of the eighteenth century), are square arms, a fence the same length as the body, and thumbscrews to lock the arms in place. Courtesy, Robert Wheeler Collection.

was much more commonly used here than in Britain, if not actually designed here. These were quite common by the end of the eighteenth century. Another example is the "Yankee" plow (fig. 8), using thumbscrews rather than wedges to hold the arms in place, and having square rather than round-topped arms (again perhaps a bit of Dutch influence), and a fence the same length as the body rather than longer. Crown or cornice molding planes like the "stick and rabbet" were used much more widely on this side of the Atlantic. In fact, the few British crown molding planes that we have seen appear to be later than and copied from the American style.

The stamps on the ends of the planes can in some cases be useful in determining the chronology of a maker's products (fig. 9). Francis Nicholson's earliest planes, probably made in Rehoboth before 1728, are stamped with a large period after the F. Very few examples of this mark are known. Most of his planes have a sort of star after the F, a reworking of the stamp by adding rays to the dot. John Nicholson used his father's LIVING IN and WRENTHAM stamps when he began making planes about 1733. When he moved in 1746 to the disputed Attleboro Gore area of Wrentham, which was to become Cumberland, Rhode Island, he had a stamp made with only the word IN since he was not actually dwelling in Wrentham. When Cumberland was founded in 1747, he used the IN with a new CVMBERLAND stamp, and when he moved back to Wrentham after his father's death, he had become a gentleman farmer, and we have no evidence of his making any more planes. Cesar Chelor was using Francis's LIVING IN and WRENTHAM stamps in his own shop by then.[8]

As fashionable moldings became more complex, planes were made to create them. The moldings that could be made were limited by the types of planes available to make them, however. Thus, planes both followed and shaped the style changes in house joinery and furniture. Trim details such as beaded clapboards and molded window headers and sills tended to be more decorative on urban houses than on those in rural areas. The elegant

Fig. 9. The same location stamp was used by different members of the Nicholson "family" of Wrentham, Mass. Authors' collection.

style of mid-eighteenth-century Newport, Rhode Island, house joinery con-
trasted with the plainer detail in the rural towns. The Newport style was followed during the building boom in the nearby town of Providence in the 1780s
and 1790s, and this helped drive the market for wooden planes. Newport, of
course, is noted as a center of cabinetmaking in the latter half of the eighteenth
century, and yet there were no major planemakers there; cabinetmakers would
probably have made their own planes to suit the job or built up moldings from
basic shapes like hollows and rounds.

Indeed, the surviving examples of eighteenth-century planes seem to indicate that planemakers produced more tools—sash planes, cornice moldings,
beads, rebates, etc. —for housewrights than for cabinetmakers. Cabinet moldings by the early makers are scarce and are usually without spring (the angle at
which a molding plane is held on the edge of a board). There is no evidence of
these American makers offering York or steeper-pitched irons for use on hard-
woods as did the British. By the last quarter of the eighteenth century, major
planemakers were producing some unique planes, probably special orders. An
unusually small bead plane by Joseph Fuller shows a consistency of style in
wedge and chamfer details, even though the plane was most likely a "one off"
for one customer.

The second section of this paper addresses the production and marketing
of planes in the eighteenth century. In New England at least, planemaking
was not a full-time occupation but was shared with farming, joinery, and/or
blacksmithing. Although there was clearly considerable production by the prolific early makers, there apparently was no need for machinery or water power.

By the 1820s and 1830s, men with substantial planemaking businesses were
making full use of the power supplied by the Connecticut River tributaries. In
the eighteenth century, however, even though the timber for planes could have
been sawn in an up-and-down sawmill powered by water, this was not done on
the premises of the planemaker. Some of the makers who certainly had the
skills to have helped build mills were part owners of mills of other kinds. For
example, Francis Nicholson owned a gristmill,[9] and Jonathan Ballou of Providence a paper mill.[10] From the land deeds and buildings we have studied, however, there is no documentation that eighteenth-century makers who had
property near streams used water power in the production of planes. To further support the theory that planemaking was a part-time occupation, even in

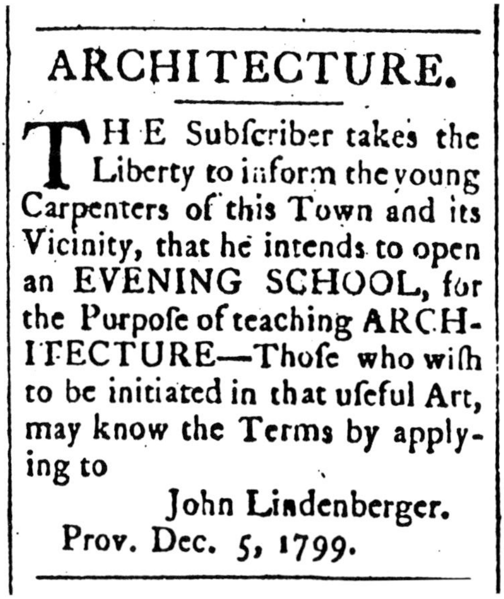

ARCHITECTURE.

T H E Subfcriber takes the Liberty to inform the young Carpenters of this Town and its Vicinity, that he intends to open an EVENING SCHOOL, for the Purpofe of teaching ARCH-ITECTURE—Thofe who wifh to be initiated in that ufeful Art, may know the Terms by apply-ing to

John Lindenberger.

Prov. Dec. 5, 1799.

Fig. 10. Providence planemaker John Lindenberger (1754–1817) also taught architecture at night school. U. S. Chronicle (Providence, R. I.), Dec. 19, 1799. Courtesy, Rhode Island Historical Society, Providence, R. I.

the town of Providence, John Lindenberger was a blacksmith as well as a teacher of night school[11] (fig. 10)!

Other planemakers were also blacksmiths, Henry Wetherel of Norton, Massachusetts, and Chatham, Connecticut,[12] and Aaron Smith of Rehoboth among them. Since the irons in their planes are unmarked, we cannot prove but assume that they made their own irons. The 962 molding plane irons in the inventory of Lindenberger's estate indicate that he must have been selling them to other local makers as well.

Certain makers used numbers to mate the fitted wedges and bodies so they would not get mixed up while other finish work was taking place. Some planes by Wetherel bear marks like those on timber-framed members; others by Fuller have numbers written in India ink. Lindenberger used a numbering system as well. This indicates production in at least small batches.

The market simply did not exist, however, for a man to spend his entire working day making planes before the Revolutionary War. The earliest New England makers were listed in legal documents as yeomen, carpenters, housewrights, joiners, or shop-joiners, with only a few being identified as toolmakers. Because rural access to imported planes was limited and timber was easily obtained, they were able to make a few planes for themselves and their neighboring fellow craftsmen. This was probably done during the winter months when they were more free from farming and house-building jobs. Stamping the name and town on the end of the plane ensured that a potential customer would be able to identify the maker and come to him to purchase more.

An example is Francis Nicholson, who had worked on the church in Rehoboth in 1716–1717. Based on the size and population of Rehoboth, word of his ability probably spread, and it is likely that he helped to build the Wrentham church in the 1720s. Realizing there was a market for some of his planes, he settled in Wrentham, right on the post road that ran from Boston to Providence.

About ninety American eighteenth-century planemakers have been documented by location and approximate dates.[13] Of them, perhaps twenty-five can be considered major, relatively prolific, makers. And of these twenty-five, only about fifteen stamped their planes with the name of the town in which they were working. We have come to the conclusion that, in general and of course with exceptions, men making planes for a primarily urban mercantile market such as Philadelphia felt no need to stamp the name of their town on their planes; craftsmen in the city would know where they were located or would purchase their planes at a store. Makers aiming at a more rural market, however, relied on their town stamp to enable customers to find them. Thus we find early Philadelphia makers like Caruthers and Armitage not using a town stamp; while John Nicholson in Cumberland and Jethro Jones of Medway, Massachusetts, not only stamped the town name but added a separate line to show that they were "in" or even "living in" the town. Simeon Doggett of Middleboro and E. Taft of Mendon, Massachusetts, avoided adding an extra line by elongating either the name or town stamp to include the word IN.

Joseph Fuller at first used IN PROVIDENCE, but dropped the IN because he did not need it with his local business, it took too much time to stamp, or he lost it! John Lindenberger, who most likely apprenticed in Philadelphia before moving to Rhode Island, used an italic-style name stamp (fig. 11) very similar to that of Philadelphia makers William Martin and Robert Parrish. Lindenberger did not use a town stamp until late in his career, and when he had it made, his PROVIDENCE stamp was carefully done in the italic style, unlike any other New England maker's. He apparently realized that because of competition from Fuller for the Providence market, he needed to broaden his own market beyond the town.[14]

John Lindenberger joined the American army in his native Baltimore at the beginning of the war, and appeared in Johnston, Rhode Island, in 1786. We are still trying to determine how he decided to make that move; was it

Fig. 11. John Lindenberger of Providence used an italicized stamp similar to those of Philadelphia makers. Courtesy, Rick Slaney Collection.

because of contacts that he made in the army, or did he think that the fast-growing Providence area provided better business opportunities for a young blacksmith/planemaker? Both William Martin and Lindenberger served as first lieutenants in the 4th Continental Artillery, enlisting three weeks apart in 1777 and serving in the New Jersey campaign.[15]

One can understand why Lindenberger and so many other American planemakers joined the army against the British—to be able to extend their markets unhindered. Benjamin Walton of Reading, John Sleeper of Newburyport, James Stiles of New York, and Joseph Fuller of Providence were among those who participated in the war. Thomas Grant left British-occupied New York when the Revolution began and moved to New Jersey.[16] The one Loyalist planemaker whom we have found was Simeon Doggett of Middleboro, Massachusetts (1838–1823).[17] Doggett made considerably fewer planes than the just mentioned men and evidently spent more of his time as a farmer and joiner than the others, judging from the scarcity of his planes. (He seems unique also in that he left a considerable paper trail.)

Society was not static; these early planemakers were a mobile lot. Before the Revolution, Nicholson moved from Boston to Rehoboth to Wrentham; Wetherel from Norton, Massachusetts, westward to Chatham, Connecticut; Ballou from the Cumberland area to Providence, Rhode Island; and Fuller eastward from Norwich, Connecticut, to Providence. After the Revolution, more urban planemakers moved in from rural areas: Lindenberger into Providence, Levi Little into Boston, Leonard Kennedy into Hartford, and many makers into Philadelphia. This is when advertising in newspapers really came into play, and one assumes that these men sold their planes directly from their shops in the city as well wholesaling to merchants. Even Henry Wetherell, Jr., in rural Chatham, was advertising in the Hartford newspaper (fig. 12).[18] The IN and LIVING IN disappeared from makers' stamps, but the tradition of using the town name remained.

Aaron Smith was working in Rehoboth about sixty to ninety years after Francis Nicholson, and although the town was the largest in Massachusetts in area, it was still overwhelmingly rural. The growth of nearby Providence during the war created a much readier market for his planes than for Nicholson's half a century earlier. In 1768, the entire population of Providence was less than 3,000, while by 1790 it had more than doubled to 6,650 and was growing rapidly. In fact, most of the major New England makers were within seventy miles of Providence.

The urban planemakers, like other tradesmen and artisans after the Revolution, tended to join associations promoting manufacture. Groups like the Providence Association of Mechanics and Manufacturers were formed in the late 1780s to provide for widows of members, assure some apprenticeship training, create libraries, and promote trade generally. This was an attempt at some

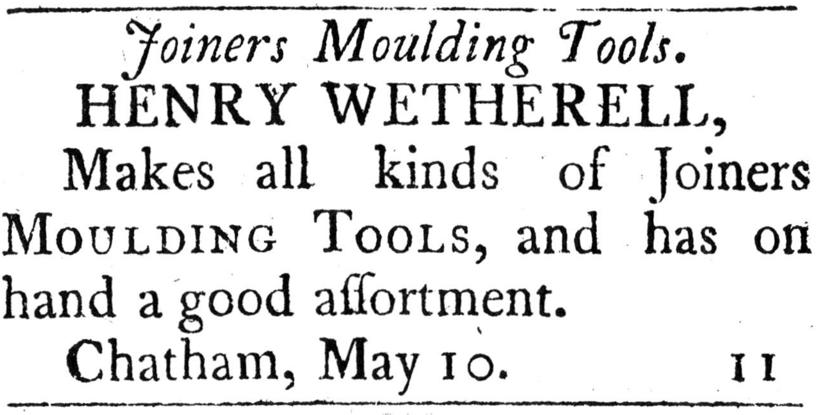

Joiners Moulding Tools.
HENRY WETHERELL,
Makes all kinds of Joiners
MOULDING TOOLS, and has on
hand a good affortment.
Chatham, May 10.   11

Fig. 12. From rural Chatham, Henry Wetherell, Jr. (1764–1840), advertised his tools in the Hartford *Connecticut Courant*, May 10, 1809.

regulation of industry, which had no history of guilds, and also an expression of patriotism for the new country. In many cities, parades of tradesmen were held, with the order of the processions published in the newspapers. The *Connecticut Courant* devoted over half a page, more than one-eighth of its total, to the Boston procession of 1788.[19] William Martin carried the banner for planemakers in the Philadelphia parade of the same year.[20]

A report to the Providence Association of Mechanics and Manufacturers in 1791 analyzing the production of the objects manufactured in the town states that "joiners' bench and moulding tools" are "made annually to the amount of $1000. . . . The particular price by reason of the great variety cannot be ascertained but are at present sold something higher than those imported—the workmen not having full employ, but the materials are so easily obtained the prices might be reduced upon par with imported tools if there was vent for large quantities."[21]

The most exciting part of our research is learning about the individual makers, which makes up the final part of this article. One begins to see these makers as departed friends, almost hearing Francis Nicholson talking to Cesar Chelor, and John Lindenberger's German accent. While trying to concentrate on the major, prolific makers, it is all too easy to become sidetracked by a "minor" maker like Loyalist Simeon Doggett. Of course, even the so-called lesser makers help to fill in the overall picture, and Doggett's papers have supported our conclusion that most woodworkers in the eighteenth century were required to make their own planes as part of their training. This would account for so many unmarked eighteenth-century planes or planes with a name or initials only. Making planes would give a lad experience in mortising, chamfering, fitting, using floats, making special jigs, finishing, etc., and the apprentice would end up with a usable tool.

We would like to find direct lines of planemakers, such as the Granford-Wooding-Phillipson line and the Madox-Mutter-Moseley-Marples line in England.[22] Without those helpful Guildhall records, though, this is not easy! We do think that we can safely state, from the styles of their planes and their locations and dates, that Francis Nicholson taught his son John, who taught Henry Wetherel and possibly Joseph Fuller—but we have no documentary proof. A comparison of the manufacturing details of early planes enables us to make educated guesses about relationships among planemakers. Chamfering, pull holes, and wedge profiles have been discussed above. Other subtle details can help to reinforce our hypotheses about these relationships.

For example, planes made by Henry Wetherel of Norton and E. Clark of Middleboro are too much alike to be mere coincidence. The mouth openings are shaped in the same way, and the handles appear to have been made from the same pattern. The two must have been associated before 1778, when Wetherel left for Chatham, Connecticut.

Fig. 13. *Top left,* another southeastern New England characteristic was the chamfering of the front of the wedge slot to prevent the wood from splitting when tapping the wedge, as in this example by Fuller and Field of Providence. *Bottom left,* float marks are clearly visible in this plane by S. Dean of Dedham, Mass. (probably Samuel Dean, 1700–1775). *Bottom right,* this wedge by Henry Wetherel (ca. 1729–1797) of Norton, Mass., clearly shows the use of a chisel in forming the relief on the back. Authors' collection.

The Nicholson-Providence group of planemakers chamfered the front of the wedge slot to prevent splitting (fig. 13) while others did not. Some makers consistently left tool or float marks on their planes. The slightly relieved wedge finials of Henry Wetherel and others are distinguished by their chisel marks as the maker pared the shape to his pattern. Heel numbering and letter stamps on irons also help to make associations among certain makers.

One can really become involved in little details in this research, particularly locating landholdings and home sites. Very few houses belonging to the planemakers are still standing, and pinpointing the exact locations of them is fascinating detective work. The shops and homestead sites of Ballou, Fuller, and Lindenberger have all been obliterated by urban growth. The survivors tend to be in areas which are still relatively undeveloped—Wetherel in Chatham (now East Hampton), Connecticut; Smith in Rehoboth, and Nicholas Taber in a historic neighborhood of Fairhaven, Massachusetts. Spending the time poring over deeds and maps is worthwhile; the more we know about the location of these makers' land and shops, the more we can learn about their "overhead" and how the site affected their production and marketing. The rural setting of Chatham, Connecticut, was quite different from urban Providence; thus, Joseph Fuller could devote much more time to making and selling planes than the Wetherels, who had to be farmers as well as artisans.

By studying eighteenth-century planes and their makers, one can follow an entire industry, from its beginnings as a cottage industry, through its more urban production and marketing, to a highly mechanized operation in the nineteenth century. The same pattern applies to toolmaking in general, and, indeed, to most American manufacturing. Having the satisfaction of discovering and becoming acquainted with a previously unknown planemaker can contribute toward a better understanding of American social and economic history.

1. John S. Kebabian, "Eighteenth Century American Planemakers," *Chron. Early Amer. Industries Assn.*, XXIII (1970), pp. 52–53; John S. Kebabian, "More Eighteenth Century Plane Makers," *ibid.*, XXIV, pp. 25–26; John S. Kebabian, "More on the Eighteenth Century Plane Makers of Wrentham, Mass.," *ibid.*, XXV (1972), pp. 15–16.

2. Carington Bowles, *New Pocket Map of the Most Inhabited Part of New England in 1780* (London, ca. 1780). Reproduced from a map in the Library of Congress, courtesy, Historic Urban Plans, Inc., Ithaca, N. Y.

3. Goodman, *British Planemakers,* 3rd ed., rev. Rees and Rees, p. 464.

4. Donald and Anne Wing, "Joseph Fuller of Providence: An Update," *Plane Talk,* XV (Fall 1991), pp. 352–355.

5. Donald and Anne Wing, "Aaron Smith of Rehoboth, 'a worthy and industrious citizen,' and his Three Planemaking Sons," *ibid.,* XV (Winter 1991), pp. 372–376.

6. *Connecticut Courant* (Hartford), Jan. 18, 1796.

7. Donald and Anne Wing, "Planemaking in Early Hartford: A Family Affair," *Plane Talk,* XIV (Winter 1990), pp. 285–292.

8. Kebabian, "More Eighteenth Century Plane Makers," *Chron. Early Amer. Industries Assn.,* p. 25; Donald and Anne Wing, "The Nicholson Family—Joiners and Plane Makers," *Mechanick's Workbench Catalogue,* XII (1981), reprinted in *Chron. Early Amer. Industries Assn.,* XXXVI (1983).

9. Wing and Wing, unpublished research.

10. Donald and Anne Wing, "Jonathan Ballou: On the West Side of the Great Bridge," *Plane Talk,* XV (Summer 1991), pp. 334–336.

11. Donald and Anne Wing, "John Lindenberger and his Descendants," *ibid.,* XIII (Fall 1989), pp. 185–190.

12. Donald and Anne Wing, "The Wetherel(l)s, Father and Son," *ibid.,* XIV (Spring 1990), pp. 225–230.

13. Emil Pollak and Martyl Pollak, *A Guide to American Wooden Planes and Their Makers,* 2nd ed. (Morristown, N. J., 1987).

14. *U. S. Chronicle* (Providence, R. I.), June 14, 1787.

15. Francis Bernard Heitman, *Historical Register of Officers of the Continental Army During the War of the Revolution, April, 1775, to December, 1783* (Washington, D. C., 1914; reprint, Baltimore, 1982).

16. Pollak and Pollak, *Guide to American Wooden Planes.*

17. Wing and Wing, unpublished research.

18. *Conn. Courant,* May 10, 1809.

19. *Ibid.,* Feb. 18, 1788.

20. Pollak and Pollak, *Guide to American Wooden Planes,* p. 252.

21. Manuscript Records of the Providence Association of Mechanics and Manufacturers, Oct. 10, 1791, Rhode Island Historical Society, Providence, R. I.

22. Goodman, *British Planemakers,* 3rd ed., rev. Rees and Rees.

The Joiner's Trade and the Wooden Plane in Eighteenth-Century New England

By Ted Ingraham

Perhaps no tools used by early American woodworkers are more appealing to collectors than wooden planes. Planes survive in an infinite number of shapes and sizes with a never-ending list of makers' and owners' marks. Their study could easily be pursued as a vocation. One area that has not been seriously addressed, however, is the plane's historical importance. By examining some of the products planes were used to produce and the making of planes themselves, I will attempt to describe the vital role these tools played during the eighteenth century and how American craftsmen adapted their wooden planes from English predecessors.

Prior to the Industrial Revolution, almost every trade that processed wood into some type of finished product used planes. The most familiar trades were those of the carpenter, joiner, and cabinetmaker. The list, however, also includes coopers, instrument makers, coachmakers, printers, and even shoemakers. Regardless of the trade that used them, all planes can be classified into one of three basic groups. The first, called bench planes, is a relatively small group of planes that were used to prepare and surface rough sawn wood. This group also includes planes used on the bench to adjust wooden surfaces during construction. The most notable members of the bench plane group are the jack plane, the trying plane, the jointer, and the smooth plane. All had straight-edged or slightly curved irons of varying widths. The second group, the joint planes, are those planes used to cut mechanical joints for assembling multiple pieces of wood. Their shapes ranged from the common rabbet and half-lap planes to the plow, sash, and tongue planes. The last and largest group are molding planes. Their primary function was to ornament, and they were produced in literally thousands of configurations. The forms most commonly found in woodworkers' tool kits were graduated pairs of hollow and round planes. The simple side bead was the next most common, followed by more complex moldings like the common ogee and ovolo. Molding planes were made to cut moldings in sizes ranging from $1/8$ inch to more than 4 inches in the case of large architectural cornices. What was once the plane's primary function, dressing and joining wood, has now been transferred almost entirely to machines. Now, if used at all, planes are called upon simply to fit and adjust woodwork.

I have limited my examination to the trade of the house joiner as practiced in New England during the eighteenth century. The house joiner was chosen since he was the single largest consumer of processed wood products and also the tradesman who used the greatest number of wooden planes.

The New England region was unique in colonial America, primarily due to its economy. Unlike its neighbors to the south, New England lacked commodities that could be directly exported to England for credit. As a result, the New England colonies attempted to meet the needs of their population by developing an intercolonial trade network and a domestic manufacturing infrastructure.[1] In short, the New England craftsman was forced to become more self-sufficient and less dependent on imported tools than his counterparts in the Middle Atlantic and southern colonies.

From the early decades of the eighteenth century, the New England population expanded at an average rate of more than 26 percent per decade. By the end of the colonial period, it was estimated to have been more than 700,000.[2] Dividing the total population with the conservative estimate of six occupants per household suggests that somewhat more than 116,000 dwellings had been built in New England by 1780, not to mention churches, public buildings, barns, shops, and outbuildings. Most structures were built entirely of wood, New England's most abundant resource, which was processed by the numerous water-driven sawmills that dotted the New England landscape.[3] Practicing the trade of house joiner in the eighteenth century meant beginning work with rough lumber direct from the seasoning pile. Preparing all the lumber they used by hand was the only option available to tradesmen until well into the nineteenth century. Although mechanical planers that used power to dress lumber were developed during the eighteenth century,[4] it was not until machines like those patented by William Woodworth and T. E. Daniels became available during the first half of the nineteenth century that the planer received widespread acceptance.[5]

In an effort to convey some idea of the enormous amount of plane-processed lumber that was required in the construction of a typical eighteenth-century dwelling, it is perhaps best to look at a surviving example. The Lowell-Whittier House was built in 1787 by David Whittier, a "gentleman" from Metheun, Massachusetts. The house and its barn comprised a portion of a saw- and gristmill complex Whittier built in the northeastern Vermont town of Danville, which at the time was still considered part of the New England frontier (fig. 1). Built in an architectural form commonly referred to as

Fig. 1. Lowell-Whittier House, Danville, Vt., ca. 1787, photograph ca. 1900. Author's collection.

Fig. 2. Front parlor, paneled room end, Lowell-Whittier House.

a "cape," this house has survived more than two hundred years with few alter-
ations and most of its original woodwork. The ground floor consists of two
formal parlors with paneled room ends divided by a massive center chimney
and a narrow entrance hall (fig. 2). The rear of the house is dominated by a
large keeping room, several small storage rooms, and a rear entry hall. A narrow stair off the back hall leads to an unfinished attic space and two finished
bedchambers. The total living space is about 1,750 square feet.

    Using scale drawings, photographs, and molding samples, a detailed list
was prepared of every piece of wood, from the interior trim to the siding, that
in some way had been dressed or shaped by a plane. Final tabulations revealed
that the completed house required more than 7,500 board feet of white pine
lumber, which was surfaced on one side only. This material was used primarily for flooring, panel walls, and siding. The doors, window sashes, and trim
required an additional 2,000 board feet of pine, which had to be dressed on
both sides. Therefore, the total amount of plane-surfaced lumber prepared by
the builders of the Lowell-Whittier House was in excess of 11,000 square
feet. Since the iron of a typical trying plane, the plane used to prepare most
wood surfaces, was only about 2½ inches wide, it was necessary to make from

six to eight passes in order to plane dress each square foot. This means that the joiner, or more likely his apprentice, would have had to push his trying plane at least 66,000 linear feet, or more than twelve and a half miles, just to prepare his stock prior to actually building with it.[6]

While by far the greatest volume of surface-dressed lumber was used in floors and siding, it was the material that was used to fashion the interior wall coverings and trim that underwent the largest number of transforming operations by the plane. The walls surrounding the massive chimney stack, as well as all the interior and exterior doors and the window shutters in the front parlors, were of panel-and-frame construction. Every linear foot of the stiles and rails, the frame in which the panels were set, required two separate planing operations. First, a ⁵⁄₁₆-inch groove was cut along the edge of the stock using a plow plane. This was followed by a ½-inch thumbmold applied to the face. Once the framework of the stiles and rails had been joined, panels were cut to fit, and their edges were "raised" with a 1½-inch panel plane (fig. 3). The three separate operations necessary to fabricate all the panel-and-frame components required more than 3,600 linear feet of plane-shaped moldings and joints.

The remaining walls not covered with lath and plaster were made up of wide pine boards planed on one or both sides. They were joined together with a half-lap joint and decorated with a ³⁄₈-inch side bead (fig. 4). This interior

Fig. 3. End view of a section of raised panel similar to the type used in the Lowell-Whittier House.

Fig. 4. End view of a section of half-lap and beaded wall-boarding like that used in the Lowell-Whittier House.

wallboarding accounted for an additional 1,900 linear feet of planed joints and 950 linear feet of ³⁄₈-inch side beading. The twenty-one double-hung windows, ranging in size from twelve-over-twelve on the front to four-light sash in the garret, required more than 1,100 linear feet of sash molding as well as 352 mortise and tenon joints. The exterior trim alone accounted for an additional 1,000 linear feet of various sized planed moldings.

In all, the 11,000 square feet of lumber the builders initially prepared were further shaped by 8,400 linear feet of joints ranging from a simple bevel, used on the siding, to the multiplane joints of the raised panel work. Their work was trimmed with more than 5,000 linear feet of moldings ranging from a ³⁄₈-inch side bead used on the wallboards and casing to a 3-inch cornice-and-bed molding applied under the eaves.

While the examination of the Lowell-Whittier House provides a valuable insight into the amount of labor and materials that were required to build a typical center-chimney dwelling, it also sheds some light on the number and types of planes required to construct a well-appointed house. During construction, the builders used at least four different bench planes, including the jack plane for initial surfacing, the trying and smooth planes to produce finished surfaces, and the jointer to straighten and square the edges of the stock. Prepared stock was assembled using six different types of joint planes: a ½-inch halving plane, a moving fillister, a skewed rabbet plane, a plow plane with a ⁵⁄₁₆-inch iron, a 1½-inch panel raising plane, and a ³⁄₈-inch ovolo sash plane. Their work was embellished using twelve molding planes including a ³⁄₈-inch side bead, a ³⁄₈-inch thumbmold, a ¾-inch and a 1-inch common ogee, and several sizes of hollow and round planes.

A similar exercise was performed on the Kelsey House of Berlin, Connecticut, built circa 1769. In spite of the fact that the two-story Kelsey House was substantially larger than the Lowell-Whittier House, the planes used during construction of both houses were almost identical in size and type.

Planes were such an essential part of the joiner's trade that understanding how to adjust, use, and maintain them was as important as learning how to use saws and chisels. After dressing and molding thousands of feet of lumber, an apprentice learned the secrets of the plane, and would be barely one step away from making his own. Contemporary documents, such as the indenture agreement between Major John Dunlap, a cabinetmaker from Goffstown, New Hampshire, and William Houston of Bedford, dated 1775, clearly indicate

Fig. 5. Wood tools made and used by carpenters and/or joiners from the mid-eighteenth to the early nineteenth century. Author's collection.

that knowledge of toolmaking was to be included as part of the training: "Aforesaid John Dunlap is to Dismiss the said William from his service and help him to make the Wooden part of a set of tools fit for the trade."[7]

The "wooden part" refers to the large number of tools that a joiner was able to make for himself out of wood, including squares, gauges, clamps, braces, and, of course, the bodies of wooden planes (fig. 5). The process of master/apprentice or father/son transfer of craft skills was, without question, the most common method by which woodworking and in turn toolmaking skills were transferred throughout New England during the eighteenth century. A skilled joiner could make most types of planes in as little as two or three hours, using no more than the tools commonly found in his tool chest. However, in spite of their ability to fashion their own wooden tools, both urban and rural craftsmen usually relied on imported English edge tools or tool steel from which to make them. Even the early plane irons made in New England by local smiths in all likelihood had cutting edges of English tool steel.

Those craftsmen who turned their hand to making planes for others developed a number of specialized tools and templates to speed their work. The most notable were "mother" or "master" planes, which were used to cut the

Fig. 6. Eighteenth-century "mother" plane and the torus nosing plane it was used to produce. Courtesy, Granick Collection.

soles of molding and joint planes, thus reducing the amount of hand shaping and ensuring consistency (fig. 6).[8] The planemaker's float, which was simply a modified version of the cabinetmaker's tool, was used to smooth the wedge mortise, throat, and escapement of a plane. Numerous templates, patterns, and preset gauges also were used to speed layout and production (fig. 7).

Joseph Howard, a cabinetmaker from Suffield, Connecticut, was a skilled woodworker who supplemented his income by making tools for others to use. Entries in his account book during 1806 and 1807 indicate that Howard made and sold to John Parmele no fewer than eighteen wood planes, including molding, joint, and bench planes. Howard's entry of August 20, 1806, illustrates the diverse nature of his planemaking skill.

To a Cornice and bedmold	10s
To a Dubell oiorn plain [double iron plane]	6s
To a Seat for Doors [set for doors]	3s[9]

The number and type of planes sold to Parmele are similar to those used in the construction of the Lowell-Whittier House and may indicate Parmele's trade as a house joiner.

In addition to making planes, Howard also taught Parmele architecture and sold him a copy of "Langly's Architecture" for 15s., the same price he charged for making a plow plane and a jointer.[10] Howard fits the profile of most American planemakers who worked in New England during the eighteenth century; their planes were simply a byproduct of their trades as housewrights, joiners, or cabinetmakers. It was not until the late eighteenth century that the demand for "ready-made" planes increased to the point that craftsmen were able to abandon their original trades and make a living as full-time planemakers. This appears to have been the case with well-known planemaker Aaron Smith of Rehoboth, Massachusetts, who was initially referred to as a housewright.

As the American population expanded through the eighteenth century, the demand for skilled labor to provide housing and furnishings placed constant pressure on the trades. As a result, apprentices were given their freedom with ever-decreasing years of training. By 1780, the average term served had been reduced to three years or less. Faced with chronic labor shortages and inadequately trained workmen, joiners were quick to accept any innovations that would facilitate their production. Several types of planes that were preferred by American joiners may well have been chosen because they could be used effectively by less skilled workmen. American joiners seem to have preferred using a wide, single-iron plane with a tote or handle to cut large architectural moldings, while the English workman relied on his set of hollows and

Fig. 7. Wood patterns typical of the types that would have been used by a plane-maker to lay out stock. Made by the author.

Fig. 8. End view of an architectural
crown molding plane with a single iron.
New England, last quarter of the
eighteenth century. Author's collection.

Fig. 9. Pair of hollow and round
planes showing how they were used
to shape a portion of a large
architectural molding. Author's
collection.

rounds—and a fair degree of skill—to perform the same task (figs. 8 and 9). This assumption is based partly on the large number of surviving examples of early American planes of this type and their relative rarity in England.

One of the more tedious jobs the joiner had to perform was producing window sash stock. It was crucial that the stiles, rails, and muntins be planed to uniform thickness. Traditionally, English joiners, as well as their early American counterparts, prepared their sash stock using two planes. First they cut a rabbet to receive the glass using a rabbet or fillister plane, then they molded the other side with a sash molding plane. Around the middle of the eighteenth century, New England joiners appear to have developed a plane that has come to be called a "stick-and-rabbet" or combination sash plane. By combining a common rabbet plane and a sash molding plane in one plane body, they were able to rabbet and mold their sash stock in one operation (fig. 10). Not only did this plane save time, it was far easier to use. The earliest datable American combination sash plane seen by the writer is an ovolo sash plane by

Cesar Chelor of Wrentham, Massachusetts. Chelor was the slave of Francis Nicholson, who has been identified as the earliest documented American plane-maker.[11] Chelor was freed upon Nicholson's death in 1753 and continued to practice the trade of planemaker. Therefore, it is possible that combination sash planes may have been developed either by Nicholson sometime before the middle of the eighteenth century or by Chelor shortly thereafter.

Another specialized plane that appeared in the tool chests of New England joiners during the eighteenth century was the sash coping plane. American joiners used this plane to cope (shape) the ends of sash rails (the top and bottom of a sash frame) to receive the molded surfaces of the stiles (the sides) (fig 11). English joiners, on the other hand, used a sash gouge and template to perform the same operation. The coping and combination planes enabled a less experienced workman to produce a quality sash frame. These assump-

tions again tend to be supported by the lack of English examples and the large number of surviving early New England stick-and-rabbet and coping planes. Another instance where the American joiner

Fig. 10. American "stick-and-rabbet" sash plane from the last quarter of the eighteenth century. Author's collection.

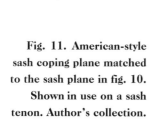

Fig. 11. American-style sash coping plane matched to the sash plane in fig. 10. Shown in use on a sash tenon. Author's collection.

Fig. 12. Early American plow plane using wedges to secure its arms. Ca. 1740–1760. Author's collection.

Fig. 13. A "Yankee"-type plow plane with thumbscrews used to secure its arms. New England, mid-eighteenth century. Author's collection.

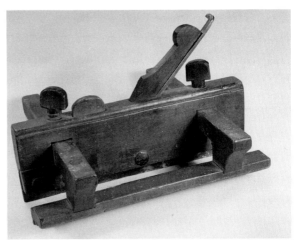

used a combination plane was in the operation of "sticking-up," or planing, the stiles and rails for door and panel work. They combined a fixed plow plane and a thumbmold plane into one easy-to-use plane.

Plow planes were one of the more important planes in the joiner's chest. The English plow and the early American version relied on wooden wedges to secure the fence arms (fig. 12). At some point around the middle of the eighteenth century, American plow planes using wooden thumbscrews to secure the arms began to appear (fig. 13). The English plow continued to make use of wedges throughout the nineteenth century. (Once again, the earliest datable examples of thumbscrew arm, or "Yankee"-type plows, are those made by Francis Nicholson who died in 1753.) American joiners actually seem to have tried to put adjustable arms like those on their plows on an assortment of planes including large moving fillisters, fillisters, tongue planes, and slitting planes.

While American woodworking was born of English traditions, the native New England joiner was exposed to a number of other influences that would ultimately leave their mark on the way he practiced his trade. From the time of the earliest settlements in New England, there was constant exchange between English settlers and settlers from the neighboring European colonies. The Dutch established settlements in the Hudson Valley and on the southern end of Long Island. French Huguenot immigrants, who were regarded as the elite of the French artisans, settled in Rhode Island and New York. English settlements along the coast of Connecticut and Massachusetts, as well as in Rhode Island, freely interacted and traded with both the Dutch and Huguenots. Since the furniture and architecture in those border regions clearly demonstrate that they were influenced by cross-cultural exchanges, it stands to reason that a mechanic's tool chest would reflect the same influences. Perhaps the most characteristic feature of eighteenth-century New England planes is the small notch that was cut in the plane body just in front of the wedge. In all likelihood, it was put there in an attempt to keep the body of the plane from splitting when the wedge was tightened or removed. This wedge notch is never seen on English planes or planes made in American cities like New York and Philadelphia, which more closely followed English patterns. Dutch planes, however, exhibit the same notch, suggesting again the contact between American and European craftsmen.

The English traditionally made their planes of beech. Why the early southeastern New England joiners selected birch for their planes is not clear. It may have been a result of their contact with French Huguenot craftsmen. The French held beech in low esteem, preferring instead hornbeam, fruitwood, or oak. Birch, which more nearly resembles hornbeam in grain and hardness, is also more difficult to work than beech.

The population of New England during the eighteenth century was almost entirely of English descent, so it would seem logical to expect colonial craftsmen to follow the traditional English craft model. However, due in part to unprecedented growth, chronic shortages in skilled labor, and cross-cultural exchanges, the New England craftsmen developed their own craft traditions. For nearly a century, scholars have published volumes on the architecture and furniture of the early American colonies and have brought to light many unique examples of American design. Unfortunately, very few attempts have been made to link these treasures with the workaday lives of the individuals who created them. Studying the tools and methods used by craftsmen and their regional variations will add another important facet to the understanding of life in preindustrial America.

1. John J. McCusker and Russell R. Menard, *The Economy of British America, 1607–1789* (Chapel Hill, N. C., 1985), p. 92.

2. *Ibid.*, p. 103.

3. Charles F. Carroll, "The Forest Society of New England," in *America's Wooden Age,* ed. Brooke Hindle (Tarrytown, N. Y., 1975), p. 29.

4. Patents for planing machines were granted in 1776 to an inventor named Hatton, and in 1791 to Sir Samuel Bentham. M. Powis Bale, *Woodworking Machinery, Its Rise, Progress, and Construction, with Hints on the Management of Saw Mills and the Economical Conversion of Timber* (London, 1880; reprint, Lakewood, Colo., 1992), pp. 70–71.

5. Nathan Rosenberg, "America's Rise to Woodworking Leadership," in *America's Wooden Age,* ed. Hindle, p. 48–49.

6. These calculations are based on planing modern, band-sawn white pine, which can be surfaced using only a trying plane. Lumber sawn by a traditional up-and-down sawmill with a coarse blade had a rougher surface. Dressing this material probably required jack planing as well as final surfacing, and the task of planing would be doubled.

7. *The Dunlaps & Their Furniture,* catalog of an exhibit, Aug. 6 to Sept. 16, 1970, Currier Gallery of Arts, Manchester, N. H., p. 53.

8. Both of these terms, coined in the last few years, have been used to describe planes of reverse profile. Since this paper was presented in 1994, research by Mr. Pat Lasswell has uncovered a contemporary reference to these planes as "counter planes" in an advertisement placed by planemaker Samuel Caruthers in the *Pa. Gaz.,* Sept. 13, 1764. See Lasswell, "The Catalog of American Wooden Planes" (June 1996), p. 7, fig. 3.

9. Joseph Howard, Account Book, 1783–1866, Kent Memorial Library, Suffield, Conn. The last entry probably refers to a plane that enabled joiners to cut in one operation both the groove and a molding on the stiles and rails. It may also include the plane used to raise panels. See the description of sticking-up planes, p. 148.

10. *Ibid.* "Langly's Architecture" refers to one of several architectural pattern books by Batty Langley (1696–1751).

11. John S. Kebabian, "More Eighteenth Century Plane Makers," *Chron. Early Amer. Industries Assn.,* p. 25.

THE RELATIONSHIP OF TOOLS
TO WORK AND PRODUCTS

Apprentices

By Harold B. Gill, Jr.

One of the features of British colonization in North America was the intention to re-create English society in the wilderness. To accomplish this end, many English institutions were imported into the New World.[1] County courts were one of the most obvious transplants with monthly meetings, justices of the peace, headboroughs, and sheriffs. Among the institutions imported almost with the beginning of settlement was the custom of training youngsters in skilled work by apprenticing them to master workmen. The instructions to Virginia Governor Wyatt in 1621 included the requirement that he put "prentices to trades, and not let them forsake their trades for planting tobacco, or any such useless commodity."[2] Ten years later, the English Statute of Artificers was declared to be in effect in Virginia. This statute, designed to regulate the trade of England and control the quality of products produced, allowed local officials to apprentice poor orphans to skilled artisans.[3]

Because so many people died young in the colony, there were numerous orphans. Many had no relatives in the country, and the estates they inherited were too small to support them. To ensure that such orphans were taken care of, the legislature allowed the local vestries and county courts to bind them out as apprentices to responsible people.

153

Even though it was never specifically stated, the apprenticeship system established in Virginia was based on English convention, especially on the "Custom of London," which was somewhat different than the practice in the English countryside. The "Custom of London" allowed children at the age of fourteen to bind themselves to tradesmen by indentures, which were contracts as binding as if the child were of legal age. This was a significant difference from the general English practice, which did not recognize as binding a contract entered into by anyone under twenty-one years of age.

The London practice, which was adopted in Virginia, required the apprentice to complete at least a seven-year apprenticeship. Virginians lowered the term to only five years, probably because of the scarcity of skilled workers as well as the fact that children might be orphaned in their late teens. London custom also allowed an apprentice to be transferred from one tradesman to another. In such cases, the indenture remained in effect as if the apprentice were serving his original master.[4] This practice, too, was not allowed under the general English procedure but was followed in Virginia.

London custom required boys to serve until age twenty-four and to serve at least seven years. Male apprentices in Virginia were bound until age twenty-one, and females until age eighteen. The length of service in Virginia varied widely—some served only a couple of years while others served much longer. In fact, John Anderson, whose father the court thought was "incapable of bringing him up," was apprenticed at age two years, six months. He was bound to a weaver for eighteen and one-half years.[5] This was not an unusual case. Many very young children were apprenticed. The practice provided the orphan with a certain standard of care, kept him from being a charge to the parish, and provided him with a means of supporting himself when free.

London custom allowed a son to practice his father's trade without serving a formal apprenticeship. It also allowed a tradesman's widow to practice his trade if they had been married at least seven years. It is not known whether or not these practices applied in Virginia, but they probably did, because no records have been found where sons were formally apprenticed to their fathers. However, there are examples of some boys being apprenticed to artisans who engaged in the same trades as their fathers.

With Virginia's population doubling every twenty years, and in some areas tripling in ten years, there was obviously a great demand for house carpenters and makers of at least basic household furniture as well as other products. In a society experiencing such growth, there was a constant shortage of labor, especially skilled labor. The need made it important to apprentice youngsters to working craftsmen in order to increase the supply of trained workers and ensure the continuation of skills to a new generation. County courts and church vestries had the responsibility of binding out orphan children and the children of parents who were unable or unwilling to provide for them. The York County court went so far as to assert that it was the "father of orphans."[6] There are instances in local records of county justices removing an apprentice because, for one reason or another, the apprentice was unsuited at the first trade. The courts took their responsibilities for orphans seriously.

Apprenticeship indentures customarily followed a standard format, and often printed forms were used. The indenture was a legal contract and imposed obligations on both the apprentice and the master. The master was obliged to feed, clothe, and house his apprentice and provide him with enough education so that he could read and write and cipher—often to perform mathematics as far as the Rule of Three.[7]

The master, of course, was obligated to teach his apprentice his trade. The apprentice was bound to obey his master, to protect his goods and trade secrets, not to get married, and generally to behave himself. At the end of the term, the master paid him his freedom dues, which in Virginia meant the same as a servant's freedom dues.

The customary freedom dues for a male servant or apprentice consisted of "ten bushels of indian corn, thirty shillings in money, or the value thereof, in goods, and one well fixed musket or fuzee." For a female, the freedom dues were "fifteen bushels of indian corn, and forty shillings in money, or the value thereof, in goods."[8] Sometimes the freedom dues were spelled out in the indenture, and they often varied. When George Taylor was bound to William Tutt to learn the trade of a house carpenter, the freedom dues were specified in the indenture as "a Suit of Clothes of the Value of Five pounds and likewise Five pounds Current Money."[9] When Henry Johnson was bound to Nathaniel Hook of York County in 1709 to learn the trade of a carpenter, his freedom dues consisted of "one Broad axe, one hand saw, three augurs, one gouge, three chissells & three planes all new tools together with a good new suit of serge apparell."[10]

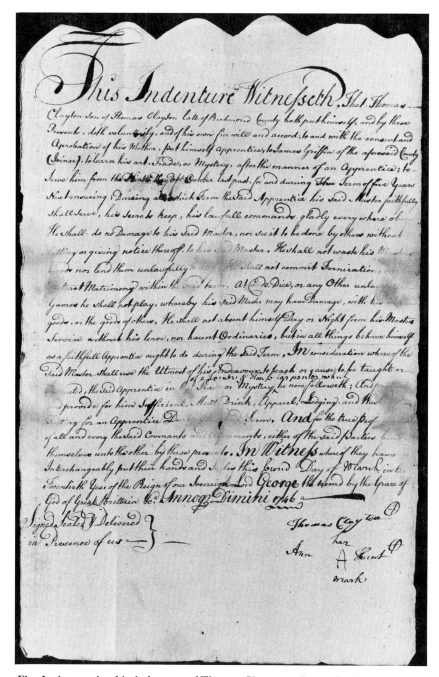

Fig. 1. Apprenticeship indenture of Thomas Clayton to James Griffin to learn the "Trade or Mystery of a Joiner & House Carpenter," Richmond County, Va., Mar. 2, 1746. CWF.

In 1727, John Parish sued his former master for his freedom dues, and the court ordered that he receive "a new suit of Cloaths of the value of two pounds nineteen shillings & nine pence and a set of Carpenters tools for course [coarse] work" consisting of "a good froe, broad ax, handsaw, adz, Inch auger, hamer, drawing knife, two Chizells, gouge, a rule & pr of Compasses, & two gimblets."[11] Another young man, who must have been sixteen years old, bound himself to Thomas Green of Amelia County to learn the carpenter's trade. In lieu of customary freedom dues, Green agreed to give him at the end of his term, in this case five years, "as many carpenter tools as will build a rough house."[12] Most apprenticeship indentures, however, only required the master to pay "lawful freedom dues" or dues "as is appointed for Servants by Indenture or Custom."

Apprentices usually received a certain amount of formal education as part of their training. The master himself might not teach his apprentice to read and write. The indenture sometimes read that the master was to "teach or cause him to be taught reading and writing." Virginia law required that both male and female apprentices be given enough education so that they could read and write. Indentures usually specified a certain number of years of schooling the apprentice was to receive. In 1707, for example, the Petsworth Parish vestry in Gloucester County bound out a girl and a boy who each were to receive three years' schooling. Several years later, the same vestry declared that if any child they bound out could not read by age thirteen, he or she was to be released of the indenture.[13] If a child could read and write when he was apprenticed, the education clause was usually omitted. Some indentures specified that the apprentice was to be sent to night school in order to cause less interruption of his daily work.

Some youngsters received at least part of their education before they were apprenticed. Matthew Hubbard, who died in 1744, specified in his will that his son be kept at school until age sixteen and then bound to some trade.[14] In her will dated in 1774, Jane Howard requested that her son "may be bound out to learn any trade or occupation he may like best after his schooling is finished."[15]

Most indentures required the master to provide clothing for the apprentice, but that clause was negotiable too. Sometimes the parents or guardian agreed to supply the apprentice with clothes during his apprenticeship.

Apprentices sometimes ran away, and the advertisements for their return indicate that most were well dressed, some even wearing wigs.

Because skilled labor was usually in short supply, the master needed his apprentice in order to meet his obligations. Most masters offered substantial rewards for the return of runaway apprentices and even promised good treatment if they returned voluntarily. In one case, the master promised not to give his runaway apprentice "the least correction" if he would return of his own accord.[16] Some masters, however, were not anxious for the return of a runaway and offered rewards ranging from half a gill of buttermilk to a handful of shavings and no thanks. Philip Mallory advertised for his runaway apprentice and described him as having "a Scar on the Top of his right Foot, which he got by the Stroke of an Adze."[17] There are few such examples indicating an apprentice was hurt on the job, but such injuries must have been fairly common.

If one party to an apprenticeship indenture did not live up to its provisions, the other could go to the county court for redress. Most cases involved apprentices suing their masters because of alleged ill usage, failure to provide an education, or failure to teach the trade. The details of the cases are seldom included in the record, but the court either released the apprentice from his indentures or sent him back to his master. Sometimes the apprentice was ordered to return to his master, who was admonished not to mistreat him and to provide the required training.

Unfortunately, we know very little of the daily lives of apprentices in colonial Virginia. Most apprentices lived with their master's family and expected to be treated as a member of that family. One guidebook reminded apprentices, "As to the Time of your going to Rest and Rising in the morning, the Hours of Working or Business, Holidays or Sparetime, and the like, you are wholly to be govern'd by the Rules of the Family into which you are transplanted: And remember that an exact Conformity to such Rules, for the Ease and Quiet of your Master, is your bounden Duty, and will be your future Benefit."[18]

Several handbooks, such as the *Young Man's Companion* and *A Present for an Apprentice,* served as behavioral guides for apprentices as well as others. One such book reminded the apprentice that his indentures required him not to "absent himself from his said Master's Service Day nor Night," and he "has no Time that he can properly call his own, but is accountable to his Master for every Hour."[19] Another pointed out that the time of his apprenticeship was "the most critical time of life, and the most necessary time for a young man to acquaint himself with business; and, if this be lost, it is irrecoverable."[20]

In 1750, the Carpenters' Company in London published "Instructions for Apprentices" that were applicable in Virginia as well as in England.

Instructions for the Apprentices
of the Company of Carpenters, London.

> You shall constantly and devoutly, on your Knees, every Day, serve God, Morning and Evening, and make Conscience in the due Hearing the Word preached, and endeavour the right Practice thereof, in your Life and Conversation; you shall do diligent and faithful Service to your Master for the Time of your Apprenticeship, and deal truly in what you shall be trusted. You shall often read over the Covenants of your Indenture, and see and endeavour yourself to perform the same to the utmost of your Power. You shall avoid all evil Company, and all Occasions which may tend to draw you to the same, and make speedy Return when you shall be sent on your Master or Mistresses Errands. You shall avoid Idleness, and be ever employed, either in God's Service, or about your Master's Business. You shall be of fair, gentle, and lowly Speech and Behaviour to all Men, and especially to your Governors. And according to your Carriage expect Reward for Good or Ill, from God and your Friends.[21]

We know almost nothing of methods used in training the apprentice. We can only guess how the master went about it, and the guess would probably be about right. Concentration on learning the names of tools and the jargon of the trade, and simple chores to start with and increasingly difficult ones added until the apprentice became proficient was probably the usual routine. How soon he acquired enough skills to earn his keep and produce some income for the master probably varied widely and depended on the individual. There is some evidence that many skills could be learned very quickly. Long apprenticeships were supposed to safeguard the quality of goods produced, but, in fact, they were a source of cheap labor for the master artisan. Apprentices performed tasks that journeymen were too highly paid to do but nevertheless needed to be done. Some believed that even highly skilled occupations could be learned in less than a year.[22] Long apprenticeships did not guarantee quality work. In one advertisement for a runaway apprentice, the master claimed the boy had "served about four Years to the Business of a House Joiner, but knows nothing of it."[23] In another case, a twenty-year-old runaway apprentice was able to pass for a journeyman carpenter.[24]

An apprenticeship indenture from western North Carolina, dated 1777, specified that the master would assist the apprentice in "making the working Tools belonging to the said Trades" of wheelwright and joiner.[25] This example is highly unusual and probably an aberration. Of the thousands of apprenticeship indentures examined that date before 1800 in Virginia, none has been found indicating the tools were homemade. Perhaps the North Carolina example is the result of the isolated location remote from retail stores or of scarcity caused by disruption of trade during the Revolution. On the other hand, the practice of making one's own tools may have been more common than records indicate. However, we know of one man who traveled from New Bern, North Carolina, to Virginia in order to buy carpenter's tools that were unavailable nearer his home.[26]

At the end of his term of service, it was the custom for an apprentice to have a party, called a "freedom frolic," for all of his friends. By that time he was able to go out on his own as a journeyman or set up shop for himself. It is surprising how many people fresh from their apprenticeships set up in business right away. Peter Powell finished his apprenticeship with the Yorktown wheelwright Mathew Burt in 1757 and, within a couple of years, had established his riding chair business in Williamsburg.[27] Richard Tankersley, too, wasted no time in going into business for himself. He was apprenticed to a joiner in King George County for five years in 1759. His apprenticeship ended in 1764 when he was twenty-one years old. One year later, Tankersley died, leaving an estate valued at over £150 including two turner's lathes, three joiner's workbenches, a variety of joiner's tools, and some unfinished furniture.[28]

The tools apprentices received as freedom dues must have given them a good start. The opportunities for skilled workers were almost unlimited, and success depended more on their own abilities and reliability than on anything else.

1. David W. Galenson, *White servitude in Colonial America: An economic analysis* (Cambridge, 1981), pp. 6–7.

2. Hening, ed., *Statutes at Large*, I, p. 115.

3. *Ibid.*, p. 167; Donald Woodward, "The Background to the Statute of Artificers: The Genesis of Labour Policy, 1558–63," *Economic History Review*, 2nd Ser., XXXIII (1980), pp. 32–44.

4. *Laws concerning Masters and Servants*, 2nd ed. (London, 1768), pp. 136–139.

5. Shenandoah County, Va., Records, Orders, 1781–1784, p. 15.

6. York Co. Recs., Deeds, Orders, and Wills, VI, 1677–1684, pp. 340–341.

7. The Rule of Three, also known as the Golden Rule or Rule of Proportion, is a method of determining a fourth number when three are known.

8. Hening, ed., *Statutes at Large*, III, p. 451.

9. King George County, Va., Records, Order Book, II, 1735–1753, p. 173.

10. York Co. Recs., Deeds, Orders, and Wills, XIII, 1706–1710, pp. 242–243.

11. Lancaster Co. Recs., Order Book, VII, p. 229.

12. Amelia County, Va., Records, Deeds, II, 1742–1747, p. 222.

13. C. G. Chamberlayne, ed., *The Vestry Book of Petsworth Parish, Gloucester County, Virginia, 1677–1793* (Richmond, Va., 1933), pp. 91, 193.

14. York Co. Recs., Wills and Inventories, XX, 1745–1759, pp. 7–8.

15. Isle of Wight County, Va., Records, Wills, VIII, 1769–1779, p. 455.

16. *Va. Gaz.* (Rind), Mar. 25, 1773.

17. *Ibid.* (Purdie and Dixon), Sept. 5, 1771.

18. Samuel Richardson, *The Apprentice's Vade Mecum* (London, 1734; reprint, Los Angeles, Calif., 1975), p. 35.

19. *Ibid.*, pp. 7, 9.

20. *The Compleat Compting-House Companion: or, Young Merchant and Tradesman's Sure Guide* (London, 1763), p. 72.

21. B. W. E. Alford and T. C. Barker, *A History of the Carpenters Company* (London, 1968), illustration opposite p. 105.

22. John Rule, *The Experience of Labour in Eighteenth-Century English Industry* (New York, 1981), pp. 99–100.

23. *Va. Gaz.* (Purdie and Dixon), Dec. 2, 1775.

24. *Ibid.*, Apr. 7, 1774.

25. Braty apprenticeship indenture, Rowan Co., N. C., Court of Pleas and Quarters.

26. Jacques Fontaine, *Memoirs of a Huguenot Family,* trans. Ann Maury (New York, 1852; reprint, Baltimore, 1967), p. 336.

27. York Co. Recs., Deeds, V, pp. 351–352; Elizabeth City County, Va., Records, Deeds, Wills, E, 1758–1764, pp. 161–162.

28. King George Co. Recs., Deeds, IV, 1752–1765, p. 388; Inventory Book, II, 1746–1765, pp. 257–259, *ibid.*

In Search of the
Colonial Woodworking Shop

Benches, Shops, and the Woodworking Process

By Scott Landis

W e can tell a lot about work life by looking closely at the mundane details
of shop construction. The configuration of benches and vises, for example, points to the kinds of tools used and the nature of work that took place
in the shop. The size of the windows and their relationship to the benches suggest the quality of the work environment. Were the windows glazed or were
they open and unshuttered? Was there a source of heat? Even wear patterns on
the floor and the bench can provide telltale clues about a craftsman's occupation.

When it comes to colonial American workshops and assessing the work
life they encompassed, we are faced with a major handicap: they don't exist.
Unlike hand planes and even some benches, eighteenth-century workshops
have long since been dismantled and dispersed. We have a few buildings without tools and a few sets of tools without buildings, but I am unaware of a single
eighteenth-century American woodworking shop that still stands in its original environment with its walls, floor, roof, and many of its original tools intact.

Making sense out of the chaos of an abandoned workshop or the mismatched tools in an old chest presents a formidable archaeological challenge. Unfortunately, colonial craftsmen themselves offered few clues. The eighteenth-century French encyclopedist, Denis Diderot, explained the attitudes of his contemporary craftsmen this way: "People who continually busy themselves with something," he complained, "are equally disposed to believe either that everyone knows those things which they are at no pains to hide, or that no one else knows anything about the things they are trying to keep secret. The result is that they are always ready to mistake any person who questions them either for a transcendent genius or for an idiot."[1]

Falling somewhere between Diderot's "transcendent genius" and the "idiot," I will do my best to resurrect from the midden of woodworking tools and craft traditions an impression of the eighteenth-century workshop and the work life that surrounded it. In the process, I will focus much of my attention on the workbench.

The workbench was the central tool in the preindustrial woodworker's shop. More than that, it remains the unifying craft artifact; no other fixture so thoroughly reflects all the other tools and traditions of the shop and craftsman. The workbench has assumed many forms—from the bodger's humble shaving horse to the most decorative and highly carved cabinetmakers' benches. Each device is well suited to the principal tools and tasks for which it was designed—the bodger's bench for the drawknife and spokeshave and the traditional cabinetmaker's bench for the hand plane.

To one degree or another, the craftsmen who used these benches were artisans manipulating tools on a piece of wood, held fast by some form of vise. That essential relationship, best described by David Pye as the "workmanship of risk," defined most craft production until the nineteenth century.[2]

When woodworkers began carrying wood to machines, their intimate relationship with bench, tools, and material began to change from one characterized by risk and by their skillful manipulation of tools on wood to one of greater certainty and predictability. Ever since, the workbench has become less central in the woodworker's shop, if it hasn't disappeared entirely. (This "evolution" of benches, shops, and craft practice is far from linear. Indeed, there are craftsmen practicing today who would be right at home in the eighteenth century.)[3]

Some of the most interesting and unexpected information about these craft traditions may be gleaned from the background of photos and illustrations that depict old shops. The tools on the walls—even the scraps beneath the bench—can provide a key to the work life of the period. For example, the familiar image of an eighteenth-century Paris joiner's shop illustrated in André Jacob Roubo's *L'art du menuisier* (Paris, 1769–1775) illuminates several layers of detail about the working environment of the period (fig. 1).

Roubo is a gold mine of information because he was one of the few eighteenth-century chroniclers of the woodworking trades who was himself a woodworker. This firsthand experience imbues his writing with a degree of accuracy

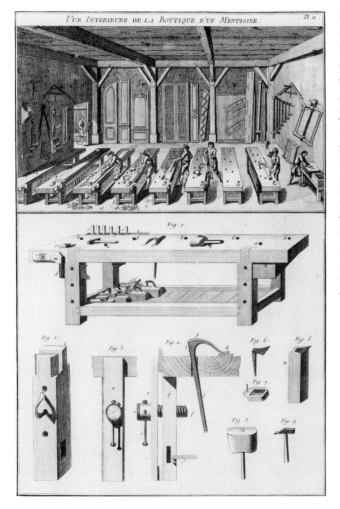

Fig. 1. Roubo provides one of the most thorough descriptions ever written of an eighteenth-century joiner's shop and the joiner's workbench. "Vue Interieure de la Boutique d'un Menuisier," in André Jacob Roubo, *L'art du menuisier* (Paris, 1769–1775), I, pl. 11. Courtesy, Winterthur Library.

and professional insight lacking in most other documents of the period. Roubo's artistic abilities (or those of his illustrator) may leave something to be desired, but his detailed treatment—in both text and illustrations—is explicit and acute.

Roubo describes everything from the length of the joiners' benches—nine feet—to the grain orientation in their tops—heartwood up. He even specifies an optimum shop ceiling height of twelve feet, which is high enough, he contends, to allow the joiners to turn a long board end-over-end. The benches in Roubo's illustration include no attached vises. Instead, the workers rely exclusively on iron holdfasts, bench hooks, and the wooden hook or *crochet* at the front left corner of each bench to secure the long, straight stock of the joiner's trade.

The work arrayed around the shop walls is the product of an eighteenth-century architectural "millwork" shop, and the craftsmen at the bench appear to be young—probably apprentices performing the "machine-like" functions of their status. There is a sharpening table on the right, and, in the very back of the shop, Roubo shows a worker carrying a steaming glue pot. The fact that the glue pot was being carried in from outside the shop indicates that the shop had no source of heat. It also suggests that glue was more of an occasional requirement than a full-time critical ingredient in shop practice.

The documentary record is clear on one point: there was extensive differentiation between the woodworking trades during the seventeenth and eighteenth centuries in England and Europe. Separate woodworking guilds delineated the functions and rights of many carpenters, joiners, and, eventually, cabinetmakers.

Two engravings from Diderot's *Encyclopédie* (fig. 2), published just prior to Roubo, clearly illustrate this distinction. The joiner's shop (top), shows an open, unembellished space; indeed, the shop appears to have been set up on the job site. It is an open-air environment, with shavings and scraps on the floor and only iron holdfasts—no vises—on the benches.

George Sturt, in his 1923 book *The Wheelwright's Shop*, described a similar work environment in England: a shop with shuttered window openings, bolted at night for security but wide open to the elements during the day. Sturt wrote: "With so much chopping to do one could keep fairly warm; but I have stood all aglow yet resenting the open windows, feeling my feet cold as ice though covered with chips. To supply some glass shutters for day-time was one of the first changes I made in the shop."[4]

Fig. 2. The illustrations of Diderot's joiner's and cabinetmaker's shops afford a striking comparison between the divergent work spaces and holding devices of these distinct trades, reflecting the different tools, materials, and skills employed by these artisans. *Top:* "Menuiserie." *Bottom:* "Ebénisterie et marqueterie." Denis Diderot and Jean d'Alembert, eds., *Encyclopédie, ou Dictionnaire Raisonné des Sciences, des Arts et des Métiers, par un Société de Gens de Lettres* (Paris, 1751–1765), pls. II and I.

By contrast, Diderot's depiction of a cabinetmaking workshop (fig. 2, bottom) shows a dedicated workspace with tools on the wall, a formidable bank of glazed windows, and a variety of work-holding devices in operation.

Modern woodworkers are loosely and often interchangeably referred to as carpenters, joiners, or cabinetmakers. But in seventeenth- and eighteenth-century London, distinctions between the powers and privileges of these three branches of woodworking were as clear as they are in Washington today between our three branches of government. Benno Forman's book, *American Seating Furniture,* contains the following reference to a 1632 proceeding in the Alderman's Court of the City of London: "It appeareth that the Comp[an]y of Turners be grieved that the Comp[an]y of Joyners assume unto themselves the art of turning to the wrong of the Turners." The court resolved "that the arts of turning & joyning are two several & distinct trades and we conceive it very inconvenient that either of these trades should encroach upon the other . . . by custom . . . the turning of Bedposts Feet of tables joyned stools do properly belong to the trade of a Turner and not to the art of a Joyner."[5]

Joinery is an ancient craft that relied heavily on the use of riven, or hewn, green wood and little, if any, glue. The staple joint in both the carpenter's and joiner's repertoire was the draw-bored mortise and tenon, which, in furniture, formed the essential component of frame-and-panel construction.

Cabinetmaking is a younger and more refined occupation than joinery, and it seems to have migrated to England in the sixteenth century from Northern Europe. In place of narrow, riven stock, cabinetmakers employed wide, dry boards, usually dovetailed together at the corners. They were more likely than joiners to use sawn softwoods, veneers, and complex mechanical and decorative elements. With the declining popularity of the draw-bored mortise-and-tenon joint and its great mechanical strength came an increased reliance upon dry wood, veneers, and joints secured by gluing. (This shift in woodworking design and technology may also have been influenced by the declining availability of local raw materials and the increasing trade in imported, exotic woods.)

The "German" cabinetmaker's bench (fig. 3), which is illustrated in Roubo's third volume, includes several sophisticated innovations not found on the earlier Roubo benches. The most conspicuous addition is the screw-operated tail vise found at the right corner of the bench, which was designed to be used in conjunction with a row of dogholes. Absent are the metal bench hook

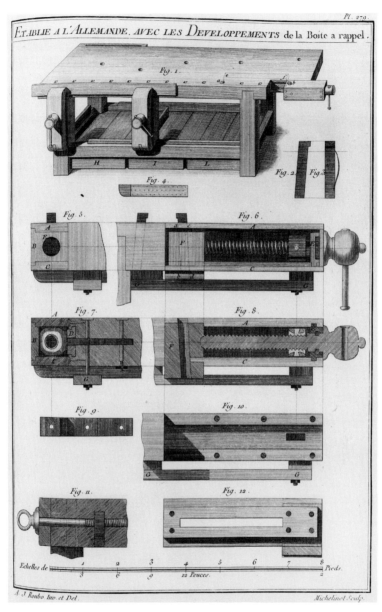

Fig. 3. The so-called German bench, shown in Roubo's third volume, introduces several sophisticated holding devices apparently unknown to Roubo when he wrote his earlier volume. The tail vise, dog holes, and adjustable leg vises would have made life easier for a cabinetmaker working extensively with thin, dry stock and veneer. "Etablie a l'Allemande avec les Developpements de la Boite a rappel," in Roubo, *L'art du menuisier*, III, pl. 279. Courtesy, Winterthur Library.

and the wooden hook that appeared in Roubo's original bench. These are replaced with a twin set of rather fancy vertical leg vises. Holdfast holes remain.

Roubo's German cabinetmaker's bench represents significant technological innovation around the third quarter of the eighteenth century. Even today,
it pretty much defines the form. But it is not necessarily a better bench. Roubo
doesn't say much about the use of this bench, except that it is handy for holding small work. That much may also be gleaned from the root of the French
word for cabinetmaker—*ébéniste*—for whom Roubo says this bench is intended.
Ebony and the other precious woods employed by high-style cabinetmakers of
the period would have been applied in thin sheets of veneer that required considerably more specialized holding and gluing devices than those found on a
standard joiner's bench.

Many familiar workshop elements can be found in the seventeenth-century relief-carved panel in figure 4 and the eighteenth-century Delft plate in
figure 5: a basic bench, saws, chisels, brace and bits, along with the ubiquitous
ax. The so-called "Stent" panel (fig. 4) depicts a joiner and a turner working
side by side in the same shop, and the work-holding method employed by the

Fig. 4. This bas-relief wooden panel depicts the diversified production of a
seventeenth-century joiner's shop in England or northern Europe. Rural economies
could not support the rigid structure and specialization fostered by the urban guilds.
Courtesy, Duncan McNab.

Fig. 5. The ax shown in
this 1769 Delft plate was a
ubiquitous splitting,
shaping, and trimming tool
in the preindustrial joiner's
shop. Courtesy, Sorber
Collection, photograph by
George Fistrovich.

Stent joiner is the same as that found on the Roubo joiner's bench—an iron holdfast and bench hook.

In the 1769 Delft plate (fig. 5), no vise is shown on the bench, although the three vertical boards riddled with holes are the kinds of adjustable board supports that usually accompany a leg or face vise. In this plate's painted scene—as in practically every seventeenth- and eighteenth-century illustration extant—we find one tool that has disappeared from most modern workshops: the ax. At times, the ax was used to rough-shape turning billets or to shave work in the manner of a large chisel or slick. The illustrated ax has a full-length handle, and the worker on the right is using it to trim a plank on the floor.

The earliest North American furniture was built in the joiner's tradition. The London Company broadside (see page 26) and colonial inventories listed axes, saws, chisels, and other tools that might be equally useful in building houses as well as joined furniture. (Smoothing planes were conspicuously absent.) This was more a function of simple economics and necessity than of trade guild restrictions, since trade guilds never took hold in the colonies as they did in England. Cabinetmaking could thrive only in an established and secure community in which sufficient capital was available to invest in dry wood or in green wood that could be set aside for seasoning. Evidence of the first

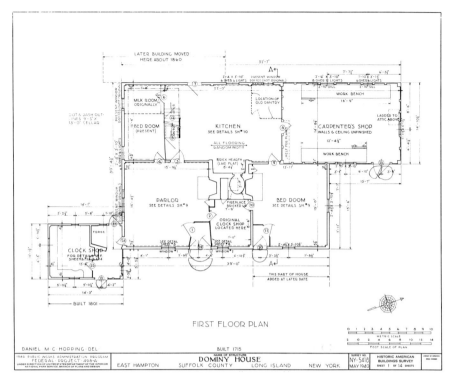

Fig. 6. Nathaniel Dominy and several generations of his descendants worked in a small woodworking shop adjacent to the kitchen of their East Hampton, Long Island, home. The Dominys were prolific and versatile rural craftsmen who specialized in making clocks, but were also engaged in a wide variety of furniture making, construction, and repairs. Historic American Buildings Survey, 1940, reproduced from the collections of the Library of Congress.

American cabinetmakers does not appear until the late seventeenth century, with the listing of glue pots and veneering materials in Boston inventories.[6]

Modern woodworkers typically set up shop in three different locations: inside the house, perhaps in the basement or a separate room; in an attached structure or ell; or in an entirely separate, purpose-built space. Likewise, colonial woodworkers employed all three. The Old Stone House in Washington, D. C., is the site of Christopher Layman's eighteenth-century woodworking shop. The shop occupied the first floor of his family's bluestone house, along with the kitchen, while Layman lived directly above with his wife and two sons.

Like the Layman shop, the woodworking shop in Nathaniel Dominy's East Hampton, New York, house was also adjacent to the kitchen (fig. 6). In this case, the loft area above the shop was reserved for wood storage. The Anthony Hay shop, shown in figure 7, which was built in Williamsburg, Virginia, in the mid-eighteenth century, illustrates an entirely separate structure, built specifically as a workshop.

Then, as now, the issues that determine a craftsman's preferred location probably relate to a combination of factors. These include the number of workers and whether those workers were family members, employees, apprentices, or slaves. Location must also have been influenced by the prosperity of the craftsman and the nature of his business. Forman pointed out that "the shops of rural craftsmen were often in their own houses, whereas Boston craftsmen often rented shop space in other, more centrally located buildings particularly after 1660."[7] Nina Maurer, in her study of Adam Kersh's nineteenth-century cabinetshop in the Shenandoah Valley of Virginia, also notes that the form of a building is dictated partly by necessity and the availability of resources, partly

Fig. 7. The reconstructed Hay's Cabinetmaking Shop and wareroom at Colonial Williamsburg.

by function, and partly by psychological reassurance—what seems comfortable and familiar.[8] (I would add that those last qualities—the comfortable and the familiar—are important factors in the design of a workbench.)

While no more than two or three Dominy family members shared space in their woodworking and clock shops, the Anthony Hay shop was operated by at least four different masters who employed professional carvers and made numerous appeals for journeymen cabinetmakers, chairmakers, and apprentices.

Until now, I have focused mainly on documents. But I have derived many vivid impressions of eighteenth-century workshops from historic reconstructions, like the Hay's Cabinetmaking Shop at Colonial Williamsburg and the Dominy workshop at the Winterthur Museum in Delaware. Because the Hay shop is essentially a modern interpretation, it leaves a number of questions unanswered.

The modern Hay's Cabinetmaking Shop was constructed in the 1960s on the excavated site of the original building, which was erected downhill from Hay's home between 1740 and 1755. The Colonial Williamsburg excavation yielded an assortment of hand tools and hardware and some information about basic shop structure, such as the perimeter of the brick foundation, the two-story chimney, and the presence of an addition that was made to the west of the main work space.

As indicated in the plan of the Hay house, shop, and kitchen (fig. 8), the workshop extension was built over a stream bed that had been diverted around the main shop's foundation. The archaeologists who excavated the Hay shop hoped to find signs of a water-driven lathe, which would have explained the building's midstream location, but no evidence was unearthed.[9]

Unfortunately, other crucial questions were left unanswered, and much of the appearance of the present-day shop is based on conjecture. For example, we don't know anything about the size or placement of doors and windows or the height of the ceiling in the original shop—not to mention the location of benches and tools.

From time to time, Colonial Williamsburg reinterprets its trade shops to reflect changing perceptions about historical "reality." In 1987, musical instrument making was moved out of the shop extension and integrated with the rest of the shop activity. (There is no evidence of a separate musical instru-

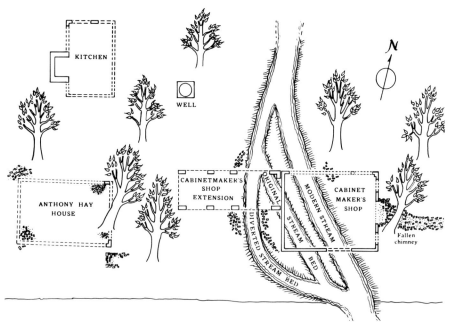

Fig. 8. This archaeologist's site plan shows the orientation of Hay's
Cabinetmaking Shop, the shop extension, and Anthony Hay's residence.
The location and diversion of the stream and their relation to the shop
remain an enigma. Ivor Noël Hume, *Williamsburg Cabinetmakers: The
Archaeological Evidence* (Williamsburg, Va., 1971).

ment shop, but public notices during the eighteenth century indicate that at
least one of the shop's masters—Benjamin Bucktrout—made and repaired instruments.[10]) In its place, a sales or "ware" room was installed. The extension
is also used for finishing and upholstery.

This arrangement bears some relationship to the high-style Chippendale
and Linnell shops in London of about the same period, but the wareroom is
still a matter of debate. Its presence suggests an inventory or some speculative
work. Although records of several late eighteenth-century eastern Virginia cabinetmakers indicate substantial quantities of ready-made furniture for sale, there
are no documented warerooms in conjunction with pre-Revolutionary Virginia
workshops.

Around the same time that musical instrument making was moved, the
German-style workbenches that originally had been installed in the

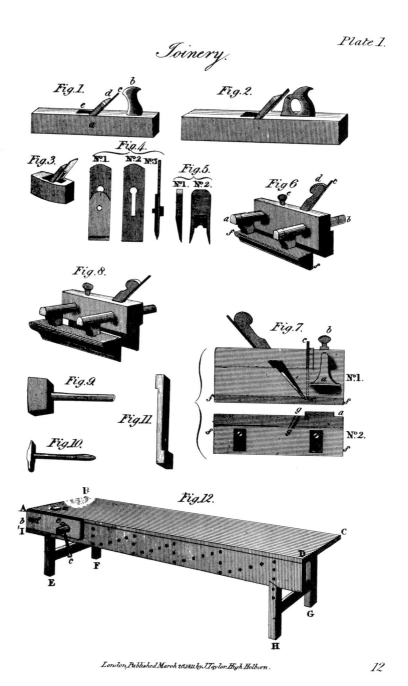

London, Published March 26.1811 by J.Taylor High Holborn.

Fig. 9. This early nineteenth-century English-pattern bench employs a horizontal face vise. The front apron is bored to receive support pegs for a range of work. Peter Nicholson, *Mechanical Exercises* (London, 1812).

reconstructed shop were replaced with English-pattern benches. These were fashioned after one illustrated near the beginning of the nineteenth century in Peter Nicholson's *Mechanical Exercises* (fig. 9).

As the modern master of the Hay shop, Mack Headley, demonstrates in figure 10, there is plenty of natural light and access to tools when the "business end" of the bench is located near the wall and windows. There are about seven benches in the present-day shop. Two of them are placed against the wall, but the others stand out in the room, with the leg vise situated near the wall and windows. According to Headley, the cabinetmakers have moved their benches all around the shop and found this to be the best setup. Using the same layout with the German benches, they discovered that the tail vise was too far from the windows to light their work adequately.

The Dominy workshop was built around the same time as the original Hay shop in a farming community near the eastern tip of Long Island, New York. Its preserved remains, which include more than a thousand tools, provide the most complete combination of artifactual information about an eighteenth-century American workshop. Even more than the Williamsburg

Fig. 10. In a work space with no artificial light, like Hay's Cabinetmaking Shop at Colonial Williamsburg, windows provide a crucial source of illumination for shop master Mack Headley.

Fig. 11. Both Hay's Cabinetmaking Shop and Nathaniel Dominy's Long Island workshop were without power or artificial light. The more rustic Dominy reconstruction at the Winterthur Museum reflects the less formal environment one might expect to find in a rural workshop attached to a private residence. Courtesy, Winterthur Museum.

cabinetmakers, the Dominys were versatile craftsmen who engaged in all sorts of woodworking, construction, and repair.[11]

The Winterthur reconstruction (fig. 11) does not incorporate any walls, windows, or flooring from the original structure, but most of the tools and equipment, including benches, vises, and some shelving, and their placement are derived from the Long Island shop. The placement of patterns and augers and their relationship to the benches was deduced from contemporary views in the Roubo and Diderot encyclopedias.

In general, the Dominy and Hay shops functioned with a similar level of technology as illustrated by the Dominy workbenches, which are also in the English style. Like most eighteenth-century shops, neither the Dominy nor the Hay shop had any source of power. Until the nineteenth century, apprentices or slaves took the place of machinery in many woodworking shops. They sometimes slept in the shop and were fed, clothed, and often educated by the master. In exchange, they performed most of the rough, repetitive operations that would nowadays be done with machinery.

In the absence of power, two things—heat and light—were of paramount concern. Cabinetmakers in the Hay shop could have used the fireplace to warm glue and materials, but there was no stove in the Dominy shop until the 1840s or 1850s. Apart from the obvious discomfort of winter work in an unheated Long Island shop, one wonders how the Dominys glued and finished their work. Did they heat the shop from the kitchen next door, or did they haul their furniture into the house?

Perhaps the Dominys relied more heavily on mechanical joinery than on glue, and they certainly used a good deal of green wood in their turning. As Charles Hummel has suggested, it is also probable that their tasks were highly structured. By building some of their furniture from component parts, they could comfortably rive wood in winter and save the assembly and finishing for warmer weather. In any event, like many rural craftsmen even today, they engaged in considerable seasonal activity.[12]

Perhaps the most striking difference between the Dominy and Hay installations is in their atmosphere. Although neither shop had any form of artificial light, the cheery hearth, large windows and whitewashed wainscoting of the Hay shop create a warm and favorable impression of eighteenth-century craft life. It would be comfortable to work—or even live—in such a place. By contrast, the dingy, exposed-frame walls, low ceiling, and small windows of the Dominy workshop contribute to a decidedly more rustic environment.

It would be tempting to say that the Hay shop is "prettier" than reality, but it is difficult to make that judgment with any certainty. As Mack Headley pointed out during one of my visits to the Hay workshop, in the context of the quality of work and the upscale bustle of the Williamsburg capital, the current interpretation may not be that farfetched.

In concluding my search for the eighteenth-century workshop, it seems appropriate to close with a comment written in 1846 by a Shaker brother, Thomas Damon, regarding the construction of a desk. "You will please suit yourself as to size and formation," Damon wrote, "'for where there is no law there is no transgression.'"[13]

1. Denis Diderot, "The Encyclopedia" (1755), in *Rameau's Nephew and Other Works*, trans. Jacques Barzun and Ralph W. Bowen (Indianapolis, Ind., 1964), p. 303.

2. David Pye, *The Nature and Art of Workmanship* (Cambridge, 1968), pp. 4–8.

3. Scott Landis, *The Workbench Book* (Newtown, Conn., 1987); Scott Landis, *The Workshop Book* (Newtown, Conn., 1991).

4. George Sturt, *The Wheelwright's Shop* (Cambridge, 1923), p. 13.

5. Benno M. Forman, *American Seating Furniture, 1630–1730: An Interpretive Catalog* (New York, 1988), pp. 44–45.

6. *Ibid.*, pp. 40–49.

7. *Ibid.*, p. 58.

8. Nina Maurer, "Limits of Conservatism: Cabinetmaker Adam Kersh" (master's thesis, University of Delaware, 1992), p. 39.

9. Ivor Noël Hume, *Williamsburg Cabinetmakers: The Archaeological Evidence* (Williamsburg, Va., 1971).

10. "MR. ANTHONY HAY having lately removed to the RAWLEIGH tavern, the subscriber has taken his shop, where the business will be carried on in all its branches. He hopes that those Gentlemen who were Mr. Hay's customers will favour him with their orders, which shall be executed in the best and most expeditious manner. He likewise makes all sorts of *Chinese* and *Gothick* PALING for gardens and summer houses. N.B. SPINETS and HARPSICORDS made and repaired. BENJAMIN BUCKTROUT." *Va. Gaz.* (Purdie and Dixon), Jan. 8, 1767.

11. Hummel, *With Hammer in Hand.*

12. Personal communication from Charles Hummel to Scott Landis.

13. Thomas Damon to George Wilcox, Dec. 23, 1846, Shaker Collection, Western Reserve Historical Society, Cleveland, Ohio.

Using Tools to Earn a Living and the Dominy Family of East Hampton, Long Island

By Charles F. Hummel

Between 1750 and 1946, seven generations of the Dominy family lived in a two-story farmhouse located in East Hampton, New York, on the road that led from the town to Three Mile Harbor and Long Island Sound. But only three generations contained woodworkers who earned a living as craftsmen during the eighteenth century. They were Nathaniel Dominy III (1714–1778), a carpenter and surveyor, his son, Nathaniel IV (1737–1812), and, in turn, his son, Nathaniel Dominy V (1770–1852). Little is known about the life and work of Nathaniel Dominy III. It is highly likely, however, that about 1750 he added the woodworking shop to the family home, a structure originally built in 1715.

By 1940, the house and shops were in terrible condition. Declared unfit for habitation in 1946, they were torn down, providing an opportunity for Winterthur to acquire the Dominys' tools and equipment in order to reconstruct their shops between 1957 and 1960.[1] With completion of a new exhibition building at Winterthur in 1992 and 1993, the Dominy Woodworking

Shop was reconstructed, once again, in space that permitted a more accurate display of the two shop structures (figs. 1 and 2).

The woodworking tools and equipment seen in the new setting were used primarily by Nathaniel Dominy IV and his son, Nathaniel V, to earn a living fashioning wood as cabinetmakers, house and mill carpenters, wheelwrights, turners, and toolmakers. Of the tools they used to earn a living in the eighteenth and early nineteenth

Fig. 1. View of Dominy Woodworking Shop, Henry S. McNeil Gallery, Winterthur Museum. Exterior reconstructed 1992–1993; interior equipment, ca. 1750–1840. Courtesy, Winterthur Museum.

Fig. 2. Partial interior view, Dominy Woodworking Shop, showing arbor and cross for turning table tops, work benches, shingling horse, bow saw, and other shop tools and equipment, 1750–1840. Courtesy, Winterthur Museum.

centuries, more than eleven hundred have survived. Fifty-six are stamped with their date of manufacture or acquisition. Another fifty-nine tools bear the initials or name of one or another of the Dominy craftsmen.

This makes it possible to date many of the unmarked tools by comparing them to dated examples used by the Dominy craftsmen during their working years. For example, Nathaniel Dominy IV's initials and the date 1765 appear on a round plane, while Nathaniel Dominy V's name stamp appears on an ovolo or quarter-round plane with the date 1800 when he made the stock for its blade (figs. 3 and 4).

Fig. 3. Round plane, birch stock and wedge, East Hampton, N. Y., dated 1765. Front of stock also stamped 7, conjoined initials ND for Nathaniel Dominy IV. L. 11⅜"; H. 6³⁄₁₆"; W. ⁷⁄₈", 57.93.20. Courtesy, Winterthur Museum.

Fig. 4. Ovolo or quarter-round plane, American beech stock and wedge, East Hampton, N. Y., dated 1800. Front of stock stamped DOMINY in serrated edge rectangle for Nathaniel Dominy V. L. 7¼"; H. 4⅞"; W. ¹¹⁄₁₆", 57.93.88. Courtesy, Winterthur Museum.

Fig. 5. Molding plane (bead, hollow, groove, reverse ogee), American beech stock and wedge, soft maple fence, East Hampton, N. Y., 1750–1800. Incised initials IM on left side of stock, possibly for Jeremiah Mulford; initials ND for Nathaniel Dominy IV stamped on front of stock. L. 11"; H. $6^{5}/_{16}$"; W. $1^{5}/_{8}$", 57.93.91, gift of Robert M. Dominy. Courtesy, Winterthur Museum.

A plane that produces a bead, hollow, groove, and reverse ogee molding (fig. 5) bears the initials IM of its first owner, who may have been Jeremiah Mulford, a carpenter working in East Hampton as early as 1725. At any rate, Nathaniel Dominy IV added his initials to the stock when he acquired it and modified it by adding a ¼-inch fence fastened with rose-headed nails. In a letter to the author, W. L. Goodman suggested that the plane may have been modified to make looking glass frames. From the extensive business records kept by the Dominys and at least one surviving example, it is known that they did make looking glasses.[2]

Many of the Dominys' tools also help to document woodworking technology in Western Europe that was transferred to colonial America. A wrought-iron ax (fig. 6), about two feet long, stamped IC in a shield, its maker's initials, was probably owned by Nathaniel Dominy III. He may have acquired it about 1750, when a woodworking shop was added to his dwelling. In *With Hammer in Hand,* I speculated that the ax was of English origin and perhaps used for carpenter's or wheelwright's work. About ten years after my book was published, Winterthur acquired the entire photograph collection assembled by Josef Greber for his book, *Die Geschichte des Hobels.*[3] In that collection is a photograph of a wood engraving printed in a Carmelite manuscript of about 1500, showing a carpenter using an identical ax to trim a floor board (fig. 7). We know that the artisan in the woodcut is a carpenter because the rest of the composition depicts the holy family. The source of the manuscript is listed by Greber as a monastery near Brussels. The ax, therefore, may be from continental Europe rather than from England.[4]

This tool would have been useful not only to Nathaniel Dominy III, but also to his son and grandson. In the Dominy manuscripts is a plan and elevation drawn about 1762 by Nathaniel Dominy IV for a house probably built for Joseph Ellis. In the accounts, under Ellis's name, is an entry, "To work Building House, Viz geting timber, hewing, framing and covering in all 24½ days at 4s-6d" for a total of £5 10s. 3p. The house was built over a total of seventy days between March 30 and June 7, 1762. Both Nathaniel IV and Nathaniel

Fig. 6. Carpenter's trimming ax, wrought iron, probably The Netherlands, 1725–1750. Blade stamped with maker's initials IC in a shield. Probably owned by Nathaniel Dominy III. L. 9" (handle); 7¾" (blade); W. 6⁹⁄₁₆" (blade), 57.26.280. Courtesy, Winterthur Museum.

Fig. 7. Detail depicting the Holy Family at Vilvoorden, near Brussels, Belgium. Wood engraving, paper, ink, Carmelite MS, ca. 1500. Josef Greber Photograph Collection, Decorative Arts Photographic Collection. Courtesy, Winterthur Museum.

ıstructed sawmills and windmills. In 1770, Nathaniel IV's journey-
...... jeremy (who may have been an Indian or a black) spent four and a half
days at 3s. per day working "on floors." Among the mills constructed by
Nathaniel V was one built for Captain William J. Rysam of Sag Harbor that
was disassembled and shipped to Honduras to saw mahogany in a grove owned
by Rysam.[5]

A frame saw in the Dominy Tool Collection is virtually identical to one
shown in Diderot's *Encyclopédie* and in Roubo's *L'art du menuisier*.[6] While the
Dominys' saw illustrates the universality of craft techniques and equipment in
the Western world, it was not necessarily used by them to perform the function of cutting veneer as shown in the French encyclopedias. Before cutting
veneer strips, posts for bedsteads, or drawer bottoms for large case pieces,
woodworkers used a chalk line to snap markings on logs as a guide for the
sawyers. In 1767, Nathaniel IV credited Aaron Isaacs for £23 of chalk. But
the Dominys didn't produce veneered furniture. It is much more likely that
this saw was used to cut posts for the seventy-three bedsteads listed in their
accounts between 1768 and 1833, or stock for the large number of case pieces,
at least 108, made between 1768 and 1833. The point is that the same woodworking tool was often used by craftsmen for different functions or tasks.

The sources from which the Dominys obtained their woodworking tools
were similar to those used by other craftsmen. Artisans in both cities and villages whose shops were near navigable water were able to buy cheaper and
well-made English tools through suppliers in nearby port cities or by trans-
shipment from major ports. Yes, there were colonial American toolmakers supplying colonial American craftsmen. But in the eighteenth century, their
products never rivaled the volume of European tools that were imported or
sold on these shores. As noted in *With Hammer in Hand*, nearly every one of
the 170 joiner's tools in the chest imported in 1760 by William Wilson of
Philadelphia had a counterpart in the Dominy Woodworking Shop. The same
is true of a "complete set" of 166 carpenter's and joiner's tools listed by the
Falmouth, Virginia, merchant, William Allason, in 1769, as recorded in Volume I of Colonial Williamsburg's *Historic Trades*.[7]

A birch square was made in the Dominy Woodworking Shop, probably
by Nathaniel III, about 1760. It is stamped NATHANIEL DOMINY in script,
the only tool surviving in the collection with that mark. A bevel square also

was made in the shop, but by Nathaniel V in 1810. Most chisel and gouge blades owned by the Dominys were made in England with their handles, all of American woods, fitted in the Dominy shop. A combination marking/mortising gauge, of American cherry, was produced in 1765 by Nathaniel Dominy IV.[8]

Between 1765 and 1798, Nathaniel IV and Nathaniel V purchased many gimlets from Aaron Isaacs, who sailed weekly between East Hampton and New York City. A large English gimlet with a boxwood handle is an example of one of those tools. Gimlets also were supplied by customers as a means of paying for some of the products or services offered by the craftsmen. Plane irons, files, and "gimblets" were the most frequently mentioned types of tools used by customers to repay sums owed to the Dominys. At least one nose auger could have been supplied by an East Hampton blacksmith like William Hedges, Samuel Sherrill, or Deacon David Talmage, all of whom made a variety of new woodworking tools for the Dominys or repaired older, worn examples. Typical of the mixture of native woods used to make many of their tools, one of several braces or bitstocks was made by Nathaniel IV of American beech with a soft maple cap. An English nose bit, however, was fitted into a hickory block.[9]

A small bow or frame saw like the one made by Nathaniel IV or Nathaniel V of American cherry is similar to one illustrated in Roubo's *L'art du menuisier*. It is an excellent example of craftsmen improving on a tool design in use for centuries. On their frame saw, the Dominys substituted a threaded bolt and nut for rope and a winding stick. The rivets holding the saw blade ride loosely in mortises and respond to pressure on the frame to change direction in cutting wood. Instead of one hand holding a blade handle and the other the saw frame, both hands grasp the frame and provide better control. It was that kind of control that was necessary to follow template designs for furniture parts scratched on wood with an awl.[10]

Backsaws, like an English tenon saw bought by Nathaniel IV from Aaron Isaacs in 1765, are illustrated in the Dominy Tool Collection by an English dovetail saw, with fifteen teeth to the inch, that Nathaniel V probably bought and handled circa 1790. Its handgrip is birch. The pattern for the handle of the handsaw survives in the Dominy Collection. A handsaw was bought by Nathaniel IV from Aaron Isaacs in 1770 at a cost of 8s., slightly more than the 7s. daily wage rate charged by Nathaniel IV for his time. It is more likely that the Dominys' surviving handsaw was a replacement bought by Nathaniel V about 1800.[11]

While the plane irons found in their bench planes could have been obtained from their customers, local blacksmiths, or purchased for them in New York City, there is no doubt that the handles, stocks, and wedges of their bench planes were made by Nathaniel IV or Nathaniel V between 1763 and 1793. First-pass, rough smoothing of sawn boards was accomplished by a fore plane with its slightly convex sole and blade. It was made by Nathaniel IV about 1765 and used so extensively that its mouth became so wide that it had to be discarded in 1792. Nathaniel IV also made an almost three-foot-long jointer in 1766 and a satinwood smoothing plane that has a stamped inscription on its stock noting that it was made on Christmas day, 1763. A strike block plane, used by woodworkers for short joints or bevels and miters, was also made by Nathaniel IV in 1793.[12]

Fig. 8. Molding plane (ogee, reverse ogee, bead, and quirk), white oak stock, dogwood addition to sole, maple wedge, East Hampton, N. Y., 1740–1770. Stamped ND in rectangle for Nathaniel Dominy IV. Probably made or acquired by Nathaniel Dominy III. L. 12"; H. 3¾"; W. 2½", 57.93.100, gift of Robert M. Dominy. Courtesy, Winterthur Museum.

One of the oldest molding planes in the Dominy Collection is a white oak example bearing the initials of Nathaniel Dominy IV (fig. 8). W. L. Goodman indicated in a letter that, because the plane has a crude European-type horn at the front, it might be Dutch in origin. It would not have been difficult for Nathaniel IV to buy or accept this plane as barter from a customer. It has a 2-inch-wide blade and a ½-inch-wide fence. The complex molding it produces may have been used to make moldings for doorways or looking glass frames. Its blade has a common pitch, forty-five degrees, indicating its use on soft wood.

This molding plane has a dogwood patch or addition made by Nathaniel IV. Its sole may have been so worn at the time he acquired it that he had to make a patch for it, or he may have added the dogwood section to the sole in order to convert it from one purpose to another. Worn files, saw blades, and planes were often converted as "make-dos" to other kinds of tools.

Eighteenth-century woodworkers had to have planes that could cut grooves in wood. Like the Dominys, they usually had universal planes—plows—with six to twelve cutting irons or two pairs of matched grooving planes. One such plane was obtained by Nathaniel Dominy IV in 1772. A sash fillister plane of American cherry was made by Nathaniel IV in 1765. Basically a type of skew-rabbet plane, the Dominys used it to make window sash, listed frequently as a source of carpentry income in their accounts.[13]

Unlike their urban counterparts, country woodworkers often included a lathe or two in their shops. Furniture produced by rural cabinetmakers relied heavily on molded, sawn, and turned decoration. The lathes in the Dominy shops were extremely important to their livelihood. Of the 936 pieces of furniture made in the Dominy Woodworking Shop between 1760 and 1840, at least 738 were made up in full or in part of turned sections.

A pole lathe (fig. 9) was incredibly useful in a small shop because products could be made on it by one person without the aid of an apprentice. Using green wood, not only furniture but large workbench screws, pump-box pipe, mill shafts, wagon hubs, and hubs for spinning wheels or reels could also be turned by the Dominys. Five six-foot-high columns for the portico of Clinton Academy in East Hampton were turned on this pole lathe by Nathaniel V in 1802. The length of their pole lathe bed measures 6½ feet, more than 1½ feet longer than the bed of their great wheel lathe.

Fig. 9. Pole lathe, ash pole (original), white oak bed, base, supports; red oak tool rest, East Hampton, N. Y., 1750–1775. Made by Nathaniel Dominy III or IV. L. 77⅝"; H. 32⅝"; W. 34½" (base), 9½" (bed), 57.26.372. Courtesy, Winterthur Museum.

When Nathaniel IV and Nathaniel V had an apprentice or journeyman available, they undoubtedly preferred the continuous cutting, choice of speeds, and greater productivity of their great wheel lathe. Its wheel is more than five and one-half feet in diameter and is closer to those shown in Diderot's *Encyclopédie* than it is to illustrations in the earlier volume of Plumier or the later book on turning by Salivet.[14] A great wheel lathe was available to Nathaniel IV by 1776 because in that year he charged Abraham Mulford, Jr., 1s. 3p. for the use of "gun bit and great wheel."[15]

Figure 10 represents the most important piece of lathe equipment to survive in the Dominy Tool Collection. None of the eighteenth- or nineteenth-century source books for tools and craft technology illustrates an "arbor and cross." It was used principally by Nathaniel Dominy V to turn the circular tops of tables and stands of which approximately 130 were made between 1789 and 1833. Responding to growing demand for these products in the area served by the Dominys, Nathaniel V went to a local blacksmith, Deacon David

Fig. 10. Arbor and cross, white oak puppet, shaft; dogwood screw; hickory screw; soft maple pulley, East Hampton, N. Y., 1795. Made by Deacon David Talmage, Jr., and Nathaniel Dominy V. H. 30½"; W. 14" (cross); L. 18⅜"; Diam. 8½" (pulley), 57.26.370. Courtesy, Winterthur Museum.

Talmage, and credited him in their accounts on February 27, 1795, 6s. 9p., "By an Arbor & Cross for Turning Stands."[16] Nathaniel V then fitted a soft maple pulley and dogwood and hickory screws on a hickory puppet in order to set it in the great wheel lathe bed in a vertical position as illustrated in figure 10.

In 1800, Nathaniel V found another use for his arbor and cross when he turned the bold molding for the broken arch pediment of a desk and bookcase produced for John Lyon Gardiner of Gardiners Island. Since its recent addition to the Winterthur Collection, this piece of furniture has been studied in detail. It is clear that the molding was turned in a continuous circle and then cut to form four sections. Nathaniel Dominy V charged Gardiner £20 8s. for this, the most ambitious piece of furniture produced in the Dominys' shop. Using one-third of that price for labor, it is evident that Nathaniel V spent nineteen and one-third days, approximately twelve hours per day, to complete this piece.[17] Joinery required more time than did turning, which probably accounts for the heavy use of both their pole and great wheel lathes.

Between 1786 and 1795, when he made the arbor and cross for Nathaniel V, Deacon David Talmage made or repaired plane irons, heading tools, forging tongs, axes, chisels, bits, augers, hammers, and a drawplate for wire for the Dominys.[18]

Much of the joinery that took place in the Dominy Woodworking Shop was accomplished on a superb eighteenth-century tool, their main workbench (fig. 11). Its major surface consists of a red oak plank more than twelve feet long, one and one-half feet wide, and about six inches thick. Equipped with a double screw vise, a bench hook, holdfast, a pivoting grease cup, and a board support that slides on a track between the bench top and stretcher, its features resemble benches illustrated by Joseph Moxon in 1703 and Roubo in 1769[19] (see pages 78 and 165). Other Dominy tools seen on top of the bench are a late eighteenth-century mallet and dividers, a hickory and white oak screw tap used to thread holes to receive the vise screws of a bench, and a bone spokeshave made by Nathaniel V at the end of the eighteenth century.

The Dominys not only made a living by using tools, they also earned income by making tools for their customers. Nathaniel IV made a joiner's bench in 1773 for which he charged his customer 10s. In 1796, Nathaniel Dominy V charged 7s. "To cut [a] pair of bench screws" for another customer.[20] Agricultural tools such as hay forks, grain cradles, rakes, harrows, and flax swingles

Fig. 11. Workbench, red oak, East Hampton, N. Y., 1750–1775. Probably made by Nathaniel Dominy III. Equipped with double screw vise, adjustable board hook, sliding board support, and grease cup. L. 148¼";
H. 29½"; D. 28¼", 57.26.367. Courtesy, Winterthur Museum.

were made in large numbers. Handles were produced for axes, hammers, shovels, and spades. By making wood patterns for sand casting in flasks, they also produced bullet, button, and shot molds.

The Dominys illustrate the fact that eighteenth-century colonial American craftsmen used a wide variety of tools with a skill and dexterity that is difficult for contemporary Americans to understand. Some of the tools that helped to speed furniture making were patterns or templates (figs. 12 and 13). By outlining the shape of these patterns with a scratch awl on boards held on top of a workbench, the Dominys and other craftsmen used the concept of reproducible and interchangeable parts within their own shops to produce objects in quantity. More than 350 chairs were made by the Dominys between 1766 and 1840. Some of the different types they made included Windsor, child's, slat-back rocking, side, and armchairs.[21]

Fig. 12. Crest rail
and splat patterns,
white pine,
American white oak,
East Hampton,
N. Y., 1770–1830.
Made by Nathaniel
Dominy IV and V.
L. 9⅝" to 20";
W. 2" to 5",
57.26.313-314,
57.26.321,
57.26.465-466.
Courtesy,
Winterthur
Museum.

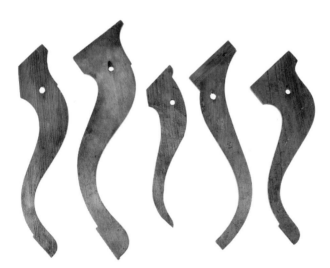

Fig. 13.
Candlestand and tea
table leg patterns,
white pine, East
Hampton, N. Y.,
1790–1830. Made
by Nathaniel
Dominy V.
H. 7⅞" to 9½",
L. 10 9/16" to 15½",
57.26.301-305.
Courtesy,
Winterthur
Museum.

The pattern used to produce the cabriole leg and pad foot for the Dominys' high chest also survives in the tool collection, as does a pattern for a dining table leg. A bracket foot pattern used for the Gardiner desk and bookcase and a variety of leg shapes and sizes for tripod-leg stands and tables also are among the Dominys' tools (fig. 13). Some of the objects made from those patterns are on view in the Henry S. McNeil Gallery of Winterthur's new exhibit building. Turned stands were produced so quickly by Nathaniel V that his charges for them ranged from 7s. 6p. to £1, the price difference often being in the wood selected by his customer—maple, cherry, or mahogany. Those pieces indicate that with the help of precut patterns, Nathaniel V never spent more than twelve hours to make his best and largest stand.

The Dominys used not only templates or patterns to speed production of furniture but they also made special tools when it was clear that orders for a particular form warranted the creation of a time-saving device. Nathaniel V found it necessary to fashion a clamp for bending slats and forcing them to retain their curve (fig. 14). This tool helped him to meet the demand for his slat-back chairs. Again, a similar tool has not been found in any literature related to craft techniques or tools. That may only mean that a clamp of this type was so commonly used by chairmakers that no one bothered to record its use in the eighteenth and early nineteenth centuries.

Fig. 14. Slat-bending clamp, tulip, white pine, red oak, East Hampton, N. Y., 1800–1840. Made by Nathaniel Dominy V. L. 27 1/16"; H. 7 1/2", D. 3 7/8", 57.26.223. Courtesy, Winterthur Museum.

Fig. 15. Turning chisel, soft maple, horn ferrule, steel blade, inlaid brass, East Hampton, N. Y., and England, 1765–1790. Made or purchased by Nathaniel Dominy IV. Made from an old sword blade dated 1660. L. 14¼"; W. ½" (blade width), 57.26.119. Courtesy, Winterthur Museum.

In this article, not all of the more than eleven hundred tools that survive in the Dominy Collection can be shown and discussed. That was not possible even in a four-hundred-plus-page book. And as Nathaniel Dominy IV stated on his watchpaper, "Time Flies." I will conclude, therefore, with an image of what is probably the most beautiful "make-do" tool to survive in the Dominy Collection. It's a ½-inch-wide, 14¼-inch-long turning chisel made by Nathaniel Dominy III or IV from the fine steel of a seventeenth-century sword blade. A flower-and-leaf design and the date 1660 are inlaid in brass on the blade (fig. 15).

The special nature of this tool, and its ability to remind us of a bygone time when craftsmen applied muscle power to handsome but useful implements in order to earn a living, was mentioned by a New York author in the 1870s. In describing the newfound playground of American artists of the Barbizon School, the author described "An old weather-beaten dwelling at the upper end of [East Hampton] village street." It was sketched and painted so often that an in joke on new artists arriving in town was "that Dominy's is going onto the canvas." After describing its already dilapidated condition, the author continued, "Two workshops, one flanking each side of the cottage, present curious interiors,—low ceilings, dusty, cobwebbed windows, tools of various callings disposed on the walls or in cribs in the ceiling, and a medley of articles scattered about,—old fashioned clocks in long cases, a photographer's camera, a Damascus blade, with gold-inlaid hilt, fashioned into a chisel."[22]

The very same chisel serves as a reminder of a time when tools were used as part of a vocation to produce objects of necessity, objects beyond necessity, and objects to earn a craftsman's bread.

1. Hummel, *With Hammer in Hand*, pp. 4–17.

2. W. L. Goodman, Bristol, Eng., to Charles F. Hummel, Winterthur, Del. [1969]. See also Hummel, *With Hammer in Hand*, pp. 234, 372, 400, 401. A looking glass made for Abraham Sherrill was acquired by the Winterthur Mus. and is now displayed in the McNeil Gallery, 92.92.

3. Josef M. Greber, *Die Geschichte des Hobels* (Zurich, 1956; reprint, Hanover, Ger., 1987) English trans. by Seth W. Burchard as *The History of the Woodworking Plane* (Early Amer. Industries Assn., 1991).

4. Additional evidence supporting a continental European origin for this tool is in a letter from Gerrit van der Sterre, Leiderdorp, The Netherlands, to Jay Gaynor, Williamsburg, Va., Aug. 15, 1994. The ax is described as a *snik* used by house carpenters but normally used by millwrights for heavy construction. Mr. van der Sterre quotes from an invoice of tools delivered in 1664 and refers to a carved stone dated 1666 in a house front in Amsterdam, which illustrates this type of ax. It is described as a *steekbijl*, or an ax "to be used in a pushing way." I am indebted to both correspondents for this information.

5. *With Hammer in Hand*, pp. 235–238. See also Dean F. Failey, *Long Island Is My Nation: The Decorative Arts & Craftsmen, 1640–1830* (Setauket, N. Y., 1976), pp. 197 and n. 14, p. 201; and Account Book B, Nathaniel Dominy IV, Dominy Family Papers, Collection 265, MS 59x9a, Joseph Downs Manuscript and Ephemera Collections, Winterthur Lib.

6. *With Hammer in Hand*, no. 102, pp. 133–134.

7. *Ibid.*, pp. 32–33; *Historic Trades*, I (1988), pp. 66–67.

8. *With Hammer in Hand*, nos. 24, 25, 36B, 40, 41, 111, 113A.

9. *Ibid.*, nos. 15A, B, C, E, 20B, 39; Account Book B, pp. 44, 47, 58, 100.

10. *With Hammer in Hand*, no. 100.

11. *Ibid.*, nos. 101, 104.

12. *Ibid.*, nos. 69, 73, 92, 95.

13. *Ibid.*, nos. 81, 90.

14. Charles Plumier, *L'art de tourneur*, . . . (Paris, 1701); Louis Georges Isaac Salivet [L.-E. Bergeron, pseud.], *Manuel du tourneur* . . . , 2 vols. (Paris, 1792 and 1796; rev. M. [P.] Hamelin-Bergeron, Paris, 1816).

15. Account Book B, p. 88.

16. *Ibid.*, p. 150.

17. *With Hammer in Hand*, no. 244, pp. 327–330.

18. Account Book B, pp. 108, 110.

19. Joseph Moxon, *Mechanick Exercises: or, The Doctrine of Handy-works*, 3rd ed. (London, 1703; reprint, Morristown, N. J., 1989), pl. 4, fig. A, p. 69; André Jacob Roubo, *L'art du menuisier* (Paris, 1769–1775), III, pl. 11.

20. *With Hammer in Hand*, no. 9.

21. *Ibid.*, nos. 180–185, 187, 191.

22. Charles Burr Todd, *In Olde New York: Sketches of Old Times and Places in Both the State and the City* (New York, 1907), p. 160.

Wing and Reed

Case Studies of Two
Early Nineteenth-Century Chairmakers

By Frank G. White

This paper contrasts the working styles of two early nineteenth-century Massachusetts woodworking craftsmen. The first is Samuel Wing, a turn-of-the-nineteenth-century woodworker, many of whose tools were included in the exhibit "TOOLS: Working Wood in 18th-Century America." The second is Elbridge Gerry Reed, a chairmaker working in central Massachusetts in the second quarter of the nineteenth century.

Born in 1774 in Sandwich, Massachusetts, on Cape Cod, Samuel Wing worked as a cabinetmaker, carpenter, chairmaker, and sawmill operator until his late thirties. In 1813, he virtually abandoned woodworking to open a cotton shirting factory with his two brothers. A century and a half later, his great-grandson donated all of the surviving material evidence of Samuel's woodworking career to Old Sturbridge Village. The collection includes more than one hundred woodworking, metalworking, and shoemaking tools, workbenches, chair patterns and unfinished parts, fragments of cabinet lumber and other supplies, and even some of Wing's shop records. His shop itself does not survive, but its size and layout were nominally recorded with rough

Fig. 1. Exterior view of the Samuel Wing house in Sandwich, Mass. His shop was at the very end of the ell accessed by the wide door. Courtesy, Old Sturbridge Village, Sturbridge, Mass.

Fig. 2. Vignette of a traditional cabinet shop in the Old Sturbridge Village exhibit "Cabinet Furniture and Chairs Cheap: Making and Selling Furniture in Central New England, 1790–1850," April 1993–December 1994. The workbench was built into Wing's shop in front of the windows just as it is here. Note the large horizontal double screw vise at the left and the sliding X-bracket that supports the other end of the board. Courtesy, Old Sturbridge Village, photograph by Thomas Neill.

Fig. 3. Wood threading tap and die set from the Wing shop with a vise screw cut with these tools. Courtesy, Old Sturbridge Village, photograph by Thomas Neill.

drawings and snapshots. This collection probably ranks second in significance to the Dominy Collection at Winterthur for what it tells us about late eighteenth- and early nineteenth-century cabinetmaking.

Wing's shop was located at the end of a long ell attached to his house that measured about twenty feet long by twelve and one-half feet wide (fig. 1). Cut around the studs of the end wall was a workbench that filled the length of the wall. It had two horizontal double screw vises, a sliding brace to support one end of a board while planing its edge, and a large wooden leg vise that was added in later years (fig. 2). Wing made this workbench himself. The large woodthreading tap and die set for cutting the threads on the vise screws and threading the holes in the bench top to receive them are among the surviving tools along with a 1½-inch screw auger for drilling the holes (fig. 3). There is also a smaller set of taps and dies and a ¾-inch screw auger for making handscrews or clamps. Interestingly, both augers are screw or spiral augers marked T. CUSHMAN and presumably date from around 1800 since Wing seemingly had his shop set up by that date.[1]

At this bench there were two good work stations in front of the windows. We know from a November 1798 contract that Wing had a journeyman cabinetmaker named Russell Blackwell working with him through the winter of that year. Blackwell was to work for three months and receive $12.00 for every $22.00 worth of work that he did. He was to take "the work as it rises Desks Tables Chairs, Clock Cases &c." Blackwell may have worked in front of one window and Wing in front of the other. How much longer than the initial three months he worked for Wing is unclear. Only one other record refers to Blackwell, a brief note dated April 12, 1799, by which he requested that Wing deliver six green chairs to Benjamin Wing (Samuel's father) on his, Blackwell's, account.[2]

Though fragmentary, Wing's daybooks reveal the kinds and quantities of furniture that he made. They also show that, like most contemporary cabinet-makers, he had to perform a range of woodworking tasks to make a living. In addition to making furniture, Wing did carpentry work and painting and even made boats for local seamen. From the accounts, it may also be possible to get a sense of his rate of production by comparing Wing's day rate for his labor to the prices he charged for the pieces of furniture he made. Entries in the day-book for labor are very scarce. In 1802, Wing charged Seth Freeman 7s. 6p. for one and one-half days' work. Other entries make it clear that this is the equivalent of $1.25, or about 84¢ per day.[3]

Using the 84¢ figure, it is interesting to estimate how long it took Wing to make chairs and some other furniture items. Of course, some allowance has to be made for material, but in most cases that is fairly nominal, especially for

chairs which were routinely made from native woods. For instance, he paid only $4.00 for five hundred feet of maple in 1796. Chair prices varied from $8.50 to $9.00 for a set of "six green chairs," but most were at $9.00, or $1.50 per chair (fig. 4). Coincidentally, contemporary woodworker Solomon Sibley of Auburn, Massachusetts, charged $1.40 for a

Fig. 4. Sack-back Windsor side chair, maker unknown, one of several chair types that Wing produced. Courtesy, Old Sturbridge Village.

Fig. 5. A single hole in each end of these unused chair stretchers suggests that Wing turned them on a pole lathe. Courtesy, Old Sturbridge Village, photograph by Thomas Neill.

"green chair" but only 83¢ for a "red chair."[4] At the 84¢ day rate it would have taken Wing around eleven days to complete the set, or just under two days per chair. Bureaus cost from $7.50 to $9.00 each and could have been made in eight to eleven days, although on one occasion a "case of drawers" cost $24.00 plus $1.25 for "casen them." A light stand, or candlestand to us, cost $1.50 and would have been made in about two days. In turning "stand posts" for Obed Nye, another local cabinetmaker, Wing charged 16.5¢ each, at which rate he could have turned five in a day.[5]

At first glance, these numbers seem quite ordinary, but when you consider the handwork that went into each piece, they become more impressive. Sawmill stock was resawn roughly to size and shape with a handsaw; it was jackplaned to remove saw marks and further smoothed with a smoothing plane; all joinery was done with chisels, mallet, bit, brace, and saw. A case piece or a table would have been scraped to render a smooth finish and then painted or stained and varnished. Turning was probably done on a treadle-driven, spring pole lathe. The presence of a single center point on either end of surviving turned stretchers virtually confirms this assumption (fig. 5). Before being turned on a pole lathe, billets had to be roughed to shape by hand. Edward Hazen in his *Panorama of Professions and Trades* observed that "when the

material to be turned is wood, it is cut to the proper length with a saw, and brought to a form approaching to the cylindrical by means of an axe or drawing-knife."[6]

With these numbers in mind, let us look in more detail at some of the chair forms that Wing produced and how he made them. From surviving evidence, we know that he made at least five different types of Windsor chairs with several variations in ornamentation and detail. He was able to fill orders for chairs quite promptly because he stockpiled many of the parts. Quantities of chair parts survive from Wing's shop. Stretchers, and probably legs and posts (pillars), were turned in quantity out of green wood and then set aside to season. Back spindles were first roughed out of green wood with a drawknife, seasoned for a time, and then brought down to nearly finished form with a spokeshave (fig. 6). Stock for Windsor chair backs was cut to size, struck with a molding or grooving plane, and then bent to shape and set aside with a cleat nailed across the ends to keep it from opening up.

Fig. 7. Chair seats made by Wing in different stages of completion. Tool marks confirm that they were sawn to shape with a frame or bow saw, the edges were cleaned up and relieved with a drawknife, and the scoop and saddle were cut across the grain with a hollowing adze, scorp, or compass plane. Courtesy, Old Sturbridge Village, photograph by Henry E. Peach.

Wing traced patterns for chair seats and crest rails, sawed them to shape with a bow saw, beveled and cleaned up the outside edges with a drawknife, and scooped the seats with an adze, scorp, or compass plane. He probably worked up seats in advance as well since four seat blanks in different stages of completion survive from the shop (fig. 7). The seat pattern could also be used to locate the holes for the legs and lay off the center lines for back spindles and posts and the seat groove by using a pair of dividers (fig. 8). The leg positions on the pattern were found by trial and error as there are multiple holes at each position, all but one of which are plugged. This pattern is also inscribed "Russell Pattern," suggesting that it was made, or at least used, by Russell Blackwell, Wing's onetime journeyman cabinetmaker.

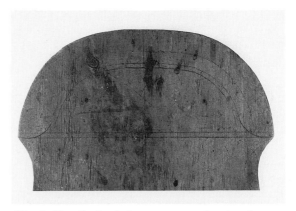

Fig. 8. Detail of a chair seat pattern showing the scribe lines for the seat groove and the center line of the back spindles. The positions of the back legs are marked by small nail holes; note a second, plugged hole beside the left-hand hole. Courtesy, Old Sturbridge Village, photograph by Thomas Neill.

Wing's practice of stockpiling chair parts was by no means unique to him. Batch production of chairs was probably routine among Windsor and post-and-rung chairmakers. The probate inventory of David Stowell of Worcester, Massachusetts, filed in 1802, includes considerable numbers of finished and unfinished chairs and chair parts and indicates a chairmaking venture of much greater scale than Wing's. At his death, Stowell had in his shop "201 unfinished dining chairs, 302 ruff bottoms for dining chairs, 242 unbent bows, 451 chair legs, 16 bent bows, 742 stretchers, 287 back flasks[?]."[7]

The other case study takes us about a quarter-century ahead to the 1830s. Elbridge Gerry Reed worked as a chairmaker in Sterling, Massachusetts, from the late 1820s to 1860 and would be just another anonymous craftsman if not for the fortuitous survival of his daybook. This daybook serves as a window into the daily work of craftsmen in the burgeoning chair trade in central

Massachusetts. Reed worked most of his life as a journeyman chairmaker and mechanic for others. At some times he specialized as a woodturner; at others he primarily assembled chairs, making large quantities that were sold far beyond his home town of Sterling. In fact, chairs produced in northern Worcester County were shipped around the world.[8]

In the 1820 *Census of Manufactures,* Sterling reported twenty-three chairmakers producing 70,000 chairs, far more than any other town in central Massachusetts. The three largest operators made 8,000, 6,000, and 4,000 chairs, respectively. In 1832, Sterling and seven other small northern Worcester County towns produced 363,000 chairs, and by 1837, those same eight towns had increased production to more than a half-million chairs.[9]

Larger chair shops were often part of a sawmill and gristmill complex that included a water-powered lathe and provided a ready supply of custom-sawn chair stock (fig. 9). The 1830 map of Sterling lists ten chair mills and seven sawmills, several of which served both purposes. Small, one-man operations were also sited on small streams to run water-powered lathes. Men who only assembled chairs had no need for waterpower and often had small shops next to their homes. The 1831 tax list for Sterling listed a shop "in or adjoining" Reed's house where he no doubt assembled chairs for other chairmakers. At other times, he turned parts on a water-powered lathe in their shops.

Reed and his fellow chairmakers made two basic types of chairs: common chairs and fancy chairs. Common chairs had pine plank seats, what we popularly call "rabbit ear" or "kitchen Windsors." Fancy chairs had rush (flag) seats and were of the traditional post and rung construction. They were distinguished by fancy turnings and different combinations of design elements. Within the two broad groups there were many variations in the design and construction of the backs and legs. All were meant to be painted and very often decorated. Common chairs retailed for 50¢–$1.00 each, fancy chairs for $1.00–$2.00. They were the cheap chairs of the early nineteenth century.

Evidence from Reed's daybook suggests that he was capable of turning from 350 to 500, and perhaps more, pieces of chair stock in a day's time. This estimate is based on his rate of 75¢ for "one days turnning" and assumes a workday of at least ten hours. By dividing his day rate into the prices for specific numbers of chair parts, Reed's average daily production of different components can be computed. For example, 716 stretchers at $1.29 yields an

Fig. 9. Re-created chairmaker's woodturning shop in the "Cabinet Furniture and Chairs Cheap" exhibit. Sawn billets of predetermined length at the left are ready for turning; quantities of turned chair parts are at the right. The original cast-iron lathe parts are mounted on a reproduction stand. Courtesy, Old Sturbridge Village, photograph by Thomas Neill.

average of 416 stretchers per day; 298 chair legs at 41¢ gives 546 chair legs per day. Reed's production rate varied with the complexity of the turnings.

Water-powered lathes, which offered the distinct advantages of sustained and continuous operation along with increased power and speed, made this rate of production possible. Even so, Reed had to be a very efficient woodturner and probably learned many of the shortcuts that are standard with production woodturners. Unlike Wing, he did not have to preshape turning stock by hand because he could knock the corners off a billet much faster in the water-powered lathe. In fact, Reed's turning squares were most likely presawn to size and length. Chairmaker Peter Pierce of Templeton, Massachusetts, had stacks of unturned, undoubtedly circular sawn, chair parts on hand when he died in 1836, including 330 unturned stretchers and 200 unturned fancy legs.[10]

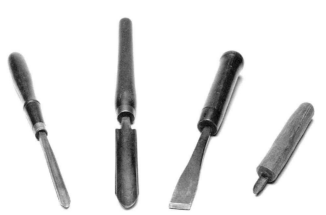

Fig. 10.
Woodturning tools
from the Old
Sturbridge Village
collections
including one large
and two small
gouges and a skew
chisel. Courtesy,
Old Sturbridge
Village, photograph
by Thomas Neill.

Reed did little or no measuring with caliper or rule but at most simply eyeballed a master pattern or finished turning. He consequently produced turnings that were visually similar but by no means identical. Variations in leg diameters of between $\frac{1}{8}$ inch and $\frac{3}{16}$ inch were routinely found during analysis of 1820s and 1830s chairs in the Old Sturbridge Village collections.[11] This range of tolerances is far greater than would be expected from the regular use of calipers or gauges. The only constants were the locations of the incised lines, or "bamboo" grooves, that registered the intersections of the stretchers. Reed's primary turning tools were a large gouge, a chisel, either straight or skewed, and a small gouge for details (fig. 10). He learned to finish the turnings with these tools alone and did little or no sanding. He was also able to replace a finished turning with a fresh billet without shutting down the lathe.

Some of this at first seems rather astonishing to amateur woodturners like myself. However, this excerpt from a description of a production woodturning shop in Wales, which supplied chair legs to a firm in High Wycombe in the 1950s, suggests that such practices were not at all unusual. The main differences between this shop and where Reed worked are the number of lathes and the motive power.

> The main equipment of the workshop was 9 lathes, 3 rows
> of 3, each row separately driven by overhead belting. All 3
> lathes in each row either stopped or ran together, and in

practice they ran all day, stopping only for lunch and tea. There was only one speed—3000 r.p.m.

Neither calipers nor setting-out boards nor form plates were used. Everything was done by eye. With the lathe in motion the operator held the end of a rough, bark-covered, blank against the spinning nose and pushed it until its weight was supported. He then used the lever to advance the tailstock until it forced the wood onto the driving lugs of the headstock. At this point the whole thing suddenly disappeared into a blur.

A thick continuous shaving erupted from a large gouge and flew over my right shoulder. . . . After the gouge had done the roughing to size and shape it was exchanged for a large chisel, 1½" wide and long-handled. Vee cuts were made for decoration and then the leg was completed by working from the centre towards each end in turn. The tools stayed sharp over a long period, and it was easy to obtain a good finish direct from the chisel. No abrasives were used at all. . . . A morning's work would completely fill the space between the lathes with moist shavings and the turners would be standing up to their thighs in them. Each man could produce 50 short legs in an hour.[12]

Reed's daybook also tells how many chairs a man could assemble, or, in his words, "fraim," in a day's time. This rate, of course, varied with the type and complexity of the chair. Common chairs, called "common mortise top" or "five rod mortise" chairs, were framed at the rate of about eleven a day. He could frame eight "turned top" chairs in a day but only four large rocking chairs that had both arms and rockers. A precise understanding of the relative rates of assembly is difficult because period chair names cannot always be matched up to known chair forms.

These production numbers are rather substantial, especially given the amount of hand work involved. The following reconstruction of the process of framing a five-rod common chair is based on descriptions of English practice in the late nineteenth and early twentieth centuries, analysis of the tools listed on almost two dozen probate inventories, clues from Reed's daybook, and a study of the chairs themselves (fig. 11).

Certain assumptions have been made about the starting point of the framing process. All the turned parts were on hand, but Reed had yet to cut the tenons on legs, stretchers, and spindles to final size. The seats were finished, but he still had to bore holes for legs and back pieces. The pillars (posts) and the crest rails were already cut to final shape, bent, and set in a form (possibly the "racks and ketches" named on inventories). There is no contemporary evidence that chairmakers had steam apparatus to aid in bending chair parts. Many chairmakers did have stoves in their shops on which they boiled chair parts to prepare them for bending. In fact, in an 1827 contract for making chairs, John Davis of Princeton, Massachusetts, granted Ezra Fay a privilege "to boil and bend stuff in the Boiler in sd. Shop," confirmation of such a procedure.[13]

All of the work necessary to bring the chair to a state of final assembly was hand work, totally unassisted by machinery. Braces and sets of bits in inventories indicate that the holes were routinely drilled by hand (fig. 12). In a five-rod

chair, there were at least twenty-four holes in five sizes. All of these holes were at odd angles to the stock, but Reed, an experienced craftsman, probably eyeballed the angles just as he did the form of the turnings on the lathe. An analysis of leg-to-seat angles on plank seat chairs in the Old Sturbridge Village collections revealed a wide range of tolerance.

Fig. 11. A five-spindle common chair made in central Massachusetts, 1820–1840. Courtesy, Old Sturbridge Village.

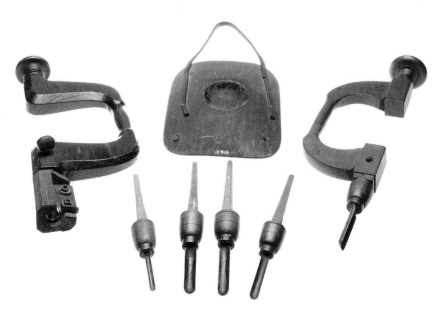

Fig. 12. Wooden braces with four "chair bits" in appropriate sizes for making common chairs. The brace at the left is fitted with a hollow auger. Wooden breast pads, so common in English chairmaking, seem to have been little used by nineteenth-century New England chairmakers, perhaps because they made pine rather than oak seats. Courtesy, Old Sturbridge Village, photograph by Thomas Neill. The term *chair bits* was used by Marshes & Shepherd in their price list for Joseph Smith's *Explanation or Key, to the Various Manufactories of Sheffield, with Engravings of each Article* (Sheffield, Eng., 1816), #504.

These angles varied on average about five and one-half degrees in the same chair with extremes of one and eleven degrees. This is a strong indication that our chairmaker drilled these holes without the aid of a preset jig.

How the round tenons on the ends of the stretchers, pillars, and rods were made is more problematic. Unlike Freegift Wells, a Shaker chairmaker, Reed made no reference to cutting these while the pieces were still on the lathe.[14] A possible allusion to this process is found in an entry for "making 2 tenanting machines" for 75¢ in 1837. At 75¢, these were clearly machines only in the most basic sense of the word. Reed's "tenanting machine" could have been a simple, wooden-stocked rounding tool that fitted into a bit brace. Perhaps it is what was also called a "wrondr" in an 1825 chairmaker's inventory.[15]

The mortises in the pillars were probably predrilled and then squared up with chisels. The corresponding tenons on the crest rails were shaped with backsaw, spokeshave, and chisel. A curious feature found in the crest-rail-to-pillar joint in all common chairs from this region clearly complicated the assembly procedure. A ¼-inch diameter tenon extends from the wide tenon of the crest rail through the pillar and then is wedged from the outside (fig. 13).

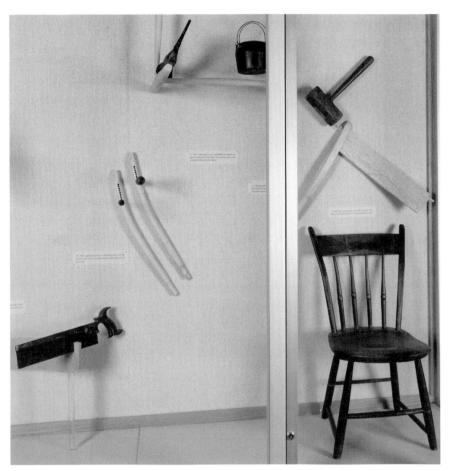

Fig. 13. Final steps in making a common chair, "Cabinet Furniture and Chairs Cheap" exhibit. At the center, mortises for the crest rail have been predrilled in the posts or pillars and are ready to be cleared with small chisels. At the upper right, wedges are being driven to secure the extended round tenon that can be seen at the other end of the crest rail. Courtesy, Old Sturbridge Village, photograph by Thomas Neill.

A nuisance to make, it helped secure the joint without needing to drive pegs or nails through the face of the pillar.

Final assembly of the chairs was done using hot hide glue, usually heated in a double boiler on top of the stove, which also heated the shop in cold weather. Reed and other chairmakers often worked year-round. In fact, in 1833 Reed framed chairs for Benjamin Stuart in every month of the year, producing 1,584 chairs. Substantial numbers of these chairs were made from December to February when he would have had to heat the shop for the gluing process, if not for his own comfort.

Although their woodworking careers were separated by only twenty-five years and they used many of the same hand tools, Samuel Wing and Elbridge Gerry Reed were poles apart in the chairmaking trade. Wing represented the longstanding woodworking tradition of the previous century, while Reed was poised on the threshold of industrialized chairmaking. Other than Reed's use of a water-powered lathe, their tools were comparable, but their production methods differed markedly. Within the next twenty-five years, however, many hand operations would be converted to machinery so that traditional woodworkers either had to adapt or drop out.

1. Thomas Cushman made augers in Kingston, Mass., for several years on Smelt Brook, a site later occupied by Cobb & Drew. D. Hamilton Hurd, comp., *History of Plymouth County, Massachusetts, with Biographical Sketches of Many of the Pioneers and Prominent Men* (Philadelphia, 1884), p. 284.

2. The contract and note are among miscellaneous Wing papers, Sandwich, Mass., Historical Society.

3. Miscellaneous papers relating to Samuel Wing's woodworking activities and his later textile business are in the collections of the research library, Old Sturbridge Village.

4. Account Book of Solomon Sibley, 1793–1840, Ward (Auburn), Mass., *ibid.* The price differential may reflect the greater amount of work involved in making a Windsor-style chair than a post-and-rung chair.

5. This figure, which presumes about two hours' labor for each post, seems a bit low even when time for preparing the billets is added to time on the lathe.

6. Edward Hazen, *Panorama of Professions and Trades, or Every Man's Book* (Philadelphia, 1836), p. 219.

7. Worcester County, Mass., Probate Records, XXXII, 1803–1804, p. 244, Worcester Courthouse.

8. Daybook of Elbridge Gerry Reed, 1829–1862, privately owned, photocopy, research lib., Old Sturbridge Village.

9. [Louis McLane], U. S. Department of the Treasury, *Documents Relative to the Manufactures in the United States* . . . (Washington, D. C., 1833; reprint, New York, 1969); John P. Bigelow, *Branches of Industry in Massachusetts, 1837* (Boston, 1838).

10. Worcester Co. Probate Recs., LXXVIII, 1835–1837, p. 471.

11. Measurements were taken from 22 chairs, which included sets of 6 and 4 chairs and several labeled chairs.

12. David Thomas, "Turning Chair Legs at Llandogg," *Tool and Trades History Society Newsletter,* IX (1985), pp. 19–21.

13. Charles Russell Papers, Box 1826–1821, folder Mar.–July 1827, Mass. Hist. Soc.

14. Charles R. Muller and Timothy Rieman, *The Shaker Chair* (Canal Winchester, Ohio, 1984; reprint, Amherst, Mass., 1992), p. 14.

15. Probate inventory of Henry Roper, 1826, Worcester Co. Probate Recs., LXI, 1825–1826, p. 211.

An Eighteenth-Century Harpsichord Workshop Contributes Two Important Technologies

By John R. Watson

Upon first glance, one might not expect to find significant new wood-working technologies coming out of the relatively small and esoteric eighteenth-century trade of harpsichord making, especially where such common tasks as mortising and shaping are concerned. Yet it was in the mid-eighteenth-century London workshop of Jacob Kirckman that several crucial components came together that greatly encouraged the development of new technologies. This article seeks to identify these technologies and the social, economic, and technological context that might have made this shop an incubator for technological innovation.[1]

As students of the history of technology, we rely on a variety of sources including, especially, old tools. We also consult period prints and written documents such as technical manuals, probate inventories, patent office records, and manufacturers' ledgers and advertisements. When investigating more esoteric trades like harpsichord making, however, we find fewer tradesmen in fewer places. No tools or catalogs of special tools can be traced, and there is not much in the way of other printed documentary sources. And so we turn to the products themselves as our primary documents.

Historical objects contain evidence that reveals in surprising detail not only the designs but also the procedures, tools, and technologies used in their making. If we do not have the tool, we at least have its effect—its footprints. Taken with existing information about other tools and trades, it is possible to reconstruct the special tools and methods of an otherwise undocumented trade or technology.

Figure 1 illustrates the mechanical action of a typical eighteenth-century single-keyboard English harpsichord. When the key is depressed, the jack rises and plucks the string with a quill. When the key is released and the jack falls back down, the pivoted tongue in which the quill is mounted swivels back, allowing the quill to fall without replucking the string. A piece of boar's bristle, bearing against the tongue at the bristle groove, acts as a spring to return the tongue to its original forward position. Precise mortises cut in the register hold the jack in the correct relationship to the string.

The harpsichord maker's craft evolved slowly until the mid-eighteenth century; a long succession of craftsmen contributed only slight improvements

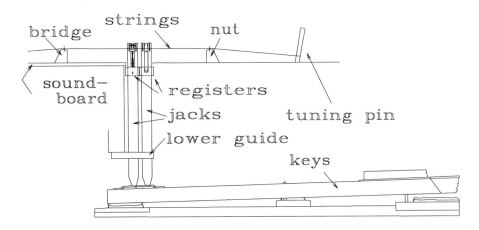

Fig. 1. **The principal mechanical parts of a harpsichord. Drawings and photographs are by the author unless otherwise noted.**

Fig. 2. A double-keyboard harpsichord made in 1758 by Jacob Kirckman of London. The harpsichord is shown with reproduction keys and jacks made by the author. The original keyboards and other mechanical parts are stored to protect them from wear during musical performances. CWF 1983-236.

to the designs, tools, and procedures of the trade. With few exceptions, mid-century harpsichord making differed little from other woodworking crafts in its reliance upon an experienced eye, a sharp cutting tool, and a steady hand to coerce from the material the intended results.

The harpsichord in figure 2 is in the Colonial Williamsburg collection and was made in 1758 in the London workshop of Jacob Kirckman. I have recently made a very close copy of this harpsichord's keyboards and other mechanical components to install in the antique. Our intention was to save the original parts from wear and tear during musical performances. Making the reproduction parts with constant access to the antique enabled me not only to duplicate Kirckman's results with some accuracy, but also to determine the tools and methods that were used in making the original; that is, to reconstruct one part of the craft tradition in which Kirckman was working.

Except for the traditional but increasing use of simple templates and jigs to improve consistency among duplicate parts, most of the workmanship could best be described as "workmanship of risk," so named by David Pye because such hand-wrought work was at constant risk of deviation from the intended

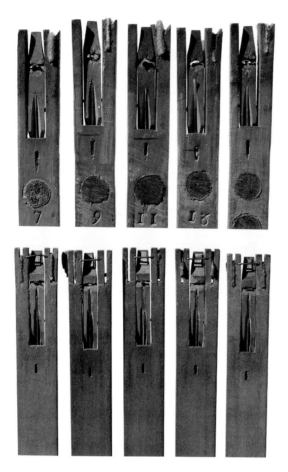

Fig. 3. A detail of jacks
from a spinet harpsichord
made in 1700 in London
by Stephen Keene.
CWF 1953–876.

Fig. 4. Detail of
Kirckman jacks.

design.[2] Figure 3 illustrates workmanship of risk in details of the mechanical action of an earlier harpsichord from 1700. Because woodcutting tools like saws and chisels were handheld, the workman's steadiness, concentration, and skill all affected how closely the final result resembled the intended design. The difference between the intended design and that of any particular piece was a function of workmanship. These resulting deviations and irregularities help make any kind of ancient artifact interesting and informative. Workmanship of risk means that each piece varies from the next, and, you might say, has a little more to tell us about its maker.

Compared to the earlier workmanship illustrated in figure 3, the harpsichord jacks of Jacob Kirckman (fig. 4) show something completely different. The variations from piece to piece are almost completely gone. During the interval between the production of these two sets of jacks, something profound had happened in the craft. The Great Divide of workmanship had been crossed into a world more like that of the machinery-dominated present. David Pye calls this "workmanship of certainty," i.e., workmanship that relies on special tools and methods that make "certain" faithfulness to the intended design. In workmanship of certainty, fidelity to the intended design is no longer controlled by the workman but by the tools. The effect was described in 1747 by Robert Campbell, who said of the workmanship in watches, "[Machines have] re-duced the Expence of Workmanship and Time to a Trifle, in Comparison to what it was before, and brought the Work to such an Exactness that no Hand can imitate it."[3]

Before turning to the evidence of new technologies found in Kirckman's work, we should consider the reasons why, more than perhaps any other harp-sichord workshop in history, his was in the right place at the right time to make significant technological contributions. Mid-eighteenth-century London was on the eve of relatively fast and radical changes in its social, economic, and technological environment. Adam Smith's 1776 economic treatise, *The Wealth of Nations,* described the scenario that was already placing England at the fore-front of what has become popularly known as the Industrial Revolution.

Among the principles extolled by Adam Smith was that of the division of labor. Allowing each workman to specialize in just one step of the manufac-turing process, said Smith, increases productivity greatly by three distinct means. First, a worker who specializes in a single task develops greater dexter-ity in performing it. Second, time is saved which otherwise is lost in passing from one species of work to another. Finally, and it is this last effect that re-sults in workmanship of certainty, such specialization leads to the invention of machines that allow one man to do the work of many.[4]

There are two principal reasons for needing workmanship of certainty. One is speed of production, and the other is precision. Mechanical action compo-nents of harpsichords require a great deal of both. Compared to the produc-tion of tables, chairs, chests, and other more ubiquitous items of furniture, the quantity of harpsichords was small; harpsichords were only to be found in some of the homes of the gentry. However, although the number of harpsichords was small, each harpsichord required 120 to 240 jacks. Even the making of a single harpsichord with its many identical jacks at least encouraged the use of mass-production techniques. Kirckman's was the most prolific harpsichord workshop before the twentieth century and is likely to have produced around eighteen thousand jacks a year in periods of peak harpsichord production.[5] Such quantities required great speed of production if the enterprise was to be profitable, and we know Kirckman to have been an astute and successful businessman.[6]

Besides extraordinary speed of construction, there was the necessity of extraordinary precision as well. While variations and irregularities caused by workmanship of risk may be charming in a set of Chippendale chairs, they are a nuisance in harpsichord jacks. To perform correctly, jacks and the register mortises in which they slide should fit together within a tolerance of a few thousandths of an inch. A too tight fit keeps the jack from falling back down, causing the note not to sound again when needed. If the jack is too loose, the note is sometimes louder and sometimes softer depending on whether the jack and its quill are leaning forward or backward in an oversize mortise. Kirckman jacks brought high-volume woodworking precision to a very early and very high pinnacle.

There are many techniques for limiting risk in executing a design, some of them predating the Industrial Revolution by centuries. But there is evidence of several kinds of risk-reducing machines in the Kirckman workshop that must have been among the first of their kind.

Simple as its task is, a jack with its tongue and register mortise is quite complex in design, requiring at least forty-eight steps in its making. Kirckman's action makers used workmanship of certainty in almost all of these steps, employing many types of jigs and other more or less traditional risk-reducing methods. But there is unprecedented evidence of at least two machines used by Kirckman that were later to become important in the mechanization of woodworking, a process that would generally not begin to occur for another half-century.

Fig. 5. Kirckman jack
tongue showing
bristle groove.

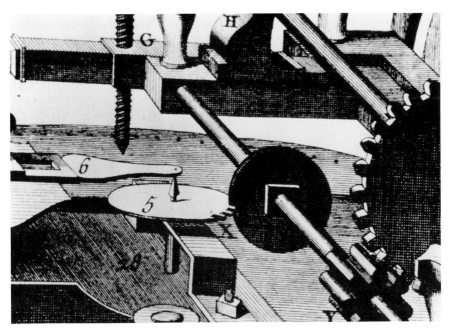

Fig. 6. "Wheel Cutting Engine," in Diderot, *Encyclopédie*, I, pl. XX.

The first evidence of a new woodworking technology is in the grooves that center the bristles against the holly or boxwood tongues (fig. 5). Earlier harpsichord makers had cut this groove with a handheld V-shaped chisel. Kirckman's bristle grooves are near perfect in positioning and consistent in length and depth. The sides of the groove at the deepest point are parallel, and there is never any sign of tear out. Hence, the bristle grooves appear to be cut, not with a chisel, but with a rotary file. Is this the earliest antecedent of the modern power shaper and router?

Rotary cutting devices for brass were already in use in the technologically advanced clock- and watchmaking trades. Figure 6 is a detail of the wheel cutting engine shown in Denis Diderot's *Encyclopédie*.

Kirckman's bristle-groove-shaping machine would have operated on the same principle, although its design probably was much simpler. It required only a stationary, hand-powered rotary file and a carriage for holding the tongue, which could be manually slid past the file in an appropriate motion to cut the groove. The result is a groove that is perfectly shaped and perfectly centered every time.

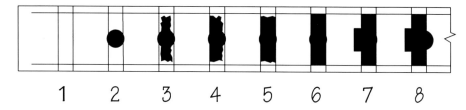

Fig. 7. Diagram showing the steps apparently used by Kirckman to form register mortises. Fixed-width scribe lines are struck in step 1. A hole is drilled in step 2 to insert a float that cuts chip clearance in step 3. The long sides of the mortise are chopped out in steps 4 and 5, and the short sides in step 6. A tongue clearance is chopped in step 7 and a bristle clearance in step 8.

Another evidence of advanced woodworking technology is in the precision of the register mortises (fig. 1). The mortises were chopped out of a solid piece of pearwood. Figure 7 shows the steps in making the register. The width of each mortise increases from top to bottom (fig. 7 pictures the mortises from the top narrower end). There is a square clearance on one side to accommodate the swiveling of the tongue, and a round clearance on the other for the bristle. What is most remarkable about these mortises is their consistency in the angle of the long side from top to bottom. The angle of the sides of these mortises varies so little as to raise the question whether the chisel cuts could have been made freehand. Although a jig guiding a hand-struck chisel could have been used, the greater force needed to drive the chisel through the entire cut in one motion and the exhausting quantity and precision of the cuts beg the use of a lever-driven machine.

The first mortising machines are generally attributed to the designs of Sir Marc Isambard Brunel as fabricated by Henry Maudslay for making blocks for the Royal Navy at the beginning of the nineteenth century.[7] These were true "machines" that operated at four hundred cuts per minute, automatically advanced the block one twenty-fourth of an inch between cuts, and automatically stopped the cutting when the block had traveled the full length of the mortise.[8]

The evidence in Kirckman's registers points to the use of some sort of simple mortising machine a half-century earlier. In its most rudimentary form (fig. 8), the mortiser could have amounted to little more than a standard chisel with its thrust provided through a lever. The work is supported at an angle appropriate for the angle of the cut. Nesting the chisel into the layout scribe line determines the precise position of the cut.

The concept of a lever-driven cutting edge was already employed in the woodworker's bench knife. However, this evidence from Kirckman's workshop suggests what may be the first use of a lever to drive a mortising chisel.

Though not substantially faster than hand methods, use of the machine took less physical effort and enabled a high level of consistency, i.e., workmanship of certainty. This would have effectively transferred much of the labor and skill from the worker to the machine.

Even in Kirckman's workshop, the potential for using such a machine for several other tasks apparently went unnoticed, probably because the particular mix of qualities needed in register mortising was not needed elsewhere, leaving little incentive to break old habits.

It is beyond the scope of this article to describe the many other steps Kirckman's workers took in producing the jacks and registers of harpsichords. The extraordinary precision achievable with these techniques resulted in another anachronistic effect, that of interchangeable parts. The effect is limited to the fit of the jacks in the registers, but it is a significant accomplishment because of the critical fit between these parts. Observations supporting this interchangeability must come from the reproduction jacks and registers rather than their antique prototypes because of the wear likely in a much-used mechanism, but the evidence is strong.

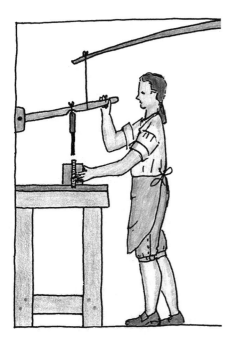

Kirckman's workshop methods are deducible from the

Fig. 8. A conjectural design for the "mortising machine" as used in the Kirckman workshop for register mortises. Drawing by John Watson and Linda Baumgarten.

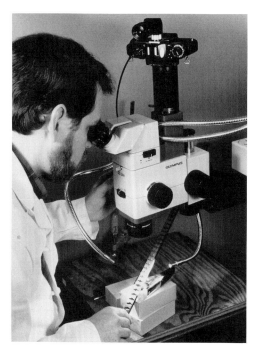

Fig. 9. An Olympus stereo-microscope was used to examine and photograph old tool marks.

surfaces left by the original cutting tools. Several modern technologies have been used in this study to help bring into focus those surfaces and the stories they have to tell. Among the most helpful has been a 10X-40X stereo microscope (fig. 9). The following photographs taken through the microscope illustrate some of the evidence on which conclusions were based.

Figure 10 shows the inside of one of the register mortises. The surfaces show that the cut was made in a continuous motion—multiple mallet strikes would have been recorded in the form of subtle surface ripples. Striations caused by minuscule nicks in the cutting edge run along the path of the chisel. The striations on the rounded portion of the mortise indicate that it was not formed with a rotary drill, as one might expect, but by a gouge (fig. 7, step 8).

Figure 11 shows the inside corner of one of the register mortises. Note where the end-grain is torn out forming a dark crevice. This shows that the narrow end of the mortise was not cleaned up with a file or float, as one might have expected, but was chopped out

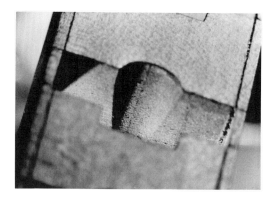

Fig. 10. The inside of a register mortise in the Kirckman harpsichord showing striations caused by the minute nicks in the gouge blade.

with a narrow chisel cutting in line with the grain; the wood fibers are thus pulled apart lengthwise, sometimes producing a very small, jagged crevice. When, for the sake of experiment, a file is used to trim the short side of the mortise, the resulting corner is slightly rounded and without such a crevice.

Of course, the tearing of the wood fibers in the corner of the mortise could also break *inside* the borders of the mortise, requiring further cleanup. Figure 12 shows evidence that this was done with a knife. That this was "workmanship of risk" is evident in the particular cut illustrated, since the first cut apparently missed the corner, requiring a second stroke to finish the job.

Among the most informative primary documents available to the historian of technology are the actual objects produced by those technologies. Early tools and contemporary descriptions of their use are often not to be found, but the evidence contained in tool marks, consistency levels, and the minute distortion

of the material from the original manufacturing processes are among the clues to the tools and methods of a historical technology. Indeed, there seems to be no limit to what can be learned from reading the sometimes

Fig. 11. A mortise corner in the Kirckman harpsichord showing end-grain tear out.

Fig. 12. The corner of this mortise in the Kirckman harpsichord was cleaned up with a handheld knife. Here, the workman slightly missed the corner and finished with a second stroke.

fine print of these non-verbal "documents," the text of which comes into focus only with just the right raking light, or under a microscope, or through an X-ray image. These methods of observation, and comparisons with the technologies employed by other period trades, reveal that the "transfer of skill" from woodworking laborer to machine got an early boost in the Kirckman harpsichord workshop, where workers were producing harpsichord actions with interchangeable parts by the mid-eighteenth century using a broad range of risk-reducing methods including mortising machines and rotary files.

1. Preliminary versions of this material have been included in papers for the American Musical Instrument Society, Bethlehem, Pa., Mar. 9, 1991, the symposium "The Harpsichord after a Century of Revival," Clayton State College, Morrow, Ga., Nov. 4, 1991, and the American Institute for Conservation, Buffalo, N. Y., June 7, 1992. I am indebted to Carey Howlett for showing this source to me.

2. Pye, *Nature and Art of Workmanship*, pp. 4–5.

3. Campbell, *London Tradesman*, p. 251.

4. These observations about the effects of the division of labor had previously been published in Denis Diderot and Jean d'Alembert, eds., *Encyclopédie, ou Dictionnaire Raisonné des Sciences, des Arts et des Métiers, par un Société de Gens de Lettres* (Paris, 1751–1765), I, p. 717, s.v. "art," as pointed out in Adam Smith, *The Wealth of Nations*, ed. Edwin Cannan (Chicago, 1976).

5. According to Charles Mould, Kirckman produced about 50 single harpsichords and 50 double harpsichords annually in the most productive periods. Allowing an average of 2.5 registers per single and 3.5 registers for doubles, that makes 18,000 jacks per year. Charles Mould, "The Development of the English Harpsichord with particular reference to the work of Kirckman" (Ph.D. thesis, Jesus College, 1976).

6. An amusing example of Kirckman's business savvy occurred when a guitar fad threatened to erode the harpsichord maker's business. His solution was to supply a quantity of cheap guitars to the ballad singers in the streets of London, whereupon the fashion-conscious ladies of the harpsichord-playing gentry class quickly returned to the harpsichord. The story is from Charles Burney's article, "Guitar," in *The Cyclopaedia, or Universal Dictionary of Arts, Sciences, and Literature*, ed. Abraham Rees (London, 1819–1820).

7. Blocks are the pulleys that are essential components of the sail-handling tackle; a single ship requires a large number of blocks. The mortising machines were part of a larger revolution of woodworking mechanization launched by Brunel and Maudslay.

8. K. R. Gilbert, *The Portsmouth Block-making Machinery*, Science Museum Monograph, HMSO (London, 1965). I am indebted to Deborah Bigelow for providing me copies of her unpublished research into the early history of mortising machines.

"The Debate of the Carpenter's Tools"

By Roy Underhill

This presentation is reprinted from *The Woodwright's Workbook: Further Explorations in Traditional Woodcraft,* by Roy Underhill. Copyright © 1986 by the University of North Carolina Press.

Annotator's Preface

AN ENGLISH ALE HOUSE, 1500

SLIDE onto a bench here at the Sawyer's Arms. Your brother carpenters have been drinking since before sunset, while you've been out hacking scarf joints in the dark. The veterans from the wars in France have already run out of stories. Give the barmaid a kiss—but check the measure of the cup that she brings. Remember at the pageant last spring? In the play *The Harrowing of Hell*, when all the souls in torment were liberated except one, wasn't it the thieving alewife that Christ left behind?

Ay, now that's better. Another pint of this and you won't care. So what if the taste comes from the stinking Dutch habit of adding hops to the ale, calling it "biere" and pretending to like it, or from the droppings of the pigeons that roost above her brewing vat. Still, another pint of this, and that fool's poem might seem funny tonight. He is so proud of his rhyme that I hear he has even had it written down. Now if only he knew how to read it! Ever since he heard the *Mystery Play of the Nativity* put on by the Wrights of Chester he thinks he can handle verse as well as he can his axe. Yea, but it's true what Joseph of Nazareth said in the play, there's no getting a better life through a carpenter's work.

> With this axe that I beare,
> this perscer and this nawgere
> and hammer, all in fere,
> I have won my meate.
> Castle, tower, nor riche manner
> had I never in my power;
> but as a symple carpenter
> with those what I might gett.

Ah, here he goes. You always hear that a bad workman blames his tools—but bad tools blaming the workman? Well, sit through it one more time. You're bound to think of something to tell your wife when you get home drunk and broke tonight. Besides, five hundred years from now—who's to know?

Note: The verse that follows is adapted from an anonymous fifteenth-century manuscript (copy in the Bodleian Library, Ashmole 61).

The "trusty hatchet" is the first to deny the carpenter and his trade. The chip axe is the functional equivalent of our broad hatchet, a "one handed plane-axe, wherewith Carpenters hew their timber smooth" (1611). The word *hatchet* was also common at this time. In the fifteenth-century mystery play *Noah and the Ark*, Cam says, "I have a hatchett wonder keene to bytte well, as may be seene; a better grownde one, as I weene, is not in all this towne." (The "sharper than thou" complex is an ancient one.) Craftsmen hewing to the lines of tradition still prefer the bare blade and "despise the saw and plane as contemptible innovations, fit only for those unskillful in the handling of the nobler instruments."

The argument is joined by the belte, the tree-felling axe. Where the chip axe says that he can do no more than keep the wright from starving, the belte believes that hard work will be rewarded in the end. Specialized forms of the axe serve for everything from tree felling to shaping elaborate scarf joints. Five of the participants in the *Debate* are variants of the axe.

The twybylle, the T-shaped narrow-bladed axe "wherwith carpenters doo make their mor-tayses" (1584), sides with the chip axe. This contrary fellow's two blades are set at right angles to one another. This would be the picklike, swung version of the two-faced tool, rather than the pushed and levered twivil. In an old German legend, the devil accidentally strikes himself with both ends of this tool on the backswing, making the sign of the cross on his forehead.

The wymbylle is a gimlet, the one-handed borer of little holes and the beginning of bigger things. An insightful theologian wrote in 1643 that "to use force first before people are tought the truth, is to knock a nail into a board, without wimbling a hole for it." The rhyme with thimble is deceptive, as gimlet is seldom so big a bore: "As the wimble bores a hole for the auger." The sound of the word and the plain imagery of the action of this tool made it popular in seventeenth-century writing. We find: "And well he could dissemble, when wenches he would wimble."

A fourteenth-century encyclopedia described how a nephew of the legendary Daedalus "made the first compas, and wrought therwith." Unfortunately, uncle "took greet envie to the childe, and threw hym doun of an highe toure, and brak his nekke." Later, in 1667, Milton wrote of God taking "the golden Compasses, . . . to circumscribe This Universe." Mortal carpenters wield small iron compasses. Large wooden ones usually belong to coopers, for tracing barrel heads. Although builders use compasses, as Joseph Moxon wrote in 1678, to "describe Circles, and set off Distances from their Rule," the compass is also fundamental to the process of "scribing." The compass is drawn along an irregular gap, transferring the contours of one surface to another. When cut to the scribed line, the two pieces fit perfectly together.

The chip ax said unto the wright:
"Meat and drink I shall thee plyght,
But clothes and shoes of leather tan,
Find them where as ere thou can;
For though thou work all that thou can,
Thou'll never be a wealthy man,
Nor none that longs this craft unto,
For no thing that they can do."

"Nay, nay," said the twybylle,
"Unreason is thy only skylle.
Truly, truly it will not be,
Wealth I think we'll never see."

"Wherefore," said the axe/belte,
"Great strokes for him I shall pelte;
My master shall do full well then,
Both to clothe and feed his men."

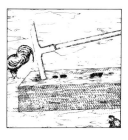

"Yea, yea," said the wymbylle,
"I am as round as a thimble;
My master's work I will remember,
I shall creep fast into the timber,
To help my master within a stounde
To store his coffer with twenty pounds."

"Nay, nay," said the compass,
"Thou art a fool in that case.
For thou speaks without advisement;
Therefore thou getyst not thy intent.
Know thou well—it shall be so,
What lightly comes, shall lightly go;
Tho' thou earn more than any five,
Yet shall thy master never thrive."

The groping iron is the first "mystery tool" of the *Debate*. One Latin lexicon defined it as the "runcina"—"that tool of the woodworker, graceful and recurved, by which boards are hollowed so that one may be connected with another." A seventeenth-century text states that "grooping is the making of the Rigget [furrow] at the two ends of the Barrel to hold the head in." So a groping iron cut a groove and is a likely ancestor of the cooper's "croze." Medieval rooms were often finished with vertical oak wainscot (split boards) joined by V-shaped tongues and grooves. The tool that cut the groove is no longer known to us, but a "grooving iron" similar to those used until recently in Germany for joining shingles together is the likely descendant of this tool.

Our medieval encyclopedia also credited the invention of the saw to Daedalus's nephew (before he was tossed from the tower for inventing the compass). "This Perdix was sutil and connynge of craft, and bethought hym for to have som spedful manere clevynge of timber, took a plate of iren, and fyled it, and made it toothed as a rugge bone of a fische, and thanne it was a sawe." Saws are difficult for smiths to make. By the seventeenth century, however, Moxon's *Mechanic Exercises* illustrated six varieties of saw, in contrast to the *Debate*'s single reference.

The Daedalus boys don't get credit for the whetstone; the fourteenth-century encyclopedia mentions only that there are "diverse maner of whetstones, and some neden water and some neden oyl for-to whette." The odd early custom of hanging a whetstone around the neck of a liar gets no play in the *Debate*. The 1418 records of the City of London state that "a false lyrer, . . . shall stonde upon the pillorye . . . with a Whetstone aboute his necke." Thomas Tusser advised husbandmen in 1550 to "get grindstone and whetstone for toole that is dull," advice heeded by Powhatan, who asked Captain John Smith for a grindstone in 1607.

Although I have counted the adze as one of the five axe variants in the *Debate*, the difference is more than just the angle of the blade. The adze is rarely used in the full-tilt chopping manner of the axe—except in the rural instance of hollowing mentioned by Tusser: "An axe and an ads, to make troffe for thy hogs." The common carpenter's use is best put by Moxon: "Its general use is to take thin chips off Timber or Boards, and to take off those Irregularities that the Ax by reason of its Form cannot well come at; and that a Plane (though rank set) will not make riddance enough with." In skillful hands the adze is an exceedingly precise tool, the craftsmen holding one end of the work "with the ends of their Toes, and so hew it lightly away."

The file, although not a proper woodworking tool, is the indispensable partner to the saw. Roman files from the first century A.D. were notched near their tang ends for use as wrests for setting saw teeth. Since files must cut other metal, they are the epitome of hardness, as in the 1484 Caxton *Fables of Aesop*—"She [the serpent] fond a fyle whiche she baganne to gnawe with her teethe." Seeing her own blood and thinking it came from the file she bit harder and harder. Moxon mentions that "coarse files" and "most Rasps have formerly been made of Iron and Case-Hardened," rather than from steel. File making is a profession unto itself. Until industrial versions of the automatic file-cutting machine described by Leonardo da Vinci in the sixteenth century were developed, each of the tiny teeth had to be cut with hammer and chisel.

The groping-iren then spake he:
"Compass, who hath grieved thee?
My master yet may thrive full well,
How he shall, I will thee tell;
I am his servant true and good,
I assure thee, compass, by the Rood,
Work I shall both night and day;
To get him goods I shall assay."

"Nay, nay," said the saw,
"It is but boast that thou dost blow,
For though thou work both day and night,
He will not thrive, I say thee right;
He lives too near the ale-wife,
And for this shall he never thrive."

Then said the whetstone:
"Tho oft my master's thryft be gone,
I shall him help within this year
To get him twenty marks clear;
His axes shall I make full sharp,
That they may lightly do their work;
To make my master a rich man
I shall assay, if that I can."

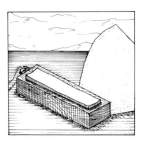

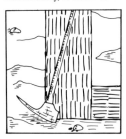

To him then said the adz,
And said: "Yea, sir, God glads!
To speak of thrift it will not be,
Wealth will our master never see,
For he will drink more in a day
Than thou can lightly earn in twey;
Therefore thy tongue I bid thee hold,
And speak no more words so bold."

To the adz then said the file:
"Thou should not thy master so revile,
For though oft he be unhappy,
Yet to his thrift thou shouldst see:
For I think, ere tomorrow's noon,
To earn my master a pair of shoes;
For I shall rub with all my might,
My masters tools to make bright,
So that, within a little space,
My master's purse I shall increase."

The carpenter's chisel is essential for cutting the mortice and tenon joints which are the basis of timber frame construction. Captain John Smith at Jamestowne in 1607 showed his priorities, writing, "As yet we have no houses to cover us, our Tents were rotten, and our cabbins worse than nought: our best commoditie was Iron which we made into little Chisels." These would be poor chisels indeed if they were all iron. Like all the edge tools of the carpenter, they require a steel bit welded to the iron body before they are hard enough to hold an edge. The chisel struck by the mallet gives both power and control, as for sculpture in stone or wood. Yet, as Shakespeare wrote, "What fine Chizzell Could ever yet cut breath?"

The line is spun linen; and the chalk, no more than a chunk of the White Cliffs of Dover. The ancient snap line appears in Odysseus: "Trees then he felled . . . and carefully He smoothed their sides and wrought them by a line." But not even Homer can talk snap lines like Joseph Moxon. "Then with Chalk they whiten a Line, by rubbing the Chalk pretty hard upon it"; then "one of them between his Finger and Thumb draws the middle of the Line directly upright, to a convenient height (that it may spring hard enough down) and then lets it go again, so that it swiftly applies to its first Position, and strikes so strongly against the Stuff, that the Dust, or Atoms of the Chalk that were rubbed into the Line, shake out of it, and remain upon the Stuff. . . . This is called *Lining of the Stuff.*"

The pricking-knife leads two lives. It follows the chalkline in the *Debate*, but is a marking tool only in one of its forms. As a scratch awl, the needle point makes indelible guidelines and dots on the wood. As a brad-awl, the end, which resembles a sharpened screwdriver blade, is used to make holes for screws and nails. Forcing it into the wood with the blade oriented across the grain, the craftsman then repeatedly twists it to push the wood aside. According to Moxon, the "Pricker Is vulgarly called an Awl: Yet for Joiners Use it hath most commonly a square blade, which enters the Wood better than a round blade will; because the square Angle in turning it about breaks the Grain, and so the Wood is in less danger of splitting."

The piercer is today's brace and bit, one of the four boring tools of the *Debate*. Two of them appear in the fifteenth-century Chester mystery play: "With this axe that I beare, This percer, and this nawger. . . ." Theory has it that the piercer/brace was introduced into Europe by returning Crusaders, for it appears suddenly in the early fifteenth century with no discernible European ancestors. The significance of this tool is that it uses full rotary motion, rather than the intermittent or reciprocating motion of the other tools. The next logical woodworking step for this crank action is credited to Leonardo da Vinci, who applied it to spinning the flywheel of a lathe. From this it was a simple progression to the increasingly complex and powerful mechanisms of industry. I am glad that Moxon illustrated this tool because in his text one finds the historian's booby prize: "Its Office is so well known, that I need say little to it." He does caution that "you must take care to keep the Bitt straight to the hole you pierce, lest you deform the hole, or break the Bitt" and that "you ought to be provided with Bitts of several sizes, fitted into so many Padds." The "padds" are the tapering square wooden shanks fitted to the ends of each bit. The padd, in turn, fits into a corresponding socket on the brace.

Than said the chisel:
"If he ever thrive, he bears him well;
For though thou rub till thy head ache,
His wealth from him it will be take:
For he loves good ale so well,
That he therfore his head will sell:
For he some days seven pence will drink;
How he shall thrive I cannot think."

Than bespake the prykyng-knife:
"He lives too nigh the ale-wyfe;
She makes oft-times his purse full thin,
No penny sometimes she leaves therein.
Tho' thou get more than other three,
Wealthy man he can not be."

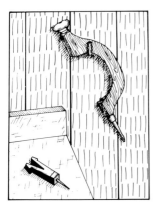

"Yea, yea," said the line and the chalk,
"My master is like too many folk;
Though he love ale far too well
To thrive, and this I shall him tell;
I shall mark well upon the wood,
And keep his measures true and good,
And so by my measures all,
To prosper well my master shall."

"Yea, yea," said the piercer,
"That which I say it shall be sure;
Why chide ye each one with another?
Know ye not well I am your brother;
Therefore none contrary me,
For as I say, so shall it be.
My master yet shall be full rich;
As far as I may reach and stretch,
I will him help with all my might,
Both by day and by night,
Fast to run into the wood,
And bite I shall with mouth full good,
And this I swear, by my crown,
To make him sheriff of the town."

What tool has a more wondrous name than the skantyllion? "And do we well and make a tower, With square and scantilion so even, that may reache heigher than heaven" (1300). It is no accident that the scantillion is paired with the square in this quotation, because they are used together in truing rectangular stock. The scantillion is the equivalent of the modern gauge, used to scribe a line parallel to an opposing surface. Stock so prepared is termed "scantling." Thus, we have from 1556 *The Spider and Flie*: "Whiche sqwyre shall sqware me, a scantlin well bent, For a right rewle, to show me innocent."

The crow is an odd bird for a simple lever. Crows have been recovered at Pompeii, some with claws and some without. Over the centuries this tool appears to have been used more for moving than nail pulling. In the mid-sixteenth century, folks called for "longe crowes of iren to lyfte great burdens." Later that same century, a player in Shakespeare's *Comedy of Errors* said, "Well I'll breake in: go borrow me a crow." (Which is also one of the earlier references to the great tradition of borrowing tools, and probably explains why the hammer is not present at the *Debate*.) A century later, Moxon illustrated a crow with a claw, but says only that they are to be thrust under the "the ends of great, heavy Timber" to lift them to put a roller underneath. No mention whatever of pulling nails.

Perhaps this is the same rule that was missing a century later at the Globe Theatre performance of *Julius Caesar*.

> *Flavius.* Speak, what trade art thou?
> *Car.* Why, sir, a carpenter.
> *Marullus.* Where is thy Leather Apron, and thy Rule?

Had this scene actually happened in ancient Rome, the tool in question might well have been a foot-long bronze folding rule divided into twelve "unciae," from which we derive our "inch." But Shakespeare wrote with his own time in mind. Thus, the rule might have been a larger and more conspicuous, ungraduated straightedge—or even the proverbial "ten-foot pole" described by Moxon for laying out house frames and ground plots. This rule makes here an early reference to "dying like a dog."

Shakespeare's Roman carpenter of two thousand years ago may also have carried a plane that could easily be mistaken for those used less than two hundred years ago. Planes recovered in Pompeii are beautifully made of wood, soled with iron. Curiously, although planes appear in many illustrations from the Middle Ages (usually of the Holy family or of Noah building his ark of "timber, i-planed wel smethe"), no planes are known to have survived from this time. The plane from the *Debate* offers to "cleanse on every side." Such carefully prepared stock reaches into the realm of the joiner, as distinguished from that of the carpenter. The distinction of the joiner's trade did exist at the time—one of the laws of Henry VIII applied to persons using "any of the misteries . . . of smithes, joigners, or coupars."

"Soft, sir," said the skantyllion,
"I think your luck be nearly done;
Ever so cruel thou art in word,
And yet thou art not worth a turd!
For all the good that thou get might,
He will spend it in one night."

Then the crow began to speak,
As if his heart was like to break,
To hear his brother so reviled,
And said: "Thou speaks like a child;
Tho' my master spend ever so fast,
Enough he shall have at the last,
Fortune he'll have as much as they,
That drank not a penny till their dying day."

"Yea, yea," said the Rule
"In faith, thou art a fool,
For, if he dies and has right nought,
Who trusts that thou will give him ought?
Thus shall he lie upon the ground,
And be buried like a hound:
For, if a man have ought before,
When he has need, it is good store."

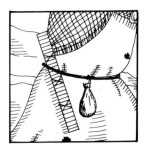

"What, sir rule," said the plane,
"Another reason I will thee say;
Tho oft my master have no stock,
Yet thy master thou should not mock;
For yet a means I shall see,
So that my master shall prosperous be.
I shall him help, both day and night,
To get him good with all my might,
I shall cleanse on every side
To help my master in his pride."

If it were not already apparent that the *Debate* is the work of a carpenter rather than a poet, this verse should make it plain. The fraternity of the broad axe and the plane is obvious only to one who is familiar with the process of hewing timbers. Most of the roundness of the log is generally chopped from the log with the same sort of axe used for tree felling; the broad axe only carefully slices off the last of the roughness. But the broad axe does indeed look like a powerful weapon. For countless years, as in a fourteenth-century poem, men have gone "to batail . . . With brade ax, and with bowes bent."

The twyvette and the twibill are often considered to be one and the same tool. Their appearance together in the *Debate* shows their individuality. The word *twivil* survives as the name of a two-headed morticing knife that is pushed and rocked, rather than swung like an axe. Both ends of a mortice are bored through with an auger and the wood between ripped out with the twivil. The larger version is a proper carpenter's tool and measures over four feet long; it uses leverage rather than velocity to attain its power. The broad chisel end of this tool is sharpened on the sides as well as on the end, so that it can cut as it levers against the top end of the mortice. In France, they are called *besaiguë* and are used with "*beaucoup d'art.*" These tools are much more common on the continent of Europe than in England. However, the Hundred Years War with France (Joan of Arc, etc.) had just ended, and it is no surprise to find French influences in the fifteenth-century English tool kit.

The block and tackle were well known to the ancient Greeks and Romans. They also knew the technique of combining them to multiply their power, and understood that "as in the lever, time is lost as power is gained." Pulleys from the Tudor warship the *Mary Rose*, which capsized off Portsmouth, were splendidly preserved in the mud. Like most tools of the carpenter, pulleys are made by a specialist. A 1568 church account notes payment "to William, torner, for turnynge of the powleys." Pulleys are essential to the carpenter raising a heavy oak timber frame. A scene from 1577 would be familiar to anyone of an agricultural persuasion: "They have a Pully . . . wherwith they hoyse up the Corne to the very Rafters of the house."

A windlass is but a lever acting on a rope, which, in combination with the block and tackle, is capable of exerting tremendous force. Chaucer tells in the "Squire's Tale" of a brass horse fastened to the ground so hard that "ther may no man out of the place it dryue For noon engyn of wyndas ne polyue." The familiar windlass is used for high lifting building materials as a structure rises—and for wells and mines where "with a wyndeles turned by fowre men they drawe vpp the coales" (1603). Horizontal pulling, however, is more commonly handled by a capstan, or "crab," with the rope winding on a vertical shaft. In 1586, forty capstans, each turned by twelve men and two horses, were employed to raise a 327-ton obelisk at the Vatican.

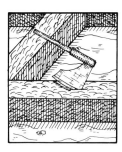

The broad ax said withouten miss,
He said: "The plane my brother is;
We two shall cleanse and make full plain,
That no man shall us gainsay,
And get our master in a year
More silver than a man may bear."

"Nay, nay," said the twyvette,
"Wealth I swear be from you fetched,
To keep my master in his pride;
In this country ye can not abyde,
Unless ye steal and be a thief,
And put many men to grief:
For he will drink more in an hour
Than two men may earn in four.
When ye have wrought all that ye can,
Still shall he never be a wealthy man."

Then be-spake the pullyff,
With great strong words and stiff:
"Hold, sir twyvette, me think you grieved;
What devil hath you so deceived?
Tho oft he spend more in a year
Of gold and silver than thou may bear,
I shall him help with all my might;
I hope to make him yet a knight."

"What, sir," said the windlass, "rule,
Me thinks thou art but a fool;
For thou speaks out of season,
It will not be, by simple reason;
A carpenter to be a knight?
That was ever against right;
Therefore shall I tell thee a saw,
'Who would be high - shall be brought low.' "

Another mystery tool. What could a rule-stone be? We already have a rule. Could that be an unmarked straightedge, and this the one that bears the measurements? But why separate rules, and why a stone? There are three clues that point to the most likely identity of this "true man." The first clue is the material—stone. Second, is the line "as I am a true man" and, third, is the absence of an essential carpenter's tool from the *Debate*. Always, "the carpenter hath his squyre, his rule and his plummet" (1553). The plummet is the plumb bob, essential to bring a structure to vertical. A plumb bob is a "true man" and, although usually made of lead, could well be stone. In any case, the rule-stone makes here the first recorded use of the expression "to rule the roost."

"The gouge" says Moxon "is a Chissel having a round edge, for the cutting such Wood as is to be Rounded, or Hollowed." One of the hollows that a carpenter needs is the shallow round pocket required to start a shell auger into the wood. Otherwise, the screwless, pikeless auger wanders about on the surface and never takes hold. More important, though, is the relationship of the gouge to the quality of fifteenth-century carpentry work. Many of the exposed timbers were being elaborately moulded and carved. The "scribing" gouge, with its bevel on the concave surface, allows such beams to be precisely fitted where they intersect. This produced expensive looking work—which often concealed inferior joints that soon failed. Carpenters were forced by the pressure of the market to cheat where it would not show.

Ropes and cables are vital to mariners, "from the anker he cutteth the gabyll rope" (1523), and builders, "at the west ende of Powlles stepull was tawed a cabell roppe" (1556). Both entrust their lives to the skill of the roper. Until recently, every community had a rope walk, just as it had a mill and a church. His waist encircled with raw hemp or flax, the roper walked slowly backwards, feeding more fiber into the lengthening yarn, which was twisted by a hook spun by his co-worker. Two of these yarns twisted together make the strands which are in turn twisted together to make a rope. When three of these ropes are twisted together, one has made a proper cable-rope. It hardly matters, but it was originally a cable, rather than a camel, that had such little chance of passing through the eye of a needle. Carpenters, however, are seldom denied passage through the Gates of Heaven on the basis of excessive wealth.

Ah, the wife. Fifteenth-century girls married who their families told them to. The idea was to unite for advantage and not for emotional attachment. Henry VIII had yet to get the divorce business under way, but husbands died earlier than wives, and after her first marriage a woman could do as she pleased. With a few years of "good marrying and fortunate dying," a woman could rise to the top of society, or even marry for love. The wife of this drunken carpenter might await just such an opportunity.

This constant guide to the angle of rightness is so characteristic of the wright's craft that from ancient times, as in the fifteenth century, "the carpenters ben signefyed by the dolabre or squyer."

"Yea," then said the rule-stone,
"My master hath many foes;
If ye would help him at his need,
Then my master should succeed;
But what so ever ye bragg or boast,
My master yet shall rule the roost:
For, as I am a true man,
I shall him help all that I can."

The gouge said: "The devil's dirt
For anything that thou can work!
For all that ever thou can do,
It is not worth an old shoe.
Thou hast been apprentice these seven year
And still thy craft have yet to learn;
If thou could work as well as he,
Our master's wealth shall never be."

"Soft, sir," said the cable-rope,
"Methinks good ale is in your tope;
For thou speaks as thou would fight,
And would, if thou had any might.
But I shall tell thee another tale,
How my master I shall avail;
Haul and pull I shall full fast
To raise houses, while I may last,
And so, within a little throw,
My master's wealth shall surely grow."

Then spake the wright's wife:
"Neither of you shall ever thrive,
Neither the master, nor the men,
For nothing that ye do can:
For he will spend within a month
More wealth than any three men hath."

The square said: "What sey ye, dame?
Ye should not speak my master shame."

Spinning yarn from wool or flax was but the most common of the trades practiced by women. Brewing was traditionally dominated by women, as was the English industry of producing cloth from imported raw silk. A merchant's wife could farm out work in the community and end up running a large business on her own. Women were active as corn wholesalers, worked in manual trades, and stood ready to continue their husbands' businesses. One popular medieval legend concerns a blacksmith who was ordered to make the nails for the crucifixion. When he pretended that his hands were injured and that he could not work, his wife quickly stepped in to do the job.

Tudor masons, too, used the square as their symbol. "I beseech you, that the stone is to be fitted to the square, not the square to the stone" (1618). A mason's square is more likely to be iron than is a carpenter's. The wright's square has a thick body, or beam, to catch on the side of the work, and a thin tongue, or blade, to stretch across it.

This debate between the defeatist faultfinders and the optimists is fueled by the valid points of both sides. Even though their power was waning, the local "guilds merchant" could still set standards for wages and quality control. Artificially low prices for fancy work forced builders to concentrate on the "skin" while skimping on the "bones" of their work. Thus a man must "steal and be thiefs." A craftsman could rise to wealth and power, not by the skill of his hands, but by connections and by increasingly controlling the labor of others. Enough to drive a man to drink.

Draught-nayle? Moxon called this tool the hook-pin. It is the carpenter's equivalent of the machinist's tapered drift-pin used to force two holes into alignment. "Its Office is to pin the Frame . . . together, whilst it is framing, or whilst it is fitting into its Position. . . . These drive into the Pin-holes through the Mortesses and Tennants," and, being tapered, pull the joint together. The carpenter will then "strike under the Hook, and so knock it out. Then if the Frame lie in its place, they pin it up with wooden Pins." In the *Debate*, as in the construction of a timber frame, it is the draught-nayle that brings the opposing sides together into a new alignment, placing the blame squarely on the carpenter's defenders.

The wage of seven pence a day is high. The fifteenth-century journeyman carpenter could expect six pence a day for summer work. This day began at 5 o'clock in the morning and lasted until around seven in the evening. The day was punctuated with a half hour for breakfast and an hour and a half for midday dinner and a nap. Winter work went from "can't see" to "can't see" (dawn to dusk), and the pay was correspondingly less. There were quite a few saint's days and festivals and market days, and work did end at about five o'clock on Saturdays. So in spite of the long hours, the carpenter's life left him ample time to drink his pay.

"Square, I have no other cause,
I swear thee, by Saint Eustase:
For all the yarn that I may spin,
To spend at ale he thinks no sin.
He will spend more in an hour,
Than thou and I can get in four."

"Yet me thinks ye be to blame
To give my master such a name:
For tho' he spend more than ye have,
Yet his worship ye should save."

"Mary, I shrew him and thee too,
And all them that do as ye do:
For his servant I trust thou be,
Therefore gain thou'll never see;
For if thou learn that craft from him,
Thy wealth I swear shall be full thin."

The draught-nail then spake he,
And said: "Dame, that is no lie,
Ye know the manner of these freaks,
That thus of my master speaks;
But listen to me a little space,
I shall now tell thee all the case,
How they work for their good,
I will not lie, by the Rood!
When they have worked an hour or two,
At once to the ale they will go,
And drink and toast there constantly:
'Thou to me,' and 'I to thee.'
And one says, 'The ax shall pay for this,
Therefore the cup once I shall kiss';
And when they come to work again,
The belte to his master will this say:
'Master, work us not out of reason,
The day is very long of season;
Small strokes let us slowly hack,
And sometimes let us ease our backs';
The wymbulle speaks softly, 'Ah, sire,
Seven pence of a day is small hire
For wrights, that work so fast,
And in our work have great haste.'
The groping iren then says full soon:
'Master, want ye this work well done?
Let us not work until we sweat,
For catching of over great heat.
For we may happen after cold to take,
Then one stroke may we not hack.'
Then be-spake the whetstone,
And said: 'Master, we want to go home:
For fast it draws unto the night;
Our supper by now I know is dyght.'
The line and stone, the piercer and file,
Say 'That is a good council!'
The crow, the plane, and the square,
Say, 'We have earned well our hire!'
And thus with frauds and falsehood
Comes many a true man to no good.
Therefore, by all that I can see,
They shall never thrive nor wealthy be;
Therefore this craft I will go fro,
And to another will I go."

Then answered the wife in hye:
"If I might, so would I,
But I am to him bound so fast,
That off my halter I may not cast;
Therefore the priest that bound me apprentice
He shall truly have my curse,
And ever he shall have, til I die,
In whatever country that he abide."

Therefore, wrights, take heed of this,
That ye may mend what is amiss,
If truly that ye do your labor
For that will be unto your honor;
And greeve you nothing at this song,
But ever make merry your selves among.
And not at him that it did make,
No envy of him should ye take,
Nor none of you should do him blame,
Because the craft hath done him shame.

Contributors

HAROLD B. GILL, JR., was a historian at the Colonial Williamsburg Foundation for thirty years. He specialized in the history of business with an emphasis on the hand trades. Mr. Gill has published numerous articles and four books, the latest of which is *Apprentices of Virginia 1623–1800*. He presently is a consultant for the Colonial Williamsburg *Journal* and continues to write about Virginia-related subjects.

JAN K. GILLIAM is Assistant Curator of Exhibits for Colonial Williamsburg, working on gallery exhibits as well as Historic Area presentations. She was a member of the curatorial team that developed the exhibit "TOOLS: Working Wood in 18th-Century America," and is coauthor of *Furnishing Williamsburg's Historic Buildings* (1991). Ms. Gilliam most recently served as curator of the exhibit "Take Joy! The World of Tasha Tudor."

NANCY L. HAGEDORN is Assistant Professor of History at St. John's University in Jamaica, N. Y. A research and curatorial fellow in the Colonial Williamsburg Department of Collections from 1989 to 1996, she was the research historian for the TOOLS exhibit, and is coauthor of *Tools: Working Wood in Eighteenth-Century America* (1993). Ms. Hagedorn has published several articles on interpreters as cultural brokers among the Iroquois during the colonial period.

DAVID HARVEY is Associate Conservator of metals and arms at Colonial Williamsburg. He served on the team that surveyed archaeological collections for the TOOLS exhibit and recently has coedited *Common People and Their Material World: Free Men and Women in the Chesapeake 1700–1830* (1995).

DAVID HEY is Research Professor of Local and Family History at the University of Sheffield, Eng. His publications include *The Fiery Blades of Hallamshire: Sheffield and its Neighborhood, 1660–1740* (1991). He is joint editor of the forthcoming *Mesters to Masters: A History of the Company of Cutlers of Hallamshire.*

CHARLES F. HUMMEL, Curator Emeritus and Adjunct Professor, Winterthur Museum, Winterthur, Del., was senior Deputy Director, Museum and Library Department. Now retired, Mr. Hummel teaches graduate courses at Winterthur and serves as a trustee of several organizations. Author of *With Hammer in Hand* (1968) and *A Winterthur Guide to American Chippendale Period Furniture: Middle Atlantic and Southern Colonies* (1976), he coauthored *The Pennsylvania Germans: A Celebration of Their Arts, 1683–1850* (1982).

TED INGRAHAM is a professional woodworker who lives in northern Vermont. He has collected, studied, and reproduced preindustrial woodworking tools and their products in an effort to understand the development of New England woodworking traditions.

PAUL B. KEBABIAN retired as Director of Libraries at the University of Vermont. A past president of the Early American Industries Association, he has written *American Woodworking Tools* (1978), coedited and contributed to *Tools and Technologies: America's Wooden Age* (1979), and published many scholarly articles on early tools.

SCOTT LANDIS, author of *The Workbench Book* (1987) and *The Workshop Book* (1991), has been working wood for more than twenty years. He is the founder of the Good Wood Alliance, formerly the Woodworkers Alliance for Rainforest Protection (WARP). Mr. Landis resides in South Berwick, Me.

JANE AND MARK REES live in Bath, Eng. Now retired from their architectural practice that specialized in the restoration and renovation of historic buildings, they research and write about the history of tools and trades. Their publications include revising the third edition of W. L. Goodman's *British Planemakers from 1700* (1993), *Tools—A Guide for Collectors* (1995), *Christopher Gabriel and the Tool Trade in 18th Century London* (1997), and many articles on tool and trade related subjects.

ROY UNDERHILL is the author of numerous articles and five books on traditional woodworking, including his latest publication, *The Woodwright's Apprentice* (1996). Mr. Underhill's television series, *The Woodwright's Shop*, has been presented for many years on PBS. He is currently developing a new living-history museum in North Carolina. Mr. Underhill lives near Jamestown, Va.

PHILIP WALKER was born in London in 1925. Throughout a varied career, Mr. Walker has enjoyed working wood by hand and developing his interests in the history of woodworking tools and techniques. He obtained his Master of Arts at Oxford and is a Fellow of the Society of Antiquaries of London. Mr. Walker has written extensively on tools. In 1983, he was instrumental in founding the Tool and Trades History Society.

JOHN R. WATSON has made thirty keyboard instruments since 1972, specializing in reproductions of particular antiques. Three of Mr. Watson's instruments, a spinet, a piano, and a harpsichord, are exhibited and played at Colonial Williamsburg. In 1986, he set up the musical instrument conservation laboratory at Colonial Williamsburg where he is Conservator of musical and scientific instruments.

FRANK G. WHITE is Curator of Mechanical Arts at Old Sturbridge Village, Sturbridge, Mass. He has curated recent exhibits on early stoves and heating practices, on nineteenth-century New England's connections with the wider world, and co-curated an exhibit on furniture making in central New England. Mr. White has written numerous articles for the *Chronicle* of the Early American Industries Association, for which he serves as a contributing editor.

DONALD AND ANNE WING, of Marion, Mass., have studied early planemakers for more than twenty-five years, documenting makers that include Ballou, Doggett, Fuller, Kennedy, Lindenberger, Smith, Taber, and Wetherel. They have written extensively on planemakers and other tool manufacturers for *Plane Talk,* the *Chronicle* of the Early American Industries Association, and *Rittenhouse.*